*Questions
for the
Movie
Answer
Man*

For Lisa

Roger Ebert

Other Books by Roger Ebert

An Illini Century
A Kiss Is Still a Kiss
Two Weeks in the Midday Sun:
  A Cannes Notebook
Behind the Phantom's Mask
Ebert's Little Movie Glossary
Roger Ebert's Book of Film
Roger Ebert's Video Companion

With Daniel Curley
The Perfect London Walk

With Gene Siskel
The Future of the Movies:
  Interviews with Martin Scorsese,
  Steven Spielberg, and
  George Lucas

With John Kratz
The Computer Insectiary

Questions for the Movie Answer Man

Roger Ebert

Andrews McMeel
Publishing

Kansas City

Library of Congress Cataloging-in-Publication Data

Ebert, Roger.
   Questions for the movie answer man / Roger Ebert.
     p.   cm.
   ISBN 0-8362-2894-4 (pbk.)
    1. Motion pictures—Miscellanea.   I. Title.
PN1993.85.E24 1997
791.43—dc21   97-5730
                                     CIP

This book is dedicated to Donna Martin,
gifted editor and steadfast friend,
who asks all the best questions.

Contents

Contents

Introduction

A lot of the answers in this book can be found in the questions. Readers write me letters and send me e-mail, and I learn, ponder, and wonder.

What is amazing is how minutely we examine the movies. Perhaps because a film is a sort of life, perhaps because while we are watching a movie we are living vicariously, we notice the smallest things. If a movie is like life, we think, then every detail should be lifelike. If a boom mike comes swinging in at the top of the screen, that's not merely wrong, it's as obtrusive as the horsemen of the apocalypse thundering in from the corners of the sky.

I began writing a Movie Answer Man column for the *Chicago Sun-Times* almost twenty years ago. I wrote them once or twice a year, and in those days the questions were all made up by me, and I didn't attribute them to anyone else. In 1990 my reviews were picked up by CompuServe, and at the same time I asked for an on-line section of my own, so I could have a dialogue with the on-line readers. I didn't want to simply publish my e-mail address; that would result in countless one-to-one communications. Instead, in a section of the ShowBiz Forum, messages could be read and replied to by others in addition to myself. I wasn't the only expert (and I wasn't always very expert, I learned).

That worked out better than I could have dreamed. ShowBiz already had a cadre of film buffs and experts on board when I joined it, and soon my section of the forum became important to my work: I got daily feedback, questions, criticisms, and observations—a running commentary on new movies and current issues. I learned.

The current form of the Movie Answer Man column developed naturally out of the CompuServe experience. I started downloading questions and answers, mixing them with snail mail, and assembling them on a monthly basis. In 1995 I made it a weekly column, carried by the *Sun-Times* and offered to my two hundred syndication clients, and also posted on CompuServe and (in 1996) on the World Wide Web. This book represents the most interesting questions of the past four years.

Are all of the questions real? No. Sometimes, when the need comes upon me to answer a question I have not been asked, I will write a question of my own. The names attached to those questions have been borrowed from characters in that timeless cult classic *Beyond the Valley of the Dolls*. My wife sometimes signs in as "Charlie Smith." All of the other names, representing probably 95 percent of the questions, are real. Contributors without towns attached sent e-mail and then didn't respond to my plea for their location. A few people have moved during the four years, and are placed in more than one town.

At the end of it all, I admit to still being defeated by a few topics. I do not feel I adequately understand *12 Monkeys* or *Usual Suspects*. I do not care as much about *Star Trek* as Trekkers feel I should. I do not know what is in the briefcase in *Pulp Fiction*. When people write me saying they hated a movie I recommended, I am not inclined to write back telling them why they're wrong—because they're not wrong. You can never be wrong about your own opinion.

Special thanks are due to friends I've made on-line over the years, whose contributions can be found in this book. They include sysop Don Devich, Andy Ihnatko, Rich Elias, Jeff Levin, Jeffrey Graebner, Gregory Soo, Rebecca Costello, Binky Melnik, Patrick Davitt, Ed Slota, Aaron Barnhart, David Bondelevitch, Thomas Alan Heald, George Alec Effinger, Margaret McGurk, Roger Avary, John Jakes, Richard Lupoff, Owen Roizman, Jim Emerson, Frank Coleman, Noel Boulanger, and many others. And a special thanks to my assistant, Carol Iwata, who tracked down the answers to some of the questions. My wife Chaz is a constant source of advice and inspiration.

The Movie Answer Man currently runs every other week, alternating with my series "The Great Movies," which re-reviews film classics. It can be found in the Sunday *Chicago Sun-Times*, many of my two hundred client newspapers, on CompuServe at GO EBERT, and on the Web at www.suntimes.com/ebert.

ROGER EBERT

Questions
for the
Movie
Answer
Man

Actors

Q. Would you agree that America has not produced a great actor since 1980? No one has emerged to unseat De Niro, Pacino, Hackman, Duvall, Newman, etc., the way they took the mantle from Brando, Clift, Tracy, etc. None among the new breed of American actors has shown the ability or the inclination to extend themselves beyond plot-based drivel. De Niro was doing *Taxi Driver* and *Mean Streets* when he was in his early thirties, and his choice of roles in the 1970s was strikingly unpredictable. Contrast that with Tom Cruise, who is regarded by some as the finest actor of this generation. He has accepted only one truly challenging role (that of Ron Kovic in *Born on the Fourth of July*) amid the numerous films of the *Top Gun* ilk. The few actors that have shown a willingness to tackle tough roles (like Tom Hanks and Denzel Washington) seem to sell out. Blaming the Hollywood establishment or the poor quality of screenwriters is the easy way out. Hollywood does seem to have room for young actors who push the envelope. It just so happens that most of them are from the United Kingdom, such as Day-Lewis, Fiennes, Oldman, Branagh. (Madhu Krishnaswamy, Edmonton, Canada)

A. Great actors are produced by great films. The early 1970s were the last "golden age" in American cinema. The careers of Scorsese, Altman, Coppola, and others were on the rise. Young directors wanted to make the Great American Film. Then came the blockbuster mentality of the post-*Jaws* and *Star Wars* era, and the newer directors all wanted to make the Great American Hit. Studios in the meantime fell under the influence of marketing "experts," who are the single most negative influence on quality because they can only recommend refinements of what has been done before. (By definition, marketing cannot discover original ideas.) Who knows what Tom Cruise might have done in the 1970s? Could De Niro have even gotten started as an actor in the 1980s? Yet we do have some strong contenders today: Not only Cruise, but such names as

Brad Pitt, Samuel L. Jackson, Johnny Depp, Matt Dillon, Val Kilmer, John Cusack, and Laurence Fishburne come to mind. And older actors like Morgan Freeman, James Woods, and Joe Mantegna all emerged in the 1980s.

Q. Dustin Hoffman's was *Outbreak*, Meryl Streep gave it a shot with *The River Wild*. Isn't it about time for Meg Ryan to stop playing the woman everyone falls in love with and start killing bad guys? (Thomas Allen Heald, Rapid City, S.Dak.)

A. I just can't see it. Somehow, that would be like handing Doris Day a howitzer.

Since this exchange took place in May 1995, Meg Ryan starred in Courage Under Fire, *taking on an enemy helicopter with her automatic weapon.*

Q. What a year! Clint Eastwood and Sharon Stone have each produced movies taking on each other's stereotypical roles. Here's Sharon shooting up the town in *The Quick and the Dead*, while Clint is rolling around on the floor in *The Bridges of Madison County*. What's next? (Bruce Henderson, Newton, Mass.)

A. The next thing you know, Meryl Streep will be shooting the rapids, while Arnold Schwarzenegger gets pregnant.

Q. Why do I get the feeling Hollywood doesn't think people know who Gary Sinise is? When *Apollo 13* came out, the advertisements told us he was also in *Forrest Gump*. Now his new HBO movie, *Truman*, is playing, and they still need to remind people that he was in both *Forrest Gump* and *Apollo 13*. It is just an insult to us and to him. (Sean Goodrich, Trophy Club, Tex.)

A. Not really. He looks so incredibly like President Truman that few people would identify him as the same actor who played Lieutenant Dan and astronaut Ken Mattingly.

Q. I read an article in the *New York Times* about box office flops like *Jade*, *Strange Days*, and *The Scarlet Letter*. It blamed the movie stars (David Caruso, Ralph Fiennes, and Demi Moore) for not pulling in the customers. It said studio executives had reached a "harsh conclusion" about Denzel Washington after *Devil in a Blue Dress* opened poorly, quoting one of them, "Denzel is not a movie star. He's a terrific actor, incredibly good-looking, but he's not a movie star." It went on to say that *Seven,* a big hit, "affirms the clout of Brad Pitt, who costars with Morgan Freeman." Do you think it is fair to review the success of these movies on the basis of their stars? (Susan Lake, Urbana, Ill.)

A. Not at all. If Brad Pitt had starred in *Jade,* it still would have bombed. If Ralph Fiennes had starred in *Seven,* he would be hailed as a rising star. One movie was bad, the other was good, and the actors were to some degree innocent bystanders. As for Denzel Washington, he is dismissed (by an anonymous source) after the box-office failures of *Virtuosity* and *Devil.* But what about Washington's success in *The Pelican Brief, Philadelphia* (with Tom Hanks), and *Crimson Tide* (with Gene Hackman)? I'm also dubious about the rush to credit Brad Pitt with the success of *Seven.* It's a hit because it's a very good movie. Pitt's star charisma didn't save *Johnny Suede, Kalifornia,* or *The Favor,* but that doesn't stop him from being called (deservedly) a star. Yet Morgan Freeman, his costar in *Seven,* is dismissed in an aside. *USA Today* called the movie "Brad Pitt's 'Seven'" and "A Brad Pitt movie," and Freeman was not even mentioned. Freeman, as the older, surer, and more experienced cop, is the dominant character in the movie, and surely had something to do with its success. As an Oscar nominee in 1994 for best actor (in *The Shawshank Redemption*) he deserves better than to be completely overlooked. The whole process is revealing: The stock of stars shoots up and down based on their latest movies, which may be good or bad in spite of their efforts.

Q. Emma Thompson not only stars in but cowrote *Sense and Sensibility.* I understand that the British don't have as high a regard for her as we Americans do. Is this true, and if so, can you explain it to me? (Art Strauss, Walnut Creek, Calif.)

A. The bashing of Emma Thompson (and to an even greater degree, her former husband Kenneth Branagh) is great sport in British critical circles. The usual explanation is that the British resent ambition, and punish anyone who makes too much of a show of it. The preferred British stance is to appear to have accomplished things by accident, without really noticing.

Q. Has something happened to all the actors in Hollywood? It looks as though there are only two actors working at the moment: Antonio Banderas and Chazz Palminteri. They seem to be in every film released (although it appears that George Clooney will be cast in every movie made later this year). A "hot" performer can be involved in so many projects, regardless of quality, that the audience will get sick of him. As a result the actor's career is over after a couple of years. This makes me wonder who they will give lifetime achievement awards to in twenty years. (Gary Currie, Montreal, Quebec)

A. An actor like Palminteri, who struggled for success for many years, can be forgiven for making hay while the sun shines. But he *has* been in a lot of movies recently: *Bullets Over Broadway, Usual Suspects, Jade, Faithful,* and *Mulholland Falls.* Sometimes it's a result of movies being made over a period of time and then coincidentally being released all at once. The last time *Variety* did a count, the busiest actors in Hollywood were Gene Hackman and Jim Belushi, but that was a few years ago.

Ads, Promos, and Posters

Q. Why is the type font for the credits of movie posters and ads so hard to read? The font is very narrow and tall. Is this some kind of standard that the industry has adopted? If so, I think it should be changed. (Don Black)

A. Those spindly, microscopic letters are the result of Hollywood contract language, according to Sherman Wolf, whose Chicago firm handles ads for many studios. "On newspaper ads that are 7.5 inches deep or more," he told me, "the rule is that the credits have to be there. If more than one actor is listed, that triggers a requirement that a lot of other names be included, like director, writer, cinematographer, and so on. Space is expensive, and they want the credits to take up as little space as possible. Contracts specify that the credits must run in a type size that is a certain percentage of the height of the title. They cannot make the words shorter, but they can make them narrower—squeezing more into a smaller space."

Q. I had the experience last evening of enduring *Bad Girls*. A totally accurate title, I might add. There is something which does rather gnaw at my consciousness, however. On the *Today* show, this movie was given a week's preview, including interviews with all the stars. The *Today* interviews were better than the movie itself. Is it possible that NBC has a financial interest in some movies—those that are promoted on the *Today* show? (Jim Croy, Midwest City, Okla.)

A. *Today* and the other morning shows promise multiple interviews in exchange for exclusivity on new movies. Sometimes they guess right (*Speed* is an example), and sometimes they guess wrong.

Q. In a theater lobby I saw the poster for the new movie *Bye, Bye Love*, and there seemed to be something uncannily wrong about it. After staring at it for a long time, I realized what. The stars of the movie are all lined up smiling, including a small boy in the second row who is giving a "thumbs-up" sign. If you compare the size of his hand with the size of the hand of the small girl also in the same row, you will see that his hand is about three times larger than her hand—almost as big as his face, in fact. Do you think this is really his own hand? Or has it been painted in by the ad agency, as a subliminal way of giving the movie "thumbs-up?" (Sheila Chesham, Chicago)

A. I checked out the poster, and you are indeed correct. Either the small boy has a very large hand, or he is wearing a flesh-colored outfielder's mitt. I talked to Nancy Meyer of Twentieth Century Fox, who said, "There is no reason behind the actor Ross Malinger giving the thumbs-up sign. He just chose to do it. He plays Ben in the movie." She has no opinion about the size of his hand.

Q. Don't we pay enough to attend the movies? More and more theaters are showing TV commercials before the previews. I used to boo during theater commercials, but my wife threatened to divorce me if I continued. Moreover, the audience, unfortunately, did not join my boos as I had hoped. I complain to theater managers, but the decision to show ads seems to be out of their control. (Larry Brown, Lincolnwood, Ill.)

A. I feel the same way, although I do enjoy the previews of com-

ing attractions, and they're commercials, too. In the old days, theaters would show cartoons and short subjects as a bonus, but these
days it's all cash-oriented. By the way, MGM has just rereleased
thirty-four of its classic shorts (by Robert Benchley and Pete Smith,
among others) on laserdisc. Those were the days. Do you ever get
the feeling that everything is just sort of slowly running down?

Q. I was watching Black Entertainment Television recently and
saw the commercial for *Dangerous Minds*. But whereas the usual
version features a white male voice-over, some sound bites from
Michelle Pfeiffer, and a few clips, this BET version treated us to a
sixty-second music video featuring the rapper who performs the
song used on both versions of the advertisement. As you observed
in your review of *Dangerous Minds*, the rap music LouAnne Johnson used as a classroom tool in real life was replaced in the movie
with the lyrics of Bob Dylan, which resonate with white audiences
but would be about as meaningful to black kids as the music of Mel
Tormé. It appears, however, that Hollywood Pictures is indeed willing to appropriate rap music—provided it is narrowcast to an
audience that may be more likely to attend a movie with a rap
soundtrack. (Aaron Barnhart, Evanston, Ill.)

A. LouAnne Johnson's original book described how she used
rap music to get difficult students involved. The movie replaced rap
with Bob Dylan. To represent *Dangerous Minds* to young black audiences as containing a lot of rap is therefore doubly ironic. But
what do you have against a great jazz singer like Mel Tormé?

*See also "Trailers and Music" for what happened to Pfeiffer's costar
in the movie.*

Q. We were at the local theater recently and saw the posters for
The Journey of August King. They show two young people in historic
times. The movie stars Jason Patrick and Thandie Newton. Both
characters appear to be black, but I told my friend that Jason Patrick
is white. Have you seen the movie? (Harris Allsworth, Chicago)

A. In the movie, Jason Patrick plays a young white man who
gives aid to a runaway slave. I checked out the one-sheet at a mul-

tiplex, and agree with you that the poster artists have subtly altered the artwork to make both characters appear black, perhaps because they think this will increase the movie's ticket sales. On a related note, the recent movie *Picture Bride* was about Japanese Americans in Hawaii. On the box of the video release, the characters have inexplicably become white. This was pointed out to me by the film's director, Kayo Hatta, who based the film on the life of her grandmother, and who is intensely unhappy about the cover art.

Q. The ads for the Cindy Crawford movie *Fair Game* say, "He's a cop on the edge!" Not long ago on the Letterman show, they had a running gag with Bruno Kirby playing a police officer who kept saying, "I'm not just a cop. I'm a cop *on the edge!*" Do movie studios honestly think we'll respond to worn-out catch-phrases like these? (John Thompson, Chicago)
A. They certainly do.

Q. Is this a new trend, or what? I'm talking about ads that appear *within* an ad for a movie. The "Moonlight and Valentino" ads feature a pitch for a discount chain and a cruise line. (Hank Ottery, Chicago)
A. It all started twenty years ago when Universal added a tag to all of its larger print ads: "When in Southern California, visit Universal Studios!" When they started adding this tag to the movies themselves, directors were bitterly opposed. I think such cross-plugs look cheap, and are a tip-off that the movie is not respected by its studio.

Q. Know what really bugs me? When studios headline their newspaper ads with "WINNER!" in very large type, followed by, in smaller type: "3 Golden Globe Nominations!" Like we're too stupid to figure out that the film has not, in fact, actually "won" anything, but has only been "nominated" for a silly award that no one takes seriously in the first place. (Ed Slota, Warwick, R.I.)
A. How about this as a suggestion:
"GOT!!!!
3 Golden Globe Nominations!!!"

Q. I rented the video of *Persuasion* because the box featured a beautiful babe in one of those Empire waistline gowns—you know, the eighteenth-century Wonderbra look, with her espièglerie at full thrust—and she's leaning in true bodice-buster style on a dashing young man with naval epaulettes. So I rent the flick thinking this is gonna be some hot evening. Imagine my surprise when the babe isn't in the movie but it's this frumpy babe instead. And as for the guy, it looks like somebody carved his face from an oak stump with a dull chainsaw. I thought the Jane Austen babe who wrote this was supposed to be really hot right now, which means lotsa sex, right? So what gives? (Rich Elias, Delaware, Ohio)

A. As Ohio's most distinguished film critic, you know perfectly well that video companies will put *anything* on a box if they think it will rent the video. Consider *Picture Bride* (see above) a heartfelt story of a turn-of-the-century romance between a Japanese "mail-order bride" and a Hawaiian farm worker. The cover shows a naked couple under a waterfall. This is sort of based on a scene in the movie—except, on the cover, they're Caucasian.

Q. I can't say I've sampled *all* the movie info hotlines in the Los Angeles area. Nevertheless, I can say that not once, not ever, never, have I called a movie theater and been given the option of Touch-Tone info such as "Press 1 for *Twister,* press 2 for *Mission: Impossible,*" etc. I always end up having to wait through long sermons of showtimes for movies that I don't want to see. In an era of digital surround sound, computer-animated acting, and lowfat buttered popcorn, where's the menu-driven movie info? (Jim Simon, Villa Park, Calif.)

A. This is an idea whose time has come. I also question why the tape-recorded announcements have to tell you who stars in the movie and add a sales pitch, since by the time you call the theater you have obviously decided which movie you want to see. My theory? The theater managers who record the hotlines are frustrated voice-over announcers.

Alan Smithee

Q. I heard at one point that when a director wants to disavow himself from a particular directing job he will use the pseudonym "Alan Smithee." Can you confirm this? I noticed that the new *Hellraiser* film has this individual credited with its direction. (Jeffrey W. Bowden, Winston-Salem, N.C.)

A. You are correct. To quote the Cinemania Web site, "Alan Smithee is nothing more than a pseudonym—a commonly used smokescreen for the identities of filmmakers who, out of embarrassment or protest over the outcome of their work, have chosen to remove their name from the official credits of a given film." And Jeffrey Graebner of the CompuServe Showbiz Forum informs me: "It is reported that the real director of the new *Hellraiser* is special effects expert Kevin Yagher, who is probably best known for designing the cryptkeeper puppet for HBO's *Tales from the Crypt* series."

Animals (and *Babe*)

Q. I saw on the news that thousands of moviegoers are swearing off of pork products after seeing the movie *Babe*. Has this sort of thing happened before as a result of a film? What do you make of it? (Mark Dayton, Costa Mesa, Calif.)

A. So who do they eat instead? Elsie the Cow and Charlie Tuna?

Q. I'd like to know your opinion on the new McDonald's Happy Meals featuring Babe and various other barnyard animals. Personally, I think if the makers of *Babe* were in on this promotion, they have destroyed the whole point of the movie (considering that cows and pigs are on McDonald's menu). As far as I'm concerned, it's disgusting. (Matt Thiesen, Maple Grove, Minn.)

A. In the movie, when Babe's fellow pigs were trucked away, he thought they were going to Pig Paradise, "a place so wonderful that nobody ever came back." I guess Pig Paradise turned out to be McDonald's. Yes, the original pigs that starred in *Babe* were sold to McDonald's, chopped up, and served as reconstituted rib sandwiches.

Footnote: Of course the pigs in Babe *were not sold to McDonald's, but my version has the stuff to become an Urban Legend. After all, since McDonald's does grind up real cows and pigs, they have their nerve using Babe as a traitor to his own kith and kind.*

Q. I work in the home video industry and recently spotted the box-art for the release of *Gordy,* upon which you are quoted as saying, "Kids will squeal over *Gordy!*" Being familiar with your writing style I find it hard to believe that you would actually say that. Tell me it isn't true! (Bret Hayden, Los Angeles)

A. I gave *Gordy* a two-star rating, adding that kids might like it. Later, after seeing and enjoying *Babe,* I wrote a footnote urging people not to mistake it for *Gordy.* As far as I can tell, I never wrote "Kids will squeal over *Gordy!*" in the past, and I am determined never to write it in the future.

Q. We had a dinner party tonight and the topic of dating came up as one of our teenage daughters is "in love." One of us said that she was "Pittatated." Another said, No! she is in fact "Twitapated." I said, You're both wrong because she is "Pitapated!" All of this because of the Disney movie *Bambi,* where the skunk was telling Bambi about love. What is the correct word? (Rick Johnston)

A. The skunk says "Twitter-pated." My thanks for this info to Richard Kinkead of Lantana, Fla.

Q. Making movies is dangerous. People have died while making movies, yet the movies still appeared in theaters. Suppose the unthinkable happens, and an animal is injured, or dies, while a movie is being made. Would the production be canceled rather than opening without the "No animals were injured" disclaimer? Would the Humane Society actually require the label, "An animal was harmed in the production of this movie?" (Dan Sachs, Merrick, N.Y.)

A. According to spokesman Jim Moore, the American Humane Association does not have the authority to prevent the release of a motion picture. The "no animals were injured" disclaimer is "not a requirement but a courtesy." When it is missing, that does not necessarily mean animals were injured. However, the AHA has an agreement with major industry unions which states that it must receive a script when animals are involved in a film, and may have an observer on the set whenever animals are used. "Last year," he says, "the AHA reviewed over nine hundred scripts and monitored 429 productions."

Q. Just read your review of *Alaska*. It's really difficult to take seriously a movie in which kids head off into the Alaskan wilderness accompanied by A Friendly Polar Bear when one has recently had the experience of sitting in an Anchorage hotel room with two fat books of nothing but stories of unprovoked bear attacks, while watching on the TV a news report of a couple mauled by bears, followed by a public service announcement reminding people that you're nuts if you go more then ten feet into the wilderness without a shotgun about the size of your leg. I don't know why the movies encourage the youth of America to horse around with bear cubs whenever the opportunity arises. They should read passages from my bear books, for example: ". . . as I felt his teeth scraping against bone, I was struck by how strange it was that I could feel it, could see buckets of my blood, and yet there was so little actual pain." (Andy Ihnatko, Westwood, Mass.)

A. Strange indeed, that the wise old Indian in the movie counsels the children, "Trust the bear!"—when such a seasoned veteran of the wilderness should probably have advised, "Get away from the bear as fast as you can!" In my defense, I must point out that my review of *Alaska* contained these words: "I started hoping for a warning to flash on the screen: *Caution! Kids! Do not try this on your next vacation to Yellowstone!* Trust the bear. But keep the windows rolled up."

Q. In your *Angels and Instincts* review, you observed that it is the first movie you can remember in which anyone is attacked by moths. How quickly you forget! There was *Mothra* and a bunch of derivative Godzilla films. (Steve Kallas, Tampa, Fla.)

A. Is it true Mothra ate holes in King Kong's coat?

Animation

Q. What will make American audiences accept animation as a form of serious storytelling? The Disney formula has drummed into us that cute animals are the criteria for good animation. Why not take a well-known novel and animate it? For instance, Stephen King's *The Talisman* has been sitting at Spielberg's Amblin Entertainment for a long time now. It could be done with half the budget of a live-action version, and with more verve and imagination. (Dimitri M. LaBarge, Nashville, Tenn.)

A. Spielberg linked up with David Geffen and Jeffrey Katzenberg—mastermind of Disney's recent animated hits—to form a new studio named Dreamworks. Katzenberg told me that in addition to making animated films for the family, he would also like to experiment with more mature animated themes—possibly including versions of Broadway musicals.

Q. In all of Disney's recent animated films, humans still animate the characters but computers are used to do all the coloring of the images as well as all the "camera moves" like multiplane shots, for example. There are no more cels used in Disney's animation, and no paint. If you walk into the animation department, all you see are animators using computer terminals. They are using CAPS, a program that was written for Disney by Pixar. This has been true for every animated film since *Rescuers Down Under.* Disney has only recently talked publicly about this. (Rob Hahn, Los Angeles)

A. In other words, the "original collectors' cels" of the more recent Disney films were not necessarily used in the production of a movie. They're more like "limited editions" from the Franklin Mint. But what I want to know is: Since *Toy Story* was created *entirely* within computers, how will Disney produce any "collector's cels" of its animation? Will they sell you a floppy disc and tell you to display it on your computer?

Q. I just saw *Mrs. Doubtfire,* and am confused by the scene in which Robin Williams starts ad-libbing while looping a cartoon. I thought the voices were done first, and animators drew to the audio track. (John Graham)

A. You are quite right. But of course a scene with Williams simply talking into a mike would not have been as cinematic as one where we can see the animated characters on the screen. Study the genie scenes in Disney's *Aladdin* for an example of animators brilliantly keeping up with Williams's verbal inventions.

Q. I don't quail at the thought of Michael Jordan appearing with the Looney Tunes characters in *Space Jam*. What I can't believe is the plot of this thing! What kind of idiot would come up with a story where Bugs and "the gang" (as if these characters were ever friends) are kidnapped by evil space aliens and need Michael Jordan's help to regain their freedom? Don't the palookas at Warner Bros. know anything about the characters they're exploiting? Making a movie where Bugs gets captured and needs a basketball player to rescue him is like making a Marx Brothers movie where Groucho bursts into tears and begs Margaret Dumont to lend him money so his wife and children won't starve. After seeing Bugs pulverize Marvin the Martian, I can't believe that he (or even Daffy) could be helpless at the hands of space visitors. If Warner Bros. thinks of Bugs and Daffy as being just objects to make Michael Jordan's debut more marketable, then maybe Bob Dole was right and they *have* sold their souls. (Sarah Weinman, Nepean, Ontario, Canada)

A. How would you feel about a plot where Michael rescues Elmer Fudd?

Are They Related?

Q. Is it true that the little boy who played opposite Whoopi Goldberg in *Clara's Heart* is really *your* little boy? (Jim Cook)

A. The little dickens sure could act!

Q. Sorry to bring you into a silly family argument, but I figured you could convince my mother-in-law (since I can't). She is absolutely positive she read that Ashley Judd and Winona Ryder are the same person. (Richard W. Emery)

A. Your mother-in-law has been doing way too much reading in the supermarket check-out line.

Q. Superman's girlfriend is named Lois Lane. The Shadow's girlfriend is named Margo Lane. Could they be related? (Nissen V. Vexler, Skokie, Ill.)

A. If they are, I'll bet they need a good support group.

Q. Last night in a bar someone made the ridiculous claim that Humphrey Bogart and Ed Sullivan were brothers. Naturally, I jumped at the chance to make back the money I had just spent on beer and pool by making a $20 bet with this sadly deluded individual. He insists he's right, but doesn't claim a source, calling it "common knowledge." And you better not come back and tell me that they were brothers, or I'll have to question the whole concept of reality and meaning in my life. (Charles Faubert, Montreal, Quebec, Canada)

A. Collect the $20. Bogart had two sisters, Frances and Catherine. Sounds like you have a sure thing with this sucker. Now bet him that Charlie Sheen and Emilio Estevez are brothers.

Q. I wonder if Nicolas Cage would ever have gotten where he is if he wasn't the nephew of Francis Ford Coppola? (Ken Felker, Oklahoma City, Okla.)

A. Hollywood is filled with failures who are the children, nephews, cousins, lovers, etc., of the great. Cage, who actually changed his name to avoid being linked with his uncle, is a capable and daring actor, who has been splendid in such widely different roles as *Birdy*, *Moonstruck*, *Honeymoon in Vegas*, *Guarding Tess*, *Red Rock West*, and *Wild at Heart*. His work in *Leaving Las Vegas* won him the Best Actor Oscar.

Q. This weekend I saw John Sayles's wonderful *Lone Star*, which shares a certain sensibility with the equally great *Fargo*. Is Chris Cooper, who plays the lead, related to Gary Cooper? There is something similar in their screen presence and (to me, at least) in their looks. My wife didn't think they looked anything alike, however. (Paul Block, Delmar, N.Y.)

A. Your wife is right. They are no relation, according to the Microsoft Cinemania CD-ROM, which says Chris Cooper was raised on his father's cattle ranch and attended the University of Missouri with a double major in agriculture and acting ("It's always best to have something dependable to fall back on, son, in case the farm fails"). He also appeared in Sayles's *Matewan* and *City of Hope.*

Q. The new edition of *Ephraim Katz's Film Encyclopedia* says that Annabeth Gish is Lillian Gish's granddaughter. Is that true? (Steven Siferd, Alpine, Calif.)

A. Miss Gish never married or had children and was said to have loved only one man, D.W. Griffith. "I am a member of a completely different Gish family," Annabeth Gish told me. "I'm no relation to Lillian or Dorothy Gish. Not even way back. But when I first became interested in acting, I wrote a letter to Lillian Gish. She wrote back, discouraging me from entering the business. 'Stay in a place where you are loved and supported,' she wrote me. 'There's too much talent and not enough work in the movies!' She said her life had been so used, since she began working at such a young age, that she knew nothing else but acting. And she wished that she did. It was kind of shattering to me that here was this wonderful actress who I respected so much, telling me such terrible things about the business. And basically what I found out was that everything she said was true."

Arnold

Q. *Junior,* the movie where Arnold Schwarzenegger gets pregnant, surprised Hollywood executives by its poor performance at the box office. We saw it and liked it a lot. Why did the public stay away? (Sheila Chesham, Chicago)

A. Beats me. I thought it would go through the roof. It's funny, it's warm, and Schwarzenegger handles the situation with great charm, on just the right note. Maybe men were turned off by the prospect of seeing Arnold pregnant? Or . . . maybe women were.

Q. We went to see *Junior* and got into a big argument afterward. In the movie, Arnold Schwarzenegger is artificially implanted with a human egg, and becomes pregnant. Is this possible? (Joe Rogers, Chicago)

A. Strangely enough, it might be. According to Victoria Weisenberg, an instructor at the St. Francis Hospital School of Nursing, in Evanston, Illinois, such an event would be known as an ectopic pregnancy: "The zygote, or egg, has little extensions named trophoblasts that implant on the womb wall. In one well-known case involving an Austrian woman with a hysterectomy, the attachment was to her abdominal wall, and the embryo was able to develop. It has not happened *yet* with a man, but is theoretically possible."

And after all, Arnold is Austrian.

Autographs

Q. I go to UCLA and live in Westwood. Obviously I live around a great number of theaters and very close to Beverly Hills, Bel Air, Brentwood, and Holmby Hills. So, when movie stars want to go to movies they go around here. I went to see *Primal Fear.* While we were in line Woody Harrelson bought a ticket and went in. Okay. Not so bad. He wasn't looking for attention but unfortunately he received it. Before my girlfriend and I got to the ticket counter, Tom Cruise and Nicole Kidman walked by (quickly) and as I watched, heads turned everywhere: in line, on the corner, and all along the sidewalk up to and I suppose in the movie they went to see *(The Birdcage).* Now for my question. They are actors, they are people, they feel, talk, dress like everyone else. People point, stare, gawk, and follow their every move. Not very conducive to a normal lifestyle. They chose that profession and are not blind to reality. They know that stars are followed, stared at, touched, etc. I would suppose two actors such as Cruise and Kidman would have the ability and sources to ask for a copy of *The Birdcage* for their personal viewing. That would allow them the luxury of never being gawked at. Yet they *choose* to go out in public. They also know the consequences. They get upset knowing they can never sit down at a corner coffee shop and drink coffee without a horde descending upon them. Should they expect a normal life? Are the outings they make an attempt to hold up the mask of normalcy or are they masochists who seek out problems with their every excursion into the land of the normal? (Frank Chartrand, Westwood, Calif.)

A. When a movie is on top of the box office charts, the studio does not have an "extra" print to send to every star who wants to see it. But setting that issue aside, I think movie stars should have the right to appear in public without being made uncomfortable by ill-mannered yahoos. A person of taste and manners will notice a star, be pleased to see the star, and grant them their privacy. A nod or a smile is fine. Shouting out their names or pointing them out to other people is a way of indicating you have not made it as far up the evolutionary ladder as you think. Asking for an autograph on any occasion other than an autograph signing is an invasion of privacy and boorish behavior. I once spent a day with Clint Eastwood during which he posed (I counted) for sixty-two photographs and signed more than one hundred autographs. For a member of the public, it only takes a moment to disturb a star's privacy. For the star, it is a lifetime sentence—a celebrity version of the Chinese water torture. No thoughtful and considerate person would ever want to contribute to that.

I got a lot of feedback over that answer. Many people told me how "gracious" stars had been when asked for their autographs, how "pleased" they were, and that if stars expect to make $10 million a picture then fame is the price they have to pay. But what does asking for an autograph say about the person doing the asking? Alan Alda, who does not give autographs, always offers an explanation about how it sets up a barrier between equals, etc. My notion is that after one reaches a certain age, say the early teen years, it is unseemly to ask for autographs. Children are privileged. Adults should be able to think of a more meaningful interaction, or allow the target his privacy. Book signings, personal appearances, fan conventions, etc., are obviously exceptions where it is appropriate to ask for autographs.

Automatic Dialogue Replacement

Q. I see almost all the latest movies and stay until the final line of the credits. Often I am the only one left with the cleaners and ushers. What is the job of ADR Voice Casting? Barbara Harris is usually listed. Is she the same actress who was in the Second City comedy troupe? (John P. Keating Jr., Chicago)

A. No, she is not "the" Barbara Harris. ADR Voice Casting stands for "Automatic Dialogue Replacement," according to Chicago film consultant Jeffrey Marden, who says: "The person holding this title brings in people to dub background voices or, in some cases, replace a lead actor's voice."

Q. The ADR Barbara Harris is—unless I'm mistaken (unheard-of)—the same woman who was Cary Grant's last wife. (Jeffrey Sweet, New York)

A. In my answer, I explained that the ADR person supervises the dubbing of dialogue replacement. Which leads me to wonder, in view of this information, if that was really Cary Grant saying, "Judy! Judy! Judy!"

Q. Don't you ever read your old issues of *Premiere?* As the enclosed clipping and photo from *Premiere* show, the ADR Barbara Harris is a black woman who started out ten years ago doing voice-overs, and now has her own ADR company, the Looping Group, which is the most successful in Hollywood. (Bill Russell, Westmont, Ill.)

A. At last we have the right Barbara Harris! The task of an ADR director is subtle but crucial: replacing movie dialogue with either improved readings by the same actors, or substitute readings by other voices if the original voices are found unsatisfactory.

B & W

Q. My wife and I were watching *The Grifters* on laserdisc last night and about ten minutes into it she remarked that it would have been much better had it been filmed in black and white. No problem, I said, and promptly turned the color off. She was right! Suddenly the atmosphere of the Jim Thompson book seemed to pop out more. We both found it greatly more enjoyable. We started rattling off a list of recent movies that would benefit from this goofy trick. (Chris Yaryan)

A. In theory I am against tampering with the original color format of a film. But it's strange how adding color to a b&w movie destroys it, while viewing a color movie in b&w often seems to enhance it. This fits into my general theory that b&w is more dreamlike and mysterious, and color is more realistic.

Although it is probably just as unethical as colorization, I sometimes experiment by turning down the color settings on a television, to experience a movie in black and white. It often seems to enhance the experience—especially with some musicals where the colors are distracting, but the songs and the choreography have held up well. Among recent movies, Fargo *is one I enjoyed in both modes.*

Q. I recently bought the sound track to *Pulp Fiction*, so of course I had to go see the movie for the third time. I noticed in the cab ride after Butch (Bruce Willis) kills the other boxer that all the scenery outside the cab is in black and white. Is there any particular reason for this? Also, did you notice that Butch put a shirt on without ever taking his cigarette out of his mouth? (Joe Long, Redmond, Wash.)

A. In old movies, the street scenes seen through the back windows of cars were usually "back projection" onto a screen behind the car window, and sometimes they didn't match—the cars outside would be fifteen years too old, or a car would turn directly from the Champs Elysses to the countryside. The autos themselves never left the sound stage. Tarantino probably made the scenery black and white to call attention to the artifice. In *Family Plot*, Alfred Hitchcock also used deliberately phony back projection through a rear car window.

Based on a True Story

Q. Recently, I rented *Dragon*, which is supposed to be based upon the life of Bruce Lee. If you read the book written by his wife you will find that the movie is essentially fiction. What do you think the responsibility of the film critic should be in reviewing these biography-type movies? The unaware viewer is likely to swallow the movie whole and to consider it to be the "truth." (Carl S. Lau, Los Angeles)

A. *In the Name of the Father* is another movie "based on fact," which nevertheless differs greatly from the real events. Moviegoers should consider such movies "inspired by" real life, but not as an accurate record. Accuracy always finishes second to the devices of drama, pacing, and storytelling. The film critic can only review the film, not the facts.

Q. I am Cheryl Sites, alias the character "Pearl" in the movie *This Boy's Life*. I take exception to your references about my father in your review. How can you state as fact incidents regarding our lives when very little in the movie is true? My father didn't die in Concrete, Oregon, and in fact we never lived in Concrete! There was no love lost between my father and "Jack" (the character based on author Tobias Wolff), but there wasn't the violent relationship depicted in the movie, either. "Jack" didn't toil at his paper route only to have my father steal his money. I shared that route. We used the money to buy what we wanted. I don't understand why it was important to portray my father as an idiot, when in fact he was an intelligent man and had a much better vocabulary than "Shut your pie hole!" I'm sorry life was miserable for "Jack," and it was, but a good deal of it was brought on my his own actions and prevarications. I don't intend to make my father a saint because he wasn't and we didn't have the *Leave It to Beaver* or *Father Knows Best* household, but it wasn't all bad, either. (Cheryl Sites, Kent, Wash.)

A. I made the mistake, common to movie reviewers, of discussing the characters in a movie as if they were real. Robert De Niro's performance as the father was obviously based much more on artistic inspiration than on fact, and as a general rule when the words "the following is a true story" appear on the screen, they're as fictional as anything that follows.

Q. You said in your review of *It Could Happen to You* that you wondered if it was from a true story. I saw it today with friends and we all swore we'd seen it in the papers. Someone said she heard that the cop had actually been a twenty-year customer at the diner and shared with the waitress as an act of generosity. Any truth to this? (Alex Fallis, Ormond Beach, Fla.)

A. Much truth. A real cop from Yonkers, New York, named Robert Cunningham, offered to split a lottery ticket in lieu of a tip, with a real waitress, Phyliss Penzo. They won, and have been splitting

$285,715 annually ever since 1984. In the movie, the characters played by Nicholas Cage and Bridget Fonda went on to fall in love, but Cunningham and Penzo remain happily married to their original spouses.

Q. Re the fact that *Fargo* is not, as it claims, based on a true story: I get a bad taste in my mouth when someone goes out of their way to assure me that something's a true story and it turns out they were just trying to manipulate me. "This is a true story" does absolutely nothing to enhance *Fargo*, and only serves to make me insert the phrase "Yeah, but remember that the first thing we see is a lie: *None* of this happened" somewhere in my mental review. I just don't think that's cricket. Sure, *suggest* that it really happened. Imply it. But when I'm told right at the top that something's a true story, I involuntarily invest more in the thing, emotionally. When I learn that was a deliberate lie, I felt manipulated to an extent. Still one *hell* of a movie, of course. (Andy Ihnatko, Westwood, Mass.)

A. I was talking the other day to the director Paul Schrader, the man who wrote *Taxi Driver* and directed *American Gigolo* and *Light Sleeper.* He said we have passed from the age of the existential hero to the age of the ironic hero: "The existential hero asks if life is worth living. The ironic hero asks, who cares?" In the new ironic movies, he said, everything has quotation marks around it. A person isn't killed, he's "killed." A few years ago, the true story line would have been intended to invest *Fargo* with extra meaning. Now it's just the Coen Brothers cocking an ironic snout at the "true story" gambit.

Q. Re the controversy over the fact that *Fargo* isn't based on a true story, although it claims to be: I remember feeling unfairly manipulated when I learned *The Texas Chainsaw Massacre*—which opens with a "this is a true story" title crawl read by John LaRoquette of *Night Court* fame—wasn't based on a true story at all, but cobbled together from bits and pieces (heh, heh) of the infamous Ed Gein story, which also inspired *Psycho*. Then I thought, hey— isn't it nice to know there *wasn't* a "chainsaw massacre"? I feel the same way about the events in *Fargo*. (Mark Verheiden, Pasadena, Calif.)

A. For that matter *Henry, Portrait of a Serial Killer* was based on a true story—sort of—and then it later turned out that Henry Lee Lucas, the killer who inspired it, had wildly exaggerated in his confessions to the police. And *The Thin Blue Line* was a documentary that created fictional scenes to reenact the events. And *From the Journals of Jean Seberg* is not based on the journals of Jean Seberg. "Truth," as Mark Twain said, "is the most valuable thing we have. Let us economize on it."

Q. I'm a freelance reader in Hollywood. Since you'll see Barry Levinson's *Sleepers* I'm writing to urge you to address author Lorenzo Carcaterra's alleged fabrication of the "true story." My work as a "story analyst" comes from one of the industry's biggest directors. *Sleepers* came his way, and therefore my way, on an "overnight read." This, boasted the agent, was a hot property—and bids would be considered first thing in the morning. I hunkered down for an all-nighter and plowed through the manuscript. Billed as a "true story," the manuscript was punchy and overwrought—and an obvious lie. That's what I reported the next morning on a conference call with the company's producers. Not long thereafter, Lorenzo Carcaterra sold the book's movie rights for a reported $2 million. I asked one of the company's producers what he thought of an obvious fraud like *Sleepers* selling for $2 million. "What fraud?" said the producer. "It's a movie."

As far as *Sleepers* living up to its billing as a "true story," the producer was unconcerned: "That's not something I obsess over." I feel strongly that billing a story as "true" to inflate its appeal is a fraudulent practice. *Sleepers* may have some merit as a revenge tale, but in my opinion, what sold the story and made Carcaterra rich was nothing less than fraud. (Name withheld by request)

A. *Sleepers* stars Robert De Niro, Kevin Bacon, Dustin Hoffman, and Brad Pitt in the story of tough New York kids who grow up and take revenge on a reformatory guard who abused them. The *New York Times* researched the Carcaterra novel at the time it was published, and concluded it was unlikely the novel could have been based on fact. Yet the new film begins with the words, "This is a true story." That seems unlikely, because the movie shows moral decisions being taken which, in the real world, would have been impossible to justify.

Before Sunrise

Q. I wonder whether you'd be interested in my story. I recently saw the movie *Before Sunrise*, where Ethan Hawke and Julie Delpy meet each other on a train, start talking, and end up spending the night walking around Vienna, Austria. Caught up in the romance of it all, I boarded a train from Philly to Charlottesville, Virginia. (I had to go there anyway.) On the train I met a woman dressed exactly like Julie Delpy and about as beautiful. So began a rather romantic trip that began with her asking me to come to Atlanta with her and ended with my return to law school two days later.

But now the story takes an interesting twist, and could probably be called *After Sunrise*. Since I had missed some school, I felt the need to explain to a professor where I had been. Unfortunately, I was too embarrassed to relate the full details, so I informed him I was sick. Two weeks later I was asked to leave the school for lying to a professor.

My legal career is probably now over. So why do I write to you? To be honest, I don't know—but the link between the movie, and my life seemed so strong I felt someone in the industry should know. Make of it what you will. (Daryl Elfield, Berkeley, Calif.)

A. I am always getting letters from people who wonder if the movies these days are not a baleful influence on young people. In your case, *Before Sunrise* sparked a grand gesture of romanticism, which would have been wonderful if the consequences had not been so dire.

Having been a college student myself, I relished the way you worded this phrase: "I felt the need to explain to a professor where I had been." My guess is, this felt need was inspired by the professor's curiosity about your absence from his classes. In a similar situation I, too, might have hesitated to reveal the whole truth. On the other hand, rules are rules. In law school I am sure it is especially important to enforce the honor code, since, as we all know, no lawyer has ever said he was sick to get out of anything.

Curious about your case, I made a few telephone calls.

The woman you met on the train was Jessica Turner, a Spanish teacher from Fryeburg, Maine. I talked to her to check out your story.

"I hadn't seen the movie when we met," she told me, "but we saw it together after we got off the train in Atlanta. I really was wearing one of those black dresses, like the woman in the movie. Actually, *I* started talking to *him*. I had stopped to see a friend in Baltimore, who packed me a bagel and wrapped it up with a note that said, 'Don't talk to strangers.' I saw Daryl sitting at the next table on the train and told him what my napkin said. We started talking, he told me all about the movie, and when we got to Charlottesville, I asked him if he wanted to stay on the train and spend some time in Atlanta.

"I feel really awful about what happened. I vaguely remember him saying that his professor would never believe his story."

Then I talked with Alison Kitch, one of your law professors, at Washington and Lee University, in Lexington, Virginia.

"I had Daryl in my contract law class last fall," she said. "I am quite sympathetic with what happened to him. But he indeed broke the rules. He got thrown out for doing what the honors book says you will be thrown out for: He lied. If he had only told his professor he missed class because he met a young woman on a train and spent two days with her in Atlanta, he might have gotten a bad grade, but he wouldn't have been thrown out of school. If you believe in the honor system, then you believe students ought to do what they sign up to do."

Professor Kitch said you are "smart and resourceful," and she is sure you will land on your feet. She added: "If you have to be stuck somewhere, Vienna seems like a better place than Atlanta."

I also talked with Eric Chaffin, who represented you before the honors committee. He confirmed the facts of the case, and added helpfully, "It's made me really want to see that movie."

Finally, Daryl, I talked with you personally. "I have a sales job right now," you said gloomily. "I'm applying to other law schools and hope to be accepted to one."

Will you see Jessica again?

"We plan to see each other in June."

"Daryl's taking me to a wedding," Jessica Turner told me. "It's in Boston. This time, he's going to fly."

Q. Just wanted to thank you for your latest "Movie Answer Man" column, about the guy who saw *Before Sunrise*, met the girl on the train, joined her in emulating the movie, and ended up being thrown out of law school. The column was as richly detailed as any movie I've seen lately, and it truly made my week. Would you be interested in knowing that *My Tutor* is based on my adventures with a well-endowed teacher who saw me through summer school? (Steve Bailey, Jacksonville Beach, Fla.)

A. No, but I think *Penthouse* Forum would.

Q. I'm glad your review of *Before Sunrise* didn't make note of the date. The action in the movie takes place on June 16, known as "Bloomsday," the day of all the action in James Joyce's novel *Ulysses*. If I wanted to stay home and read books, I wouldn't go to the movies. (Bob Kamman, Phoenix, Ariz.)

A. Too bad they cut away during the love scene in the park. For those who are curious about what happened between the bottle of wine and sunrise, the director's cut on laserdisc will include dialogue where Julie Delpy turns to stately, plump Ethan Hawke and says, "Yes I said yes I will Yes."

Billing

Q. I'd like to know why, in the movie *Hero*, Chevy Chase isn't listed in the credits. (Dan Gerson, Santa Clara, Calif.)

A. Stars sometimes pass up billing for supporting roles, as an ego thing. Hoffman costars seem to have a special fondness for the practice; Bill Murray was also uncredited for his funny work as Hoffman's roommate in *Tootsie*.

Q. How come on the *Far and Away* movie poster both Tom Cruise's and Nicole Kidman's names were featured, but this summer's poster for *The Firm* has only his name on it? I thought Gene Hackman was also in this movie. Do you have to be married to Tom Cruise to have your name on his posters? (R. Sullivan, Lowell, Mass.)

A. Yes, and that's where Hackman draws the line.

Black Themes

Q. Aren't you outraged about Spike Lee's call for all black kids to skip school and see his new movie, *Malcolm X*? (Emerson Thorne, Chicago)

A. Not particularly, since school is out before most theaters open. His comment is well within the tradition of Hollywood hyperbole which has also given us, "I laughed so hard I needed artificial respiration!" and "Mortgage your house to see this movie!" Kids usually skip school for bad reasons. If they see *Malcolm X* it might do them some good. It might even stay with them longer and be more important to them than what they might have learned in the classroom that day. That goes for white kids, too. But the most pointed observation on the subject comes from an anonymous Hollywood executive who asks, "If Spike feels that strongly, is he planning to let them in free?"

Q. I am excited about the overdue "black filmmaking renaissance" of the past few years. But have you noticed: Not one "white" film, to my knowledge, in the past twenty-five years has had a negative black character in it without somewhere in the film there also being a positive black character. However, I can name a dozen "black" films with negative white characters in them, without a single positive white character anywhere else in the film. Have you noticed this? (Brett Roth)

A. I have. But I have also noticed black-themed films like Spike Lee's *Clockers*, where the major favorable character is a white cop (Harvey Keitel). And, of course, if you go back more than twenty-five years, you get to long decades during which almost all black characters in Hollywood films were negative. What goes around, comes around.

Q. I saw *Sugar Hill* in a theater in a very wealthy, mostly white, neighborhood in North Dallas. However, I was the only white person in the theater. Do you think that white people miss out on great movies such as *Menace II Society*, *Boyz N the Hood*, etc., because they are considered "black" movies? (Dmitri Pekker, Dallas, Tex.)

A. Without a question. And that means they are missing a lot of the cutting-edge filmmaking in America today. Spike Lee is one of our best filmmakers, and the Hughes Brothers' *Menace* and John Singleton's *Boyz* are two of the most important recent American films, explaining life in the big cities in a way that headlines and newscasts cannot even approach.

Q. There was a shooting at a movie theater in Chicago last week, and a young black woman lost her life. The movie was *Set It Off*, and the anchor folks on TV mentioned that you gave it three and a half stars. I should have called that station and told them, if the movie received no stars, what difference would it make? The movie and the act of violence were totally separate incidents. Someone could have stepped on someone's toes in the theater. (Myrin New, Chicago)

A. This is a tough call, but if the title of the movie is newsworthy, then perhaps it is also newsworthy that many major critics have given *Set It Off* highly favorable reviews. I agree with you that the movie should not be held responsible for the shooting, which might just as easily have taken place during a different film.

Q. I went to the Hillside theater recently to see *Set It Off* with some friends. After paying for our tickets, we went into the theater and then noticed our stubs said *Ransom*. We asked the manager and were told to just go into *Set It Off* and not worry about it. Was this a practice to inflate the box office for *Ransom* and take proceeds from *Set It Off*? (Celeste Lengerich, Chicago)

A. Box office grosses are tabulated by computerized ticket machines. Your money was credited to *Ransom*, not *Set It Off*. It may have been a one-time error by the ticket-seller, although director Spike Lee has said in the past that some theaters act in this way to deflate the grosses of black-oriented films.

Bloopers

Q. Saw *Groundhog Day* and found a blooper. The train that pursues Bill Murray in the crazy driving sequence has a Burlington

Northern engine. Pretty slick, considering that BN doesn't get within five hundred miles of Pennsylvania. (Bill Becwar, Wauwatosa, Wisc.)

A. The movie was shot in Woodstock, Ill.

Q. In the movie *Rookie of the Year,* the twelve-year-old Cubs pitcher throws his final pitch directly underhand. In the major leagues, isn't an underhand pitch illegal? (Paul Dunn, Peoria, Ill.)

A. You know, I *sensed* there was something implausible about that plot. Thanks for pinpointing it.

Q. I saw *D2*, the *Mighty Ducks* sequel, and I think the filmmakers know next to nothing about hockey! At one point in the movie a character mentions the score of the game, and uses the word "points." Sorry, guy—anyone who has been to even *one* game knows you keep track of the score in goals. And what about the gimmick (featured in the commercials) of the puck flipping end-over-end to knock out the goalie? Pu-lease! A puck flipping like that is like a knuckleball: It doesn't fly straight, it dips unpredictably, and it comes in more slowly than usual, and certainly with less force than a regular shot. Again, anyone who's actually *seen* a puck flip would know better. (Andrew Coles, Toronto, Canada)

A. You bring up some interesting goals.

Q. In *Jurassic Park,* why do the electrically-powered cars have ignition keys and gearshifts? When T. Rex turns one over, why do you clearly see an exhaust system underneath? The one thing you *don't* see is any kind of pickup device making a connection between the cars and the rail the vehicles are supposed to run along. Somebody ought to take Spielberg for a ride on the "L" sometime, so he can learn how electric vehicles work. (Bill Becwar, Chicago)

A. Better still, in the sequel, maybe he could have one of the dinosaurs attack the "L," in the great tradition of King Kong.

Q. My wife and I just saw *I'll Do Anything.* We had a baby three months ago. In the scene where the baby in the movie is crying into the baby monitor, my wife says that the transmitter and receiver were backward! The transmitter was by the parent's bed and the receiver was with the baby. The moviemakers probably didn't think anyone would notice the difference. (Michael and Linda Hildebrand, Riverside, Calif.)

A. And the poor kid was up all night listening to its parents snoring.

Q. In your review of *Timecop*, why didn't you mention the cheeziest depiction of a futuristic automobile since something my mother hung on the refrigerator when I was four years old? This movie is set only ten years into the future. Why do all the automobiles look the same, and like they were assembled from scrap parts on a *Doctor Who* set? (John Kelly)

A. Maybe the art director traveled back in time to your mother's refrigerator?

Q. Bruce Willis's character in *Color of Night* may have a Ph.D., but he couldn't figure out that it would be quite difficult for Jane March to nail both of her hands to a chair. He should have kept an eye out for someone else in the building. (Mark Perry, Richton Park, Ill.)

A. *Ebert's Little Movie Glossary* covers this phenomenon under the entry "Third Hand": *An invisible appendage used, for example, by Rambo, in the scene where he hides from the enemy by completely plastering himself inside a mud bank. Since it is impossible to cover yourself with mud without at least one hand free to do the job, Rambo must have had a third, invisible, hand.*

Q. I didn't care much for *Kalifornia*. It wasn't the movie as much as the Kentucky license plate on the front of the car they were taking cross-country. I am from Louisville and cannot remember ever seeing anyone from Kentucky being portrayed in a movie or on television as anything but poor white trash. Wherever I travel, people find out I'm from Kentucky, and I immediately become a hillbilly. I wonder if Tom Cruise has the same problem when people find out he is from Kentucky. (David M. Geary, Louisville, Ky.)

A. I thought you were exaggerating the situation until I used a computer database to compile a list of movies set in Kentucky. It listed fourteen titles, of which four were about horses, two were about the Civil War, and eight were about hillbillies. Or maybe only seven, since I'm not sure how to classify *Return of the Living Dead.*

Q. I just saw your Answer Man complaint by David Geary about "the Kentucky license plate on the front of the car" in the film *Kalifornia,* and I'd object for another reason: We don't *have* front license plates in Kentucky! (Ed Ellers, Louisville, Ky.)

A. Nor is California spelled with a "K."

Q. In one of the opening scenes of *Nobody's Fool,* Paul Newman is told by the Melanie Griffith character that her husband, played by Bruce Willis, has just undergone open-heart surgery. In most movies, we would simply accept that. But this movie later has a strip-poker scene where Willis is wearing only his shorts, and we can clearly see that he has no visible scars from the surgery. What gives? (Douglas Brown, Chicago)

A. I think the director was counting on you to play more attention to Willis's girlfriend, sitting next to him, who is also wearing only her shorts.

Q. You had a Q&A dealing with Bruce Willis's lack of a bypass surgical scar in the poker scene in *Nobody's Fool.* You suggested that the director probably figured everyone would be too busy looking at the topless woman next to Bruce to notice that he didn't have a scar. Well, obviously *you* were too busy staring at Willis's naked companion, since he *does* have a surgery scar on his chest. It runs from his trachea to his navel. Yes, it is faded and covered by some chest hair (Okay, a lot of chest hair) but that is to be expected seven or eight months after surgery. Just felt the record should be set straight, since it seemed startling that a veteran director like Robert Benton would make such an obvious error. Next time, maybe you should look at Willis instead. (Melinda Benson, Cleveland, Ohio)

A. If you think, for even one instant, that I'd rather look at a topless woman than a surgical scar . . .

Q. My wife and I just watched *Speed* for the second time on home video, and want to know if you caught the same edit snafu as we did. Early in the movie, Keanu Reeves shoots Jeff Daniels in the *left* leg to free him from Dennis Hopper in the parking lot. The next scene shows Daniels and Reeves getting accolades from the city and Daniels has his cane in his *right* hand and a bandage on his *right* leg. At the end of the following scene (in the bar celebrating), Daniels leaves with the cane back in his *left* hand while he favors his *left* leg. (Forget that both legs seem just perfect as he enters the window to Hopper's home the next morning in full SWAT gear.) Also, why does Hopper's holding the phone with his right hand against his left ear seem so unnatural? I know his left thumb was blown off, but I've yet to find anyone who will put a phone in their right hand and raise it crossover-style to their left ear to talk. Believe me, I've been trying this on people for a few weeks! Does it strike you as odd? (Gary G., Naeyaert, Lansing, Mich.)

A. Not as odd as it probably does to the people you've been trying it on.

Q. I recall reading that Jodie Foster had *awfully* nice teeth for a backwoods girl. Just wondering if you shared this critique. (Nick Stadler, Potomac, Md.)

A. She has nice teeth even for a Hollywood star.

Q. More and more films have night scenes with steam coming from all over to emphasize the drama. Today I just got suckered and saw the film *Bad Boys,* which takes place in Miami. In the opening scene, there was steam everywhere: in the buildings, in the stairways, on the streets. I'm from Florida, but I've been gone a few years. Have they started installing underground steam-heating lines in Miami? When I lived there most buildings had air-conditioning instead of steam heat. Or, as I suspect, have the "production designers" finally lost their marbles? Come on guys, let's try to make an action movie that doesn't look like a bad MTV clip. (Richard Hubbell, Arlington, Va.)

A. That's not steam. It's smoke from the dry ice used to cool the fresh stone crabs at Joe's.

Q. We saw *The Madness of King George* the other night. Pretty good. However, the first scene showed some heavy wooden doors.

As the camera panned in you could read the graffiti carved on the doors. The most prominent was the date "1867." It bothered the heck out of me to start the movie with this obvious continuity issue. Was this a director's idea of a joke or an IQ test ? (John T. Bear, Atlanta, Ga.)

A. The scene was shot at Eton College, which is about five hundred years old, and students have been carving graffiti on that door for all of that time, according to Nicholas Hytner, director of the film: "We didn't notice the date until we were editing the film. We couldn't go back and reshoot because the actors were unavailable and college was in full session. We were confident that the credit roll at the beginning of the film would obscure some of what couldn't be hidden by editing and filters."

Q. What would you say is the all-time most embarrassing prop goof? An example: I watched *Oceans 11* yesterday and the most unintentionally funny moment in the movie was when a studious doctor told Richard Conte he might die of a serious illness. The chest X ray the doctor was studying was upside-down. (James O'Brien, Hermosa Beach, Calif.)

A. I liked it in *Jaws IV* when Michael Caine's seaplane landed on the ocean and was chewed into toothpicks by the giant shark. On board a nearby yacht, his death is mourned—until he pulls himself on board, miraculously alive. Even better, his shirt is dry.

Q. Thought you might get a chuckle out of our local news on KNBC in Los Angeles. The anchor, Chuck Henry, did a news story on the "controversial" opening of *Kids* in Florida and said that at one theater they gave away condominiums to all the attendees. When he finished, Kelly Lange advised him that what they gave out were actually condoms. (Elliott S. Mitchell, Costa Mesa, Calif.)

A. Ironic, since the whole movie is about how these kids never use condominiums.

Q. I haven't seen *Strange Days* yet, but the ad campaign is driving me nuts. December 31, 1999, is *not* the last day of the century! That distinction applies to December 31, 2000. Doesn't stuff like that get you? I hope they don't refer to that in the film itself. (David Montgomery, Bakersfield, Calif.)

A. Maybe *that* explains why the world doesn't end at midnight the way people in the movie expect! Attention, cult members: Take a long, hard look at anyone who tells you the world will end on the last day of 1999.

Q. It occurred to me while watching *The Scarlet Letter* to wonder: How many young women in colonial New England shaved under their arms, do you suppose? (Will Shank, Toronto, Canada)

A. Even more to the point, how many of them took long, luxurious baths in front of peepholes, so that other people could see if they did?

Q. In *Executive Decision,* which movie executive was responsible for only having two pilots in the flight between Athens, Greece, and Washington, D.C.? On a 747-300 or earlier, there would definitely be a captain, first officer, and second officer and possibly even a substitute pilot. I guess that wouldn't have given the cockpit a place for the hijacker to stand nor an ample bookshelf of manuals lined up like cookbooks. (Jim Simon, Villa Park, Calif.)

A. Must have been a cut-rate airline. Remember that after one flight attendant was killed in the galley, that left only Halle Berry and Marla Trump to serve those four hundred passengers.

Q. In *The Nutty Professor,* when the professor puts a frozen TV dinner in the microwave, my seven-year-old nephew noticed that he forgot to remove the foil first! Add this Hollywood mistake to the list. (Elaine Procento, Hoffman Estates, Ill.)

A. That professor, what a nut.

Q. Just saw the movie *Chain Reaction* and agreed with your assessment. You didn't mention some of the amusing "gaffes" in the script, however, which a good Chicagoan such as yourself must have noticed. For example, Keanu Reeves meets Morgan Freeman in the Field Museum and then leads a band of bad guys on a chase down a hall and into the Museum of Science and Industry. I guess when the director decided to move those two museums to Washington, D.C., he saw fit to join them together. Slick move. (Martin Densch, Janesville, Wisc.)

A. At least the chase didn't continue in the Smithsonian.

Blue Eyes

Q. Is it possible for beginning actors to "make it" in movies if they do *not* have blue eyes? It's getting so that now even black actors stand a better chance if they have blue eyes (one is the actress who played a soldier in Danny DeVito's *Renaissance Man* and is also in *Clueless*—Stacey Dash). Add to the list: Tom Cruise, Robin Williams, Don Johnson, Brooke Shields, Kurt Russell, John Travolta, Richard Gere, Jonathan Taylor Thomas, and rumor has it that Brad Pitt wore brown contact lenses in *Seven* so he wouldn't look so good. I feel the trend toward blue-eyed actors has been in place for a long time, and I just noticed it. If you are not interested in the movie, looking at eye color gives you something to do. (Don Howard, San Jose, Calif.)

A. How do you handle the black-and-white films?

Books into Films

Q. *The Scarlet Letter* has been read by everyone who ever completed a high school English Lit course. By filming a drastically-altered version of the story, the producers have set themselves up to be criticized for having changed a "classic" for the sake of "updating" the story. The amusing thing is that when this was required reading for us all, we hated the story. I recall one English instructor being quite put off when a student referred to Nathaniel Hawthorne as "a purveyor of boring drivel." Amazing how we have come to value the author with the passing years. (Larry Jones, Ontario, Calif.)

A. I don't think it's what they did, but how they did it that has audiences snickering. Few people have surpassed James Fenimore Cooper in the department of purveying boring drivel, but no one complained that *The Last of the Mohicans* was unfaithful to his book—because the movie was good. Sir Walter Scott is another unparalleled boring drivel purveyer, but the movie of his novel *Rob Roy* also escaped criticism, maybe because no one now alive has ever been able to read it. The producers of *The Scarlet Letter* committed the double error of making a bad movie about a book people have read.

Q. Though critics try to enter a theater without preconceived notions of what the film should be, what happens when a film is made from a monster best-seller that everyone seems to have read? I was working in a warehouse when *The Shining* hit paperback, and every single guy in that warehouse (except one) read the book (two copies circulated until they fell apart). My then-girlfriend worked at a T-shirt shop at a mall, and everyone *she* knew read the book. My parents read it. My grandmother read it. My best friend who does construction read it. We all went out to see the film—and thought it sucked. It was the dumbed-down version of the book. In a case like this, isn't the public better serviced by an informed critic who has read the book? (W.C. Martell, Studio City, Calif.)

A. Interesting question. I usually say I'm reviewing the movie, not the book, and that the movie's duty is to be a good movie, whether or not it's "faithful" to the book. When I know a book is going to be made into a movie, I avoid reading it, because I don't want to form preconceptions. But often I have read the book, and in those cases I can't help comparing my mental images with the screen images (I was particularly distracted during *Bonfire of the Vanities*). Not everything in a book will work in a movie, however, and in the last analysis I think it's the director's duty to keep what he can use and throw out or change the rest.

Q. I saw *Four Weddings and a Funeral*, and was very moved by the poem read at the funeral service. What is its title and author? (Susan Nolan, Chicago)

A. It is *Funeral Blues*, by W.H. Auden, and an edition of his poems, tied to the movie, has recently been published in paperback.

Boom Mikes

Q. Please tell me why in big budget movies you can often see the boom microphone in the picture. I have seen it frequently in many big budget pictures. The cinematographer must be incompetent to not notice this, along with the editors. Why do they leave it in? (Paul M. Nowak, Farmington Hills, Mich.)

A. The Answer Man gets this question about once a week, and answers it about every six months. When you can see the sound boom in a movie, it is usually not the fault of the filmmakers, but of the theater projectionist, who has framed the movie incorrectly. All movies contain more picture area than you are ever intended to see, in order to allow the picture to "bleed" over the sides of the screen. Sometimes a boom strays into the "head room," but if the projectionist has done his framing correctly you will never see it.

Q. I saw *Ransom* this weekend and was amazed by the number of times the boom mike was visible. I saw the mike twenty different times once I started counting. I could hear people in the theater commenting on it during and after the movie. I found myself relieved whenever the movie moved outside since I knew I would not have to worry about it ruining those shots. I haven't noticed anything quite like it in other movies. Sometimes there are mistakes but I have not seen one mistake repeated so often and so prominently. I just kept wondering how they missed it or if they just didn't care. (Tracey Storey, Columbia, Md.)

A. When you see a boom mike in a movie, it is almost always the fault of the projectionist in the theater you are attending, who has "framed" the movie incorrectly. However, reports of visible boom mikes in *Ransom* have been epidemic all over the country, even prompting an article in the *Los Angeles Times* where Brian Grazer, the film's producer, says the mikes will not show if the film is properly projected, but concedes the film may have cut things a little too close. For a technical explanation of this phenomenon, I turned to Jeffrey P. Graebner of Los Angeles, whose knowledge of film procedures is encyclopedic. His detailed analysis:

"A decision in the filming of *Ransom* may have caused a common projection error to be much more noticeable than usual. Standard 35mm film has an aspect ratio of 1.33-to-1, but most American films are matted in the projector to the standard 1.85-to-1 ratio. The aspect ratio of a television screen is almost exactly the same as the full, unmasked 35mm film. This means that a common compromise used when a film is later transferred to video is to simply transfer the entire frame. That's why you sometimes see more head and foot room on a video than you saw in the movie theater. If they didn't do that, they'd have to crop from the sides. In order to accommodate this practice, many cinematographers make an effort to keep the film 'TV safe.' What that means is that they still compose the film for the 1.85:1 theatrical aspect ratio, but make an effort to keep boom mikes and other garbage from showing up even in the portion of the image intended to be behind the mattes. For some reason, the makers of *Ransom* apparently decided not to bother to keep the film 'TV safe,' meaning that the boom mike frequently shows up in the portion of the image intended to be hidden behind the mattes. If the film is projected properly, this is no problem, but if the projectionist screws up the framing (causing you to see the portion of the image you aren't supposed to see), then the mikes are visible."

Box Office

Q. There was an interesting article recently comparing *Demolition Man* to *Last Action Hero*. The article pointed out that both films cost almost exactly the same and ended up with almost exactly the same final box office take. Despite this, *Demolition Man* was considered a minor hit, while *Last Action Hero* was considered a major flop. The general conclusion of the article was that it was all a matter of perceptions. (Jeffrey Graebner, Los Angeles)

A. The AP article reported that both movies cost around $70 million and grossed about $55 million. After foreign revenues and video are added in, both films may even turn a profit. Yet *Hero* was portrayed as Arnold Schwarzenegger's bomb, and *Demolition* was seen as Sylvester Stallone's comeback. The perception is probably based on the recent box office records of the two stars: Schwarzenegger was expected to break all records, while Hollywood was surprised that Stallone, whose career has been lagging, did so well.

Q. The press keeps talking about how *Jurassic Park* has outgrossed *E.T.*, and how *Aladdin* is the all-time top-selling video. If inflation would be taken into account (i.e., use the dollar value at the time of Charlie Chaplin's *Modern Times*, for instance), which film would now be the top-grossing film? Should the videocassette editions be included in the calculations? People lined up for more than a year to see *Star Wars*. *Jurassic Park* had a strong three months and then the video came out. (Sylvain DeSeve, St.-Laurent, Canada)

A. The best way to measure popularity would be by head count, but who knows how many people saw *Birth of a Nation*, or one of the many rereleases of *Gone With the Wind*? Jon Woolf of the CompuServe ShowBiz Forum points out that since ticket prices have doubled since *Star Wars* came out in 1977, it would be Hollywood's first $400 million film if it came out today.

Q. Re your suggestion of an expanded weekly movie best-seller list that would name the top foreign, art, and documentary films: an interesting idea, but it could have adverse effects. "Art" films rarely make more than $100,000 a week. Mr. and Mrs. Public, looking at the $50 million that *Batman Forever* pulls in, may regard the alternative list as a sort of consolation prize. What some magazines have started, and this may help, is a list of the Top Ten Per Screen Grosses. This is fairer to films in limited release. (David Gerrard, Chappaqua, N.Y.)

A. People likely to go to alternative films will not expect *Batman*-style grosses, but would be interested to learn that *The Postman*, *Crumb*, and *Kids*, for example, are doing susprisingly well. Still, per-screen averages would also get that across. The point is to give equal recognition to films that do not open on two thousand screens and therefore cannot ever hope to make the first team.

Q. I've noticed an interesting correlation between the films without opening credits and their box office success. Those movies without opening credits have done better than those with opening credits. For example, *E.T.*, the *Stars Wars* trilogy, and *Jurassic Park* all lack these opening credits. Maybe if all producers left the opening credits out, we would see many $300 million grosses! What do you think? (Mason Mandy, Birmingham, Ala.)

A. On the other hand, maybe if all movies were produced by Steven Spielberg or George Lucas, we would see more $300 million grosses. Another possibility: If the opening credits were left off of Pauly Shore movies, the audience might stay longer.

Q. Now that the grosses are in, it seems that *Executive Decision* is never going to be number one at the box office, despite good reviews, the best Steven Seagal scene ever put on film, and good word of mouth. Stranger still is the film that has managed to stay at number one for four weeks in a row: *The Birdcage*, set in a transvestite nightclub. Would *Executive Decision* have been a bigger hit if two of its stars, B.D. Wong and John Leguizamo, appeared in drag, as they did, respectively, in the play *Madame Butterfly* and the movie *To Wong Foo*? How long will it be before someone in Hollywood combines the bus films *Priscilla, Queen of the Desert* and *Speed*? (William C. Martell, Studio City, Calif.)

A. Did you miss the skirts in *Braveheart*?

Q. Those of us outside the movie business are both amused and confused by stories of Hollywood's "creative financing," where a movie can "lose money" while generating revenue equal to several times the production costs. In the real world, if a company were to lose money on each item it sells, that company would soon go broke and close. A movie studio can produce a number of movies in a year, each movie can "lose money" so the studio doesn't have to pay the "net participants," and the studio can somehow post a profit at the end of the year. Did I miss something? (Steven Stine, Buffalo Grove, Ill.)

A. I predict a great election victory for the first political party that puts Hollywood accountants in charge of the national debt. The country would continue to lose money, but we'd all get rich in the process.

Q. You wrote about the record-breaking opening of *Mission: Impossible,* and said the studio was surprised by the numbers. Paramount executives did as much as they could to guarantee a huge opening. The film played on well over four thousand screens, more than any film in history. There were advance showings on Tuesday—which, I gather, can be legitimately added to the Wednesday opening's numbers, therefore boosting them even more. *Twister,* by comparison, made $36 million, on about half the number of screens, so its per-screen average was much higher. And although *M:I* beat *Jurassic Park*'s record by $1 million, it had a lower per-screen average, since *Park* was shown on less than three thousand screens. (Gregory Tyler, Greenfield, Mass.)

A. Excellent point. Studio marketing strategies now depend on getting everybody into the tent right away, instead of hoping for long runs. *M:I*'s second-weekend receipts at the turnstiles were down sharply, but the movie was quickly over $100 million.

Braveheart

Q. In the ads for *Braveheart,* the following quote is used: "Every man dies, not every man really lives." Since this ad will be exposed to millions, was it really necessary to make an error in punctuation? (Ashley St. Ives, Chicago)

A. Good point. After the word "dies," it would have been acceptable to use a period, a semi-colon, or even a dash. It wasn't easy to single out an incorrect punctuation mark and use it, but the ad succeeds.

Q. I read that Paramount is rereleasing the movie *Braveheart* on September 15, 1995, for a limited time in about one thousand theaters nationwide. Is this a new precedent for a motion picture that had its premiere just two and a half months ago? I personally bombarded Paramount with fax after fax telling them that they severely "mismarketed" this brilliant motion picture. . . . I guess they finally got my message. What was their mistake? They neglected to promote the film to women. At *all* of the showings of *Braveheart* that I've attended (and there have been many), it has been *women* who have been profoundly affected by its message. Overseas, where the movie was distributed by Fox, it was marketed as a "romance." I expect some profound marketing changes with *Braveheart's* rerelease by Paramount. (Sue Ritchie, Phoenix)

A. In my opinion, *Braveheart* rather surprised Paramount, and many others in the movie business, by being as good as it was. They expected a swashbuckler, and got a sensational action and romance picture, directed by Mel Gibson with real style and vision. Although the movie is already a success, the September rerelease is intended to "reintroduce" it as part of a campaign to position it for Academy Award nominations. The ads will portray it as a classier, *Lawrence of Arabia*–type epic, rather than just an adventure.

As everyone knows, the rerelease was a stunning success, probably the linchpin in Braveheart's *Oscar campaign. Spring and summer movies are usually seen as crowd-pleasers, while the autumn releases are more often viewed as Oscar contenders. Exhibitors and distributors churn new movies so quickly that word of mouth has little time to build for hard-sell pictures;* Braveheart's *W.O.M. presumably built during its hiatus from the big screen.*

Q. You have stated that *Braveheart* is the most violent film to ever win the Oscar as Best Picture. That ignores cinema history: See *Silence of the Lambs, Unforgiven, Godfather 1 and 2*, and *Platoon.* Mel Gibson reacted with stunned aplomb to your question on TV, and rightly so. (James Buchanan, Antioch, Calif.)

A. In my opinion, *Braveheart* is at least as violent as the films you mention. Mel Gibson might agree. When the movie was released, he told me: "I wanted the audience to feel like they were in the middle of it and to experience the full hell. . . . I wanted to make it shocking, hard, and brutal, and juxtapose that against what I think is, really, a romantic picture. When we first cut the picture, it was worse. Not for me but for some guy who just came in to a test screening from eating an ice-cream cone and he was, like, he couldn't believe it, because there were brains flying everywhere. It was too much. The object is to keep the audience in the theater, in the seats, so we had to kind of bring it down a level."

Bright Ideas

Q. Here's an idea. What about starting a Movie Astrology column? People could write in with their three favorite (or most despised) movies, from which the astrologer could figure out the comings and goings of their innermost selves. (Mark Steven Heyman, Graham, Wash.)

A. How would you determine the astrological sign of each movie? By the day and time when the deal was signed?

Q. Rush Limbaugh and Howard Stern share the same birthday—and you don't believe in astrology! (Danielle D. Dooley, Santa Rosa, Calif.)

A. Even more amazing, they share it with Beavis and Butt-head.

Q. I know that you will be interested in the AAI, or Appropriate Age Index. This is a totally new way to rate movies and may well replace the outdated MPAA!

The AAI breaks every movie into six separate categories: Sexual Content, Nudity, Mature Themes, Personal Violence, Strong Language, and General Violence. Each category receives a rating from 0 to 5. A "0" would indicate that there is none of that topic in the film. A "5" would indicate a great amount. After the ratings in the separate categories are determined, they are added together to express in years the *minimum* appropriate age for that film, plus or minus three years.

There is a lot more to it, of course, but you get the idea. People who have been reading the AAI are calling it the "movie rating system for the next century"! (Tim Bonomo, Corning, N.Y.)

A. Hmmm. According to my calculations here, *Basic Instinct* shouldn't be seen by anybody under thirty. I think the system works.

Q. In your review of *Nico Icon,* you referred to the famous Andy Warhol statement, "In the future, everyone will be famous for fifteen minutes." An art history professor taught me a different perspective on Andy Warhol's prophecy that I find more meaningful. The professor argued that what Warhol meant was not that every John Doe would have his fifteen minutes, but that mankind's collective attention span would become atrophied to the point that nothing would hold our interest for over fifteen minutes, regardless of how famous or important that subject seemed. In my opinion, we are not far from there, as evidenced by the overabundance of neatly packaged TV shows that offer five-minute montages on the latest Hollywood soft news. Everything is important today. Something else will be important tomorrow, or right after these messages. What do you think? (Roberto Soltero, Guaynabo, Puerto Rico)

A. Sorry, but your question is so long that I forgot how it began.

Q. Did you hear Dick Armey's remarks about the v-chip? He's afraid that kids will be able to hack into the Pentagon computers with it!! Can you imagine that these guys are legislating this technology that they know *nothing* about? (Jill Cozzi, Fort Lee, N.J.)

A. No one should be allowed to vote on the v-chip or the Internet until he has demonstrated that he knows how to successfully get online and download tomorrow's weather report. The v-chip is a good idea if it helps parents monitor their children's TV-watching. Is Armey afraid it can also tune out violence in the Pentagon?

Budgets

Q. Kevin Costner spent $200 million on *Waterworld,* and Mel Gibson spent another fortune on *Braveheart.* Shouldn't moviegoers be protesting these gargantuan budgets? (C.H. Smith, Chicago)

A. Why? Are they billing it all to your credit cards? I've never been able to understand public indignation over big budgets. Hey, as long as they're not charging you $60 to see these films, how can you lose? The more they spend on a movie that still costs you the same ticket price, the better—right?

Q. I enjoy watching movies funded by credit cards and experimental drugs. The people who make these movies tend to have the most compelling stories to tell. Perhaps they have had these conversations and images pent up, waiting for the medium through which to express themselves. Can you please recommend some of your favorite inexpensively made films? (Douglas N. Stotland, Chicago)

A. I don't know about the experimental drugs, but some movies have been funded by credit cards, notably Matty Rich's *Straight Out of Brooklyn*, with a budget of $24,000 and much help from his grandmother's MasterCard. Other recent movies made for under $30,000 include *Clerks*, *The Brothers McMullen*, and, the champ at about $8,000, *El Mariachi*. The spiritual godfather of all of these films is John Cassavetes, who made his films with little money and a lot of help from his friends.

Canada

Q. Ever notice that if a movie is filmed in Canada every single thing that would point to the film being set there is obliterated? Do filmmakers think Americans are (a) so bigoted or (b) so stupid that they couldn't accept a film being set in Canada? Or (c) do they think American viewers would expect a line of dancing men singing *Alouette* on every corner? (Charlene Smith, Chicago)

A. (c)

Q. Saw Jackie Chan's *Rumble in the Bronx*, and couldn't help noticing that the Bronx in the movie has beautiful beaches, golf courses, and a mountain range in the background. The closing credits list several firms and organizations in Vancouver, Canada. Was the movie by any chance shot there? (Ronnie Barzell, Chicago)

A. Yes, it was. But special effects and the "blue screen" process were used in many shots to add the beaches, mountains, and golf courses so typical of the Bronx.

Candles

Q. In your review of *Two Bits*, you wrote about movie scenes in which countless candles are suddenly available, and you also cited *Taxi Driver* and *Interview With the Vampire*. There was a scene in *Waiting to Exhale* where the coffee table is covered with candles and I was thinking the same thing—whenever there are candles in a movie, there is never just one. Another film off the top of my head that had a scene with "countless candles" in it was *Mad Love* with Drew Barrymore, after the couple moves into the run-down apartment. (Tom Crosley)

A. Countless candles are often used in touching scenes involving love or reconciliation. I think the time is ripe for one of those Leslie Nielsen satires where the beautiful blonde is eager to be seduced, and he keeps her waiting for days while he lights seven thousand candles.

Cannes

Q. Is the Cannes Film Festival open to the public? I hope to attend one of these days but do not know whether I should wait until I'm actually showing a film there. If one has to be a bona fide member of the film industry (as opposed to a member in training), it'll probably be a while before I'll see the light of day there. (Michael Hidalgo, New York University)

A. Technically, it's a trade convention and not open to the public. But a limited number of seats are made available every day to the official screenings. It is sometimes possible to talk your way into the "market" screenings in the local cinemas. And sometimes you can talk people out of their tickets, or obtain invitations to special events.

Q. Since you have been covering the Cannes Film Festival— were those leopard-skin-wearing ladies there this year? (Rebecca Costello, Ithaca, N.Y.)

A. You are referring to the legendary mother-daughter team that attends every year dressed in leopard-skin dresses, and promenades up and down the Croisette, photographed by everyone simply because they exist. Yes, they were back. But this year the trade papers lamented the presence of "faux leopard-ladies"—phony leopard-lady impersonators. It is a sad commentary when even a hard-working leopard lady is ripped off by a celebrity lookalike.

Q. Often after the prizes are given out at the Cannes Film Festival, there are charges that the vote was rigged or the jury tampered with. Is there any truth to these charges? (Charles Smith, Chicago)

A. "They bent over backwards to avoid the slightest appearance of influence," jury member Greta Scacchi told me, the day after the 1996 awards were announced. "On the day of the awards, they locked us up in a villa in the hills above Cannes, and wouldn't even let us make or receive phone calls. There were armed guards at the doors. Gilles Jacob, the festival director, sat in on our deliberations, but didn't utter a single word."

Casablanca

Q. Something has been nagging me for years. In *Casablanca*, in the scene where Claude Rains arrests Paul Henreid, and Bogart pulls a gun on Rains, Bogart tells Rains to call the airport. Instead, he calls Major Strasser, the Nazi. *Why??* All through the film Rains never acted pro-Berlin unless Strasser was there, and then he "put on a show" for the Germans. Rains never would have called Strasser; there was nothing in it for him. Even if Strasser had caught Bogart, Bergman, and Henreid, he would have arrested Rains for letting them get that far. I just can't come up with a good reason why Rains called Strasser. (Barry J. Ingram, Baton Rouge, La.)

A. Maybe for dramatic reasons. If Rains had not called Strasser, Bogart could not have killed Strasser, and Rains could not have said, "Round up the usual suspects." Instead, the movie would have ended with everybody just going to the airport and getting on the plane: an anticlimax, denying us some of the best moments on the movie.

Now what *I've* always wondered is, why Bogart and Rains didn't get on the plane, too? There were only two "exit permits," yes, but with Strasser dead and Rains starting a beautiful friendship with Bogie, who was to stop them? Remember that when Henreid and Bergman walk toward the plane, there is no one left to even *care* if they have exit permits. And permits would not have been needed to land at the other end of the flight. Henreid, the noble Resistance hero, could have vouched for Bogart and Rains as the men who saved his life.

Q. Near the beginning of *Casablanca*, Peter Lorre as Ugarte is telling Rick about two letters of transit that have been stolen from

Nazi couriers who were killed in the desert. In his charmingly slimy way, Ugarte says, ". . . letters of transit signed by General de Gaulle. Cannot be rescinded, not even questioned." What? Why would Nazi couriers be carrying letters signed by the leader of the Free French? And why would those letters not be questioned by the Nazis or the Vichy French who controlled Casablanca? De Gaulle was their enemy. Anyone in Casablanca trying to use letters of transit signed by de Gaulle would be arrested and then would probably commit suicide or die while trying to escape. (Frederic Townsend, Lake Bluff, Ill.)

A. This is a real mystery. In the published version of the screenplay, the line reads: ". . . General de Gaulle [Marshal Weygand]." The Internet Movie Database says, "It sounds like Ugarte says that the letters of transit are signed by 'General de Gaulle.' leading to confusion as de Gaulle had no authority in that area at the time. Peter Lorre actually says 'General Weygand,' but his accent makes it difficult to understand." Since "de Gaulle" and "Weygand" do not sound much alike in any accent, I checked out my laserdisc of the scene. What Lorre says sounds like a cross between "jenna-rye dee-go" and "jenna-rye wee-gond." So, which is it? Probably Weygand. But why does the published screenplay give both possibilities?

Q. Re your return visit to *Casablanca* in your newspaper series "The Great Movies"—Whoa! I've seen *Casablanca* many times and never thought that Inspector Renault was homosexual. I see him as a heterosexual using his position to have sex with women, particularly young, beautiful women. I agree that he has an adolescent male crush on Rick because Rick is charming, enigmatic, heroic in control, etc. Please tell what you saw that I didn't. (Kent Westmoreland, New Orleans)

A. I said in my article that Louis Renault, the police captain played by Claude Rains, was "subtly homosexual." This generated a lot of questions, which follow:

Q. Hmm . . . I seem to remember Louie being a little miffed at Rick for his act of charity that robbed Louie of the opportunity to bed "the young girl who will do anything to help her husband." Maybe you think he was trying to bed the husband, instead? Actually, since Louie ended the film (a) acting in an admirable fashion, and (b) still being alive, by the Hollywood conventions of the era, that pretty much rules him out as a homosexual character, subtle or otherwise. (Paul McElligott, Lake Forest, Calif.)

Q. Sometimes Renault is not so subtle. "What kind of a man is Rick?" he says to Ilsa. "Well, if I were a woman, I should be in love with Rick." And remember the rejoinder Rick tosses out to the young Hungarian woman pleading for her husband's safe passage. The woman suggests her husband has had to approach Renault directly, and Rick—knowing full well what this would entail—replies, "I see Renault has become broad-minded." On the surface this seems to be an astonishing comment for a 1942 film, and for many years I thought I had simply misinterpreted it. Even when masked as a coy throwaway line, I always thought it masterful. (Kevin Hendzel, Washington, D.C.)

A. And of course there's the film's enigmatic last line, when Rick says, "Louis, I think this is the beginning of a beautiful friendship." I've analyzed *Casablanca* half a dozen times on various campuses, using the shot-by-shot stop-action approach. Each time, the audience and I have picked up on something about Renault's manner, about his speech, about certain lines of dialogue, that suggest the possibility that he may be either latently or secretly homosexual. Renault does indeed use his influence to pick up women, but the more I see the movie, the more I wonder what he does with them. The recent documentary *The Celluloid Closet* is illuminating in its study of the way Hollywood slipped homosexual characters into movies in violation of the Production Code.

In my review of Barb Wire, *the movie starring Pam Anderson Lee as a bar owner in a free city under threat from neo-Nazis, I observed how closely the movie paralleled the plot of* Casablanca. *But there was one scene missing, I said: The famous scene where the Nazis order the band to play "Wacht am Rhein," and the bar patrons drown them out with La Marseillaise. In* Barb Wire, *the bad guys are right-wing "Congressionals," and the bar patrons all wear leather and chains and are into S&M. So, I asked readers what the anthem of the villains would be, and what* song the S&Msters would sing to drown them out. *The best answer came from Andy Ihnatko, of Westwood, Massachusets:*

"For the Nazi-style government, I suggest the National Anthem of the USSR. First, because it's the most kick-butt national anthem in the world. "So-YUZ NERUSHIMI ResPUBLIC SVOBODNIK!!!" . . . no other national anthem is nearly so effective at inciting dim-witted teenaged conscripts to go off and invade whichever country you happen to think needs to be taught some manners. Second, because no one else seems to be using it at the moment. For the freedom-loving S&M people, the obvious choice is *Henry the Eighth I Am.* They'd win the challenge in a walkover, because it's perfect musical sherbet. Once you hear it, it completely smears away your ability to think of any other song at all, and after one whip-through even the Evil Government People would be belting out "SECOND VERSE, Same as the FIRST!!!"

Casting Decisions

Q. That HBO movie, *Barbarians at the Gate.* Did the producers get any heat from the wheeler-dealers who were portrayed on the screen? (Harris Allsworth, Chicago)

A. Veteran moviemaker Ray Stark, who produced the film, told me the principals were mostly content with their screen portray-als. But he got an early call from buyout artist Henry Kravis, wor-ried about how he would come across. Kravis is not the tallest of men. Stark told him: "If you don't cause any trouble, Jonathan Pryce will play you. Otherwise, I'll get Danny DeVito." That was the last they heard from him.

Q. Re the made-for-TV movie *The Late Shift*: When you make a movie about someone as entertaining as Letterman, you need to have him played by an actor who can at least approximate wit. The guy playing Leno was a little better, but neither of these guys are imaginable as great comic talents in this movie—and that is ulti-mately what it is all about. (J. Walker, Nashville, Tenn.)

A. Exactly. You can't imagine anyone bidding millions for those doofuses.

Christmas Movies

Q. Out of the countless movie renditions of *A Christmas Carol*, which version of the Dickens classic do you think is the best? Which is the worst? (Bret Wiersbe, Griffith, Ind.)

A. The best is probably the famous 1951 British version of *A Christmas Carol*, with Alastair Sim as Scrooge. The worst is probably *Scrooged* (1988), a miscalculated Bill Murray comedy that didn't quite work. The sleeper is *Scrooge* (1970), a musical with Albert Finney wonderful in the title role. You didn't ask, but my favorite holiday movie (after *It's a Wonderful Life*) is *A Christmas Story* (1983), based on Jean Shepherd's memories of growing up in northern Indiana.

Q. Saw *It's a Wonderful Life* again the other night and suddenly realized that a key scene is fundamentally silly. George Bailey stands at the bridge, determined to kill himself by jumping off. Then Clarence enters the picture . . . and George *jumps* into the river to save him, coming up unscathed! So either George is rather unskilled at choosing methods of suicide, or the entire final quarter of the film was unnecessary. Also, why is George so chilled by the fate of Mary, his intended, in the film's Alternate Reality? By all indications, she's a well-dressed, well-groomed, intelligent, and independent woman with a career and a position of responsibility in the community. What's the problem? (Andy Ihnatko, Westwood, Mass.)

A. The problem is obvious. Mary is doing so well she may not need George. All successful women make men fear redundancy. Your first question is more difficult, but my guess is, when you jump into an icy river to save an angel, somehow your own safety is guaranteed. (Be absolutely *sure* it is an angel before you jump.)

Q. Every Christmas my family and I watch *It's a Wonderful Life* and wonder if Jim Henson paid tribute to this classic by naming his characters "Bert and Ernie" after the cop and taxi driver. (Liz Taylor, Houston)

A. "No, it's just a coincidence," says Jill Silverman of Jim Henson Productions.

Cinematography

Q. I'm a photographer, and have been wondering—who started the Orange and Blue Movement? All those movies where each scene has to have something blue and something orange in it? A good example would be *Trading Moms*, with Sissy Spacek. There are lots of others in the last two years. I think it began with night city scenes mimicking neon reflections on faces. The actor usually has a warm (orange) main light on his/her face from a 45-degree angle, and has a cold (blue) kicker light skimming the shadow side of his face. Warm colors appear to move forward and cold colors recede, so it adds depth to an object. Someone grabbed this theme of color and a movement began. (Jim Langley, Phoenix, Ariz.)

A. Frankly, Jim, I thought you might be hallucinating. But I referred your question to the great cinematographer Owen Roizman, a five-time Oscar nominee. He responds:

"I don't think he is hallucinating. When we are shooting at night we have a tendency to look for reasonable sources of light to justify or enhance what we are shooting. When we are in areas that don't have many sources, we tend to turn to 'moonlight' as one of them. Some people fantasize that moonlight is blue whereas others envision it as a cold white light. Neither is correct, but that is a long story. The 'blue' believers generally use the 'moonlight' as a backlight or edge light, otherwise known as a kicker. What sets off the blue very nicely is a warm tone, such as orange. Hence the orange and blue.

"The other approach is that generally a warmer tone of front or side light is very pleasing at night, like fire or candlelight, or for that matter a dimmed lamplight. If everything is lit with just the warm tones it has a tendency to get 'muddy' looking but if some blue light is introduced somewhere, either in the shadows or backlight, etc., it gives the subject a much more pleasing quality.

"I used this approach on *Wyatt Earp* on almost all of my night work and I was very pleased with it. I must have done something right because I received a nomination for it. I know you hated the picture but I didn't write it so I'm off the hook."

Q. I understand Kodak has stopped producing sound Super-8 movie film, and the future of the entire format is in question. I think that this is a pity for us amateur filmmakers because 16mm is way too expensive for a hobby. (Alan Mark, Salt Lake City)

A. A company spokesman tells me Kodak has stopped producing *sound* Super-8 movie film. As soon as the current inventory is exhausted, sound Super-8 will no longer be available. The reason: "Environmental regulations have negatively impacted the manufacturing of sound stripping and in order to continue, it would take a substantial capital investment in order to retrofit the manufacturing area. Based on the low level of sound Super-8 film sales, together with declining sales trend, it doesn't make good business sense to make that kind of investment." He adds that Kodak is exploring alternatives, and will continue to offer Super-8 without sound.

Class System

Q. I saw *To Die For* the other day, and thought that class and ethnicity were as significant as themes in that movie as TV and the media. I have not, however, read any reviews mentioning the class dimension. I had largely the same reaction when I watched *Quiz Show* last year. Am I somehow holding repressed Marxist yearnings or has no one else noticed? (David Rhee, Berkeley, Calif.)

A. An interesting point. Nicole Kidman's ambitious TV weatherwoman looks down on her Italian American in-laws, and despises the lower-class teenagers she recruits to help with her crime; the way she puts down the Joaquin Phoenix character is especially wounding. And in *Quiz Show,* there is the subtext that the patrician WASP (Charles Van Doren) is hated by one of the Jewish characters (Herbie Stempel, the defeated contestant) and envied by the other (Richard Goodwin, the investigator), in both cases because of the world he represents. When class and ethnicity are the buried subjects of movies, critics don't always comment or even notice—perhaps because in our democracy we like to believe such prejudice doesn't exist.

Colorization

Q. Got you now, wise guy. You've been attacking colorization for years, and here's a news item that says Jean-Luc Godard, the great French director, is going to personally colorize his 1959 classic *Breathless.* What do you say to that? (Ronnie Barzell, Chicago)

A. Jean-Luc Godard has every right to colorize his film, if he wants to. He is the film's director. My argument is with third parties like Ted Turner, who have colorized other people's movies, often against their will. Godard did not, by the way, make good on his threat.

Q. What's the real story on the *Citizen Kane* affair—when Turner claimed that Orson Welles's contract prohibited him from colorizing the film? (Susan Lake, Urbana, Ill.)

A. True, it did. Turner might also have been influenced by three other factors: (1) He must have enjoyed the widespread praise he received for his restoration of *Gone With the Wind* and other films, and didn't want to reap a maelstrom of bad publicity by vandalizing *Kane*; (2) he has found that black-and-white movies on his cable stations are getting equal, or better ratings, than the colorized offerings, and (3) it's supposed to be a deep, dark secret, but the national VHS tape sales of Turner's 1989 colorized version of *Casablanca* totaled—get this—less than six hundred copies. Colorized videos are a failure in the video sales marketplace.

Q. I watched the colorized version of *Miracle on 34th Street.* What bothered me the most were the color combinations that were used. The owner of the tape replied to my inquiries by stating that the colors were the exact colors used on the sets. The colors were written down and the "colorizers" just followed the script. My problem is with some of the color combinations. The kid in the courtroom wore green pants and blue socks. In one of the last scenes, where the X-ray machine was presented, there was a green couch on a blue rug. My question is, were blue and green popular color combinations when this film was made? (Eugene Kellick, Morton Grove, Ill.)

A. Colorization is always a mistake, because the colors must be laid on top of the original black and white. Therefore, brighter colors are necessary, leading to all those men in 1930s and 1940s movies who seem to be dressed for golf. Don't believe them when they say the "original colors" were used, since the colors used for a black-and-white movie were not selected for how they looked on the set—but for how they photographed in black and white!

Comedy

Q. *Variety* reported that Trimark Pictures is planning three movies starring the comedian Carrot Top. The company's vice president, Phil Goldfine, was quoted as saying, "We think that Carrot Top is the next Pauly Shore." The *next* Pauly Shore? *Aarrgghh!!!* What do you think? (Kevin Burk, Bonney Lake, Wash.)

A. What do I think? I think Carrot Top should sue.

Q. We saw *To Die For* in a nearly empty theater. I had no trouble laughing out loud. But we also recently saw a live theater piece with no more than a dozen folks in the audience, and it was difficult to laugh out loud there, even when it was very funny. What kind of dynamic do you suppose is at work? (John Banks, Tucson, Ariz.)

A. Laughter is a form of communication, which explains why we seldom laugh at funny movies we are watching by ourselves— unless they strike us as *really* funny, in which case our laughter is accompanied by mental notes to share the joke with friends, which is a form of delayed communication. In a small movie audience we laugh so that others will hear us, but in a theater we laugh so that the actors will hear us—and isolated individual laughter in such a live situation is inhibited because it feels like a personal, rather than an anonymous, communication to the stage. While we're at it: Buddy Hackett once told me that his jokes worked better in Vegas rooms where the audience looked down at him than in rooms where they looked up at him. I have personally observed that comedies seem funnier when seen from a balcony, and dramas play better when one is looking up at the screen.

Q. I can understand your dislike for the *Kids in the Hall Brain Candy* movie (even if I don't share it). But I find it hard to believe that you didn't laugh once, especially since the film finally explained one of your favorite movie clichés: the obligatory scene in which our hero examines an abandoned house, only to be startled by a jumping, wailing cat. The movie offers a plausible explanation for the sudden appearance of these animals (and for why they only materialize at the head-and-shoulders level): The room is filled with cats, all stuck to the ceiling, and every few seconds, another one drops to the floor. Come on. You gotta admit, that's funny. (Tim Carvell, New York City)

A. I gotta admit, that's funny.

Q. Upon your recommendation we went to see *Kingpin.* The one intelligent and strong-minded woman character was in a scene in which she fought with her breasts and spent time with an abusive boyfriend. There were so many gratuitous "let's put this in because it's a cheap laugh" scenes, such as Randy Quaid's character dancing in the strip bar dressed in a bikini and glittery makeup, that ruined the movie. The filmmakers started out with a decent black comedy about prosthetics, bowling, and the Amish and just couldn't get any further. This was pure dreck. (Elisa Zuckerberg, New York)

A. I grant you the vulgarity, the sexism, the "let's put this in for a cheap laugh" scenes, and even the dreck. But I laughed. Something about the movie's heedless spirit struck me as funny, and once I got hooked, everything seemed funny. It's a strange thing about *Kingpin.* I've received a lot of mail, divided about evenly between those who thought it was hilarious, and those who wanted their money back. As a critic, I am at the service of my personal reaction. If I laughed, I have to say so. I can't suppress that information and lecture the filmmakers on their taste.

Q. Your review of *Congo* was the *most accurate* review of a movie that I can remember. I've seen it three times and have enjoyed it more with each showing. It's hysterical. There are so many inside jokes that it's tough to catch everything the first time. I've dragged friends to it who had refused to see it because it got "terrible reviews." After I told them about your review, and about how I believed your assessment was right on target, they went. *They loved it!!!* You are about the only critic in the country who "got" the movie. Thanks for putting yourself out on a limb for it. (S.W. Simmons, Jenner & Block, Chicago)

A. *Congo* is a comedy that was mislabeled as an action drama, and has suffered as a result. I still say if it had been titled *Mel Brooks's Congo*, people would have caught on.

Credits

Q. The credits at the end of films are obviously made for the big screen, and when they roll past on home video, they're too small to read. Why don't they make them bigger? (Joan Baxter, Chapel Hill, N.C.)

A. Larger titles would take even longer to roll past, and some are already approaching the ten-minute mark ("Benji's dog chow catered by . . . ," etc.). Exhibitors believe few people read the titles; briefer titles increase the time available for selling popcorn, etc. That's why some theaters close the curtains while the titles are still running. Larger titles on home video, especially collector's editions, would be a bonus.

Q. We saw *Vanya on 42nd Street* last week. The print at the Galleria 10 Cinemas had no end credits, which was a little disconcerting because we were expecting to see a cast list. I find it hard to believe that Louis Malle would make a film with no end credits, considering the film was made in New York with its strong unions. The theater manager said the print "arrived with no end credits." (R. Steven Daniels, Birmingham, Ala.)

A. We called the manager's bluff. According to Dylan Leiner of Sony Classics, "We checked with the depot at which the print that played in Birmingham is stored. The print is intact with full end credits." And no wonder, since virtually all features have end credits. Some theaters cut them off, however, to clear the house for the next crowd. Demand your money back!

Q. A credit is given to Elizabeth Stone in many of Oliver Stone's movies. She is called the "Naijo No Ko." What does that title refer to? (John L. Santoianni III)

A. The credit for Stone's former wife is a Japanese term that loosely translates as "spiritual adviser," according to Stone's assistant, Annie Mei-Ling.

Q. In the credits for *Cliffhanger* I note that it was based on a "premise" as opposed to a novel. Does that mean Sly Stallone and his pals could have written the whole thing out on cocktail napkins at a bar in Aspen? (Tom Wagenbrenner)

A. You're catching on fast.

Q. Sometimes in the opening credits all the actors are listed by name except for one who is listed along with the name of the character he plays. It even happens on television; *Seinfeld* has "Jason Alexander as George." Please tell me why they do this. It eats at me and my girlfriend every time we see it on the screen. (Sean Polreis, Saskatoon, Saskatchewan)

A. It's an ego thing. Best of all is top billing, of course. But when an actor gets aced out of the top position, his agent may angle for other special billings. For example, last billing (". . . and Sean Polreis"). Or character billing (". . . Sean Polreis as the Joker"). In France, they get really fancy ("With the kind participation of Sean Polreis"). You may have noticed that this does not eat away at you nearly as much when it's your name.

Q. How can a movie have a guest star? As a one-time event, isn't one actor in a film as much a "guest" as the next actor in the same film? (Jonas M. Grant, Bloomington, Ind.)

A. I'd never thought of it that way before, but you're absolutely right.

Q. Have you noticed movie ads on TV? They print the credits in tiny type, just like the posters in front of the movie house. Those things are difficult to read when you have time to stand there and study them. They are impossible on the TV screen with only seconds allowed. (George Bergen, LaGrange, Ky.)

A. You're right: Movie ads on TV usually end with a screen or two containing dozens of names so small no one could possibly read them—but then no one is supposed to; they're listed simply because of contractual obligations.

Q. I just rented *The Usual Suspects* and noticed it was produced by Bad Hat Harry Productions. I wonder if that's in reference to Roy Scheider's line in *Jaws,* when he tells the old man on the beach who prods him to talk about his fear of water, "That's some bad hat, Harry." No one I ask seems to even remember the line, so needless to say they aren't much help to me. Any idea? (Richard Wolfe, Turtle Creek, Pa.)

A. According to Christopher McQuarrie, the writer of *Usual Suspects,* the name for Bad Hat Harry Productions was indeed a reference to Roy Scheider's line in *Jaws.* McQuarrie says *Jaws* is Bryan Singer's favorite movie and the two of them came up with the company name.

Crying at the Movies

Q. Something happened to me when I saw *Dead Man Walking* a couple of days ago. I broke down. I could hardly contain myself in those last twenty minutes of that movie. I am a thirty-one-year-old film buff, male, "seen it all" kind of guy. But I was a withering mess at the end of the movie. Why? Have you heard from any other people who have had such an extreme reaction? I almost left the theater because I could hardly handle it anymore. Looking back on it, I don't think it was the death penalty issue. I think it was that so many of the characters were in such pain, and it was so difficult for them to express that. Just wondered if anyone else had such a reaction. (Stephen M. Carrasco, El Paso, Tex.)

A. The movie helps us identify with the inner spiritual and emotional life of its characters. It is not about plot. It is about being a person in that situation. I felt great sorrow for the condemned man, because in his talks with the nun and with his family, it became clear that life had not provided him with an education and vocabulary adequate to express what he was feeling. Now, near death, with the help of this woman, his mind is opened enough to allow him to realize the enormity of his crime. He is sorry for what he has done. And we, realizing that he only now understands, grieve for him as well as for his victims.

Q. Do you ever cry at a movie? (Richard Kuzniak, Etobicoke, Ontario, Canada)

A. Yes. Not big sobs, exactly, but my eyes do grow moist two or three times a year. The strongest emotional reaction I've ever had was after *Do the Right Thing*. Other recent movies that really affected me were *Schindler's List, Leaving Las Vegas,* and *Dead Man Walking.*

Deaths and Dedications

Q. Do you have any additional information regarding the investigation into Brandon Lee's death? I saw Steven Seagal on CNN saying that he thought it was murder. Besides that, not a word from anyone. I would think some of the celebs would be up in arms about such a tragedy and screaming their heads off. I, a moviegoer nobody, was so outraged about it. I wrote letters to Carolco and the Motion Picture Association of America. I stressed in my letter to Carolco not to have the bad taste and release this film, billing it as Brandon Lee's last. If the only way I can protest this situation is by witholding my movie dollars from such incompetent morons, *I will.* (Kimberly R. Davis, Chicago)

A. The official investigation indicates Brandon Lee's death was accidental, although negligence and carelessness are suspected. No charges have been filed. The question of taste is a tricky one. What is worse—to make TV quickies exploiting the deaths of the Waco cultists, or to release Brandon Lee's only starring role? If I were Lee, I would want my final performance to be seen.

Q. Just saw a rough cut of a trailer for *The Crow,* the movie where Brandon Lee lost his life while shooting. At the risk of sounding morose, I can't wait for this movie to be released. It looks brilliant.

The production design is somewhere between *Batman Returns* and *Blade Runner.* Lee's makeup reminds me of David Bowie's Ziggy Stardust. Loads of action, looks like some sex and a killer story. Very dark, very film noirish, based on the comic book character. Know anything more? (Sean M. Apple, Los Angeles)

A. The movie was almost completed when Lee died, and the editors were able to assemble a finished product, which is now being shopped to various potential distributors.

A decision was made to complete the film and release it.

Q. Regarding the wonderful film *Il Postino*, I understand the lead actor, Massimo Troisi, passed away just after the film was finished. Because the resolution of the plot seemed abrupt and not in keeping with the tone of the rest of the movie, I'm wondering if he died before the film was completed and the director had to improvise the ending. Anyway, a great film and a real loss of a fine talent. (Robert Hodgins, Delta, British Columbia, Canada)

A. Troisi had a heart condition since childhood and, according to *Entertainment Weekly,* needed a heart transplant, but put the movie first. He died twelve hours after finishing his last scene, and two days before he was scheduled to fly to London for the operation. The film has turned into a surprise hit on the U.S. art circuit.

Q. There were news reports of the death of Kiyoshi Atsumi, said to be the most popular actor in Japan, who played an actor named "Tora-San." Have you ever heard of any of these movies? Do they ever play in the rest of the world? (Ronnie Barzell, Chicago)

A. There are forty-eight Tora-San movies, making it history's longest-running feature film series with one actor. The beloved Atsumi, whose real name was Yasuo Tadoroko, was compared in Japan to Charlie Chaplin; he made two Tora-San movies a year until recently, when advancing age slowed him down to one a year. His films were rarely exported. I have seen only one of them. They all follow more or less the same story line, in which an everyman gets a few weeks off from his job, visits his family in their old neighborhood, doesn't get along with them very well, and then decides to go on vacation to a famous Japanese tourist area. While there, he meets a beautiful girl and falls in love with her, but the romance never works out, and he ends up helping her in some way and then returning to his lonely bachelor life. Audiences enjoyed the predictability of this plot, which was repeated with variations in film after film. In their unassuming way, these human comedies reflected the Japanese notion of "nolo con aware," or the bittersweet awareness of the transience of earthly things. Some of the "Tora-San" movies are available on video in the United States.

Q. At the end of *Dead Man Walking*, the credits dedicated the movie to Lee Robbins and Thelma Bledsoe. Who are these people? Were they in any way involved with the real-life characters in the film? (G.E. Milkowski, Chicago)

A. Thelma Bledsoe is director Tim Robbins's maternal grandmother, and Lee Robbins is his paternal grandfather, who died during the filming of *The Shawshank Redemption*. One of the reasons Robbins dedicated the film to them is that they helped put him through college.

Q. My husband and I saw *Cliffhanger* last night and we were both on the edge of our seats!! We didn't hang on to each other that much when we were going through Hurricane Andrew!!! But did you notice in the credits that one of the stuntmen, who I believe they listed as doubling for Stallone, had the film dedicated to his "memory"? And someone else was named, too. Did these people die as a result of a stunt executed during the filming? (Michelle Haber)

A. The film was dedicated to Wolfgang Gulich, Sylvester Stallone's stunt double in the climbing sequences, who was killed in an auto accident three days after shooting was completed, and to Fadel Kassar, who died of natural causes during the production, and was father of the film's executive producer, Mario Kassar.

Q. At the end of *The Shawshank Redemption*, there was a line "In Memory of Alan Greene." Can you tell me who this was? (Kenny Corber, Côte-Saint-Luc, Quebec, Canada)

A. Greene was the literary agent of Frank Darabont, who wrote and directed the film. "He was instrumental in gaining the rights, and worked with me until the last days before his death," Darabont says. "He was not only an agent but a close friend."

Q. At the end of *Dead Man Walking*, Tim Robbins cuts back and forth between the murders and the execution. Do you think he was implying a sort of equivalence between the two acts? (Raymond C. Hollenbach, Campbellsville, Ky.)

A. Well, they were both executions, with the difference that the crimes were committed by ignorant psychopaths on drugs, while the lethal injection was done by the state, in our names.

Dialogue

Q. Something has always bothered me about *Sunset Boulevard*. The second most famous line in the film (after "I'm ready for my closeup, Mr. De Mille") occurs after William Holden's character asks, "Didn't you used to be big?" Gloria Swanson's character then replies "I *am* big. It's the pictures that got small!" If she's trying to convince him that she's still big, wouldn't she say that the pictures had got bigger, and that she appears small by comparison? (John Shannon, Oceanside, Calif.)

A. Your logic seems sound. But let's see how the suggested dialogue would sound: "I *am* big! But the pictures got even bigger, and I appear smaller only in comparison." Hmmm. Know what? I actually think it plays better the way Swanson says it.

Q. How does Woody Allen do it? How does he make Helena Bonham Carter (of all people!) sound exactly like Mia Farrow, who sounded exactly like Diane Keaton? (Eric Isaacson, Bloomington, Ind.)

A. Well, I'm a verbal chameleon, and start sounding like the people I'm talking to; I'm more British in London, more southern in Virginia, etc. Maybe there's something about Woody's vocal patterns that influences his costars. One thing you have to admit: Mira Sorvino, his costar in *Mighty Aphrodite*, didn't sound like anybody he has ever worked with before.

Q. I just read your review of *Dragonheart,* which you have convinced me I would enjoy watching. I just wanted to add one point. You said that, oddly, the dragon in the movie spoke English. Probably only a geek like me would know this, but in many of the traditions that include dragons, the dragons are intelligent and very eloquent. The dragon in J.R.R. Tolkien's *Hobbit* is a prime example. So, although *Dragonheart* sounds silly, the silliness of having Draco speak is in the tradition of dragon/knight stories. (Veronica Villanueva, Washington, D.C.)

A. I was also amused that both the dragon and the knight shared the same values and worldview, and seemed to have more in common than any of the humans in the film. Strange, since I doubt they attended the same schools.

Q. In *Lethal Weapon 3,* Rene Russo's character says, "You call that close? Close is a lingerie shop without a front window." Mel Gibson's character wasn't the only one who didn't get it. I haven't been able to find a soul to explain the joke to me, even though at least one Canadian critic thought it was the best line in the movie. (Michael Meyer, Champaign, Ill.)

A. The line has the *form* of a one-liner, and so maybe it seems to demand a laugh. I didn't get it, either. But from David Simkin, who has inside knowledge, I learned:

"Being a screenwriter and actually having worked for Jeffrey Boam (*LW3*'s writer) let me explain this weird line and how things like this occur. Here's the setup. Russo is a detective. She has traced the murdered suspect's phone calls to a lingerie shop. But, upon further investigation, she discovers that the shop has no front window. She intuits that a lingerie shop without a front window is like a day without sunshine. She suspects that the place is a front. So she goes with Mel to check it out.

"Now, in the filming process (where rewriting was happening on the set before takes, during takes, and often after takes), some plot points get lost or shuffled around a bit. During a shoot as crazy as *LW3*'s was some setups got lost or entire scenes were collapsed down into one- or two-line exchanges. That results in weird narrative *burps* like this one. Now, just to cover my rear, Mr. Boam did not tell me this directly. His development director did."

Directors

Q. Who is your favorite American director currently working and why? Also, who is an up-and-comer to look out for? (Kenneth Alan Goldman, Medford, Mass.)

A. The best American director is Martin Scorsese, whose work is filled with such energy, passion, and love of film that every frame seems alive. His *Raging Bull* was voted in three different polls the best film of the 1980s, and a case can be made for *Taxi Driver* in the 1970s and *GoodFellas* in the 1990s. Among the up-and-coming directors, I like Quentin Tarantino *(Pulp Fiction)*, John Dahl *(The Last Seduction)*, Carl Franklin *(One False Move)*, Atom Egoyan *(Exotica)*, and Gregory Nava *(My Family)*.

Q. What was the first film to use the director's name in the opening credits—for example, "A film by Robert Altman"? (Bert Schneider, Tucson, Ariz.)

A. The Directors' Guild of America is stuck for an answer. David J. Korduner, its associate general counsel, told me: "I asked around the office and got assorted answers, as follows: (1) George Sidney, the distinguished director, thinks it was sometime in the 1960s, but is not sure. (2) Frank Capra had a possessive credit on *Frank Capra's Mr. Smith Goes to Washington* in 1939. (3) Norman Jewison might have had one in *In the Heat of the Night* in 1967. (4) *Birth of a Nation*, or one of the Chaplin films. (5) European directors a long time ago, like Abel Gance on *Napoleon*. (6) Some French director like François Truffaut."

Directors' Cuts

Q. On the *True Lies* laserdisc, after the credits, are two theatrical trailers with scenes not seen in the theater version. A couple look quite interesting (Arnold Schwarzenegger bedding Tia Carrere, for example). Any word of a director's cut version coming out? (R.M. Vivas, Brooklyn, N.Y.)

A. No, but given the nature of the movie—an action epic with expensive special effects—it's likely that a collector's edition will eventually be released. Previews are often made from work prints long before the final form of the movie is set, which explains why they often have shots from "missing scenes."

Q. On June 5, 1995, Warner Home Video announced that an unrated director's cut of Oliver Stone's *Natural Born Killers* would be released to the home video market. On June 8, Warner announced that the director's cut had been removed from solicitation to video stores. The director's cut was to have featured the three scenes cut from the theatrical version, plus thirty-eight minutes' worth of outtakes. No word on who exactly was responsible for pulling the plug. This whole story keeps getting curiouser and curiouser, no? (Ed Slota, Warmick, R.I.)

A. Not so curious if you reflect that the furor over the first Robert Dole attack on Hollywood's values peaked in the interim, and his chief targets were *Natural Born Killers* and Warner Bros. "We're trying to get a handle on what they're doing," Stone spokesman Steve Rivers told me. "Oliver had a conversation with [top Warner's exec] Terry Semel, who told him they were 'not withdrawing it, just tinkering with the release date.'" Warner's own home video department did not return my calls. "Director's cuts" on tape and disc are premium-priced sets aimed at serious film viewers. Since the original release date was September 1995 and no new date has been announced, the studio may be planning to hold the release until after the November elections.

The director's cut was released in the autumn of 1996.

Q. I have noticed that with a lot of movies, a couple years after they have been released on video cassette, a Special Edition is released *only* on laserdisc. Why only laserdisc? Why not VHS tape also? (Sharon Prediger, Saskatoon, Saskatchewan, Canada)

A. Two reasons: The people interested in special editions tend to be laserdisc-oriented, since that is the format of choice for buffs. Second, laserdiscs allow the parallel sound tracks on which the running commentaries, etc., are placed, and the freeze-frame capacity for the stills, etc. Tape does not offer these features, so a "special edition" on tape would be a forlorn thing.

Q. While browsing through the neighborhood video store recently, I noticed a sign advertising the pending release of the "Director's Cut" of a recent blockbuster. I have seen the term "director's cut" quite often in the last few years but, to be honest, don't understand the concept. Aren't *all* final versions of movies the "director's cut"? I thought that the picture was the director's baby, beginning to end. If this is not the case, then who does actually have the final say regarding what will end up on the big screen—the studios? producers? grips? Have you seen many (any) "director's cuts," and are they actually better than the originals? Should I devote my life to tracking these down? (Denise Leder, Las Vegas)

A. Some directors have the right of "final cut" but many do not. However, the words "director's cut" do not always mean that the theatrical version was not the director's desired cut. They may indicate that (1) if the director had his druthers, the movie would have been an hour longer, or (2) that sex was taken out to qualify for the R rating and is now back in. Even in the case of directors with enormous clout, a studio contract may specify that they must deliver an R-rated film, and so last-minute cuts are common as part of the MPAA rating process.

Directors' Inside Jokes

Q. Every film I've seen by director John Landis, from *Animal House* to *Blues Brothers* to *Coming to America,* and including even Michael Jackson's *Thriller* video, uses the phrase, "See you next Wednesday." This is obviously an inside joke, but what does it mean? (Kris Gallimore, Thunder Bay, Ontario, Canada)

A. The line was used in the telephone call from orbit in Stanley Kubrick's *2001: A Space Odyssey,* and has become a Landis calling card. Not to be outdone, Kubrick has set a scene in a bathroom in every one of *his* movies.

Q. Recently you mentioned the tags saying, "When in Southern California, visit Universal Studios," which directors used to have to stick on the end of their Universal pictures. It seems director John Landis got the last laugh. At the end of *Animal House*, when they tell what became of each character, they say Babs became a tour guide at Universal Studios. Then, after the credits, the "visit Universal Studios" tag was appended with "(Ask for Babs)." The same gag also appeared on the tag after Landis's *The Blues Brothers*. (Dan Margules, San Diego, Calif.)

A. And tell Babs, for me, that you'll see her next Wednesday.

Q. If you go back and watch any Jeff Goldblum movie, you'll invariably notice at least one scene in which Jeff is both eating and talking at the same time, or drinking and talking at the same time. It drives me nuts. Sure, we all do it on occasion. But Jeff seems to think that it's great acting. Maybe way back when, some Hollywood director said, "This kid's got talent! Look at him eat and talk at the same time. Wow, he looks so natural." Jeff should realize there are other ways to appear natural on film. Don't get me wrong, I think he's a good actor, I'm just tired of his shtick. Michael J. Fox is another great eater/talker/actor, but then again, so's my dad—no big deal there. (Steve Glasberg, Agoura Hills, Calif.)

A. I say if you can't do it as well as John Belushi did it in *National Lampoon's Animal House*, you shouldn't even try it.

Q. You mentioned that Stanley Kubrick always has a bathroom in his movies, and John Landis always uses the line "See you next Wednesday." What about Dan O'Bannon's chickens? O'Bannon started screenwriting in college with classmate John Carpenter. Their first full feature together was *Dark Star* in 1974. I haven't seen this film for myself, but I believe there is a scene in it that involves the world's crappiest joke—pulling a rubber chicken from a jacket and shaking it to make it look alive. Ever since then, Dan O'Bannon has incorporated a chicken into each of his film scripts. In *Alien* a chicken's membrane appeared on the monitor when John Hurt was being scanned. In *Blue Thunder* a missile takes out a fried chicken restaurant. In *Return of the Living Dead* the joke appeared on a billboard in the background. In *Total Recall* me and a couple of friends are pretty sure it appeared at the end of the film—the alien "handprint" on the atmosphere-creating machine being in reality a mold of an enlarged chicken's foot. (Graham Keith, Haslingden, England)

A. The scene I am waiting for is a man in a bathroom, telling a chicken, "See you next Wednesday."

Q. After seeing *The Hudsucker Proxy* this week, I decided to pull out my copy of *Raising Arizona* to enjoy some other work by Joel and Ethan Coen. Lo and behold, I noticed that a patch worn on the overalls of M. Emmet Walsh in the prologue reads *Hudsucker Industries*"! Has this corporate name appeared in their other films as a running gag, or is this a sole incident? (John Muller)

A. Frank Casey of Warner Bros. says it's not a running joke. While making *Raising Arizona*, the brothers completed the script for *Hudsucker Proxy*, and when the scene with M. Emmet Walsh came up, they just slapped "Hudsucker Industries" on his overalls patch. It was a one-time thing.

Q. Some reviews say the screenplay for Steven Soderbergh's movie *The Underneath* is by Sam Lowry and Daniel Fuchs. Others credit Soderbergh and Fuchs. Who wrote it? (Ronnie Barzell, Chicago)

A. The movie is based on a 1949 *film noir* named *Criss Cross*, written by Daniel Fuchs. Soderbergh, who made substantial changes, did not want to share credit with the earlier screenplay. When the Writers' Guild insisted, he adopted the pseudonym "Sam Lowry," the name of the hero of *Brazil* (1985), a statistician played by Jonathan Pryce. The press kit for the movie says, "Sam Lowry left his position with the Ministry of Information in order to pursue a film career."

Discreet Matters

Q. We rented *Apollo 13* on video and wondered: What happens after one of the astronauts throws up? And how does it smell? (Sean McHugh, Three Oaks, Mich.)

A. Stuart Williams of the NASA Flight Crew Operations Directorate replies: "We have a standing rule: He (or she) who loses it cleans it up! Actually, the inside of the aircraft doesn't smell any different because of the lost lunches. It does have a sort of 'old house' odor to it. The interior is padded with basically the same foam rubber that acts as a cushion in the soles of running shoes, and this foam rubber is getting kinda old, so I think that is the source of the odor."

Q. The premise of *Indecent Proposal* might not actually be as outlandish as it sounds. The next time you see *Elizabeth Taylor* give her a jolt by suddenly and unexpectedly asking her about the time *Frank Sinatra* offered to pay her a *million dollars* for a single night's roll in the hay. (Hank Cleary, White Plains, N.Y.)
A. Tell you what, *Hank.* First, *you* ask *him.*

Q. Something I've always wondered about Brian De Palma's *Body Double*: In the movie, the hero finds his girlfriend in bed with someone else. The woman is in a sitting-up position, and is clearly enjoying herself. Later, the boyfriend recounts this to another character, saying, "There she was, lying there, glowing," when she clearly *was not* lying down. My theory is that DePalma was having a little fun with his audience. What's your theory? (Jacqui Deegan)
A. My theory is the woman was having a little fun with her boyfriend.

Q. I hereby nominate *Body of Evidence* for consideration as laserdisc of the year. MGM/UA's bold, innovative decision to index the chapter stops with descriptions of the closest dirty part puts them up there with the greats. (Andy Ihnatko, Westwood, Mass.)
A. Did *Body of Evidence* have any parts that weren't dirty?

Q. I'm a theater manager and get to see movies many, many, many times. I thought I would point out a minor error in *Indecent Proposal.* Early in the movie, Woody Harrelson is shaving and Demi Moore is watching and talking to him. He shaves the right side of his face and has just begun to work on his left when (lovebirds that they are) they start smooching. When you see Harrelson again, there is shaving cream *all over his face!* In the next scene Demi Moore and Woody Harrelson make love. While they are doing this, Demi has left the iron on and Woody's pants become scorched. With Woody on top of her and the two engaged in a passionate embrace, Demi says, "Your pants are on fire!" Woody replies with an almost bashful look, "You have no idea." At this Demi lets loose with a delightful laugh that seems genuine, unrehearsed, and spontaneous. Was this a bit of improvisation on Harrelson's part? (Thomas E. Sisk Jr., Greensboro, N.C.)

A. Or was Harrelson perhaps indicating that he was indeed aroused during the scene? Shows how people's minds work. What I was wondering during the same scene was, how long can a pair of pants burn before two people in the same room smell the smoke?

Q. I think some critic should address the issue of men getting kicked in the genitals in movies. It sometimes seems that every movie has such a scene—even comedies like *Roger Rabbit.* Often they are treated as comic relief. Even children are shown getting hurt by blows to the groin. You could do a fascinating show just showing clips from movies showing males getting kicked there. I wonder what would the reaction be if women were routinely shown having their nipples pinched. (Charles Church, Walkertown, N.C.)

A. A similar thought occurred to me while watching the PG-rated *Rudyard Kipling's The Jungle Book,* in which Mowgli, the young hero, employs kicks to the groin on four separate occasions. Apparently Hollywood thinks this is hilarious, although, as any man can tell you, there is *nothing* funny about it.

Q. I'm writing from Taipei again where there's a movie playing called *Fart King.* This is the actual title as it appears in the newspapers here. That's *not* the unusual part. The *unusual* part is the banner across the bottom of the newspaper ad that promises the movie has: ACTION WITH UNNECESSARY SPECIAL EFFECTS. Question: How unnecessary does a special effect have to be before the director determines that it should be kept? (Bob Zix-Kong, Taipei)

A. Thanks for your continuing updates on cinematic developments in Taipei.

Q. In one of your articles from Cannes, you wrote about *Pom Poko*, saying: "This Japanese family film about cute animals is not likely to make a sale in the American market, since the secret weapon of the raccoons is their ability to make their testicles grow so large they can crush their opponents."

If that's all you have to say about it, that's really too bad. The film is directed by Isao Takahata, who is the world's greatest living director of animation. His movies tend to be about serious subjects. *Pom Poko* treats the subject of environmental conservation with humor and wisdom. The secret weapon of the raccoons is their ability (as in Japanese legend) to change shape, which they do to frighten away the men who are trying to change their forest home into a condo development. The raccoons change into a number of things such as ghosts, people, animals, etc.

But yes, they do in a couple of scenes attack people with their enlarged testicles, and that would make showing the film commercially in the United States a problem. I saw it at the San Francisco Film Festival, where the children in the audience didn't seem to have any trouble with it. (Robert Forman, San Francisco)

A. The Japanese are more open in their attitude toward human plumbing than we are. So are children, who would probably be delighted by the raccoon's choice of weapons if it were not for their dreary parents.

Q. Am I wrong or are there more and more movie scenes taking place in public rest rooms in recent years? (David Tatai, Chicago)

A. You are quite correct. In fact *Ebert's Little Movie Glossary* covers this in three entries. The "Bathroom Rule," contributed by Eugene Accardo, states that no one in the movies ever goes to the toilet for the usual reasons, but instead uses the room to take drugs, commit suicide, escape through the window, etc. The Timely Bladder Syndrome, contributed by Kevin Wan, observes that the hero always goes to the toilet just before the good guys attack, and thus is able to observe while hidden, and make his plans. The Mandatory Latrine Scene, contributed by Donna Martin, observes that in all movies since 1980 with office settings, all major decisions are made by men of power while standing next to urinals and washbasins in the men's washroom.

Q. Is it Hollywood's "in" thing to show men urinating? I don't watch the other guy in the men's room, so why do I want to spectate as Will Smith relieves himself? (Or the guy in *Waterworld,* although that rude scene at least had a point.) It's even more sophomoric when the guy converses with himself and refers to his activity. Does he do this when he ties his shoes or shaves? Why don't they have scenes of ladies on the pot in these movies? Doesn't this enhance the feminine mystique? I didn't think so. (Jim Carey, New Lenox, Ill.)

A. I am adding your observation to *Ebert's Little Movie Glossary* under the heading, "Tinkle, tinkle, little star." It may be related to an existing glossary entry pointing out that in movies about large corporations, most of the conspiratorial conversations take place in the men's room.

Q. I read that James Spader had a quotable answer at a press conference at Cannes when he was asked about the lack of male nudity in his new film *Crash.* But the answer was not quoted. What did he say? (Susan Lake, Urbana, Ill.)

A. Spader was asked why there was female nudity in the film but not male nudity. His reply: "The nudity takes place during sex scenes. At such times, male nudity is not visible—if you're any good at all."

Q. I read your review of *Fly Away Home,* accompanied by a photo of Anna Paquin kneeling on the grass feeding the Canada geese. How was she able to do that without getting droppings all over herself? I wonder if the movie credits list a goose cleaner-upper? Where I work, we don't walk across the grass because it is a minefield planted with green-gray goose offerings. (Robert Erck, Lombard, Ill.)

A. The movie's geese wranglers were Geordie Lishman, Greg Wells, Wayne Bezner-Kerr, and Florence MacGregor. Where do you work?

Distribution and Exhibition

Q. I would have thought *Princess Caraboo* was exactly the kind of film that would have hugely benefited from good reviews. The critics did get to see it at the Montreal festival, and it received only positive reviews. Yet I understand it was never shown to other critics, and as a result got few reviews, one way or the other. What was the studio thinking of? (Matthew Cope, Westmont, Quebec, Canada)

A. You are referring to the comedy about a mysterious young woman who appears in England in the early nineteenth century, and fascinates society. The film had a first-rate cast: Phoebe Cates, Kevin Kline, Wendy Hughes, Jim Broadbent, and John Lithgow. Yet it was not screened, and I was unable to catch it in a theater before it disappeared. Sometimes there are political reasons why a studio wants a movie to fail, because it has been sponsored by an executive whose success is not in the best interest of his rivals. Other times, the studio simply has no idea what it has. Look at the last year's case of *Tombstone*, where Disney's nonscreening policy may have cost Val Kilmer an Oscar nomination.

Q. John Candy's last film, *Canadian Bacon*, was directed by Michael Moore, who made *Roger & Me*. But it has never been released. What's the story? (Tank Drummond, Boulder, Colo.)

A. The movie is about a war between the United States and Canada. It was shelved for many months by Propaganda Films, some said because the company didn't like it, others because of its unfashionably leftist politics. I ran into Moore at the Independent Spirit Awards and he told me he has regained control of the film and, to the consternation of Propaganda, it has been accepted as an official U.S. entry at this May's Cannes Film Festival.

It was given a limited release in 1996, but was not successful.

Q. I read wonderful reviews of excellent movies and then the film vanishes. I'm dying to see *Persuasion*, so where is it? (Mrs. M. Stern, Gary, Ind.)

A. *Persuasion*, which was a much better Jane Austen adaptation than *Sense and Sensibility,* did not get much of a shove from its distributor. Theaters are often booked by computers according to cynical demographics that favor the kinds of movies that can appeal quickly to younger viewers and rack up a hot opening weekend. Films intended for older or more discerning audiences get penalized by this "top ten" mentality. A current example: *Once Upon a Time . . . When We Were Colored,* one of the best films of the year, is tailor-made for those who hunger for a film with positive, nonviolent, family-oriented African-American material. But it has a puny advertising budget, and unless audiences actively seek it out, quickly, it can be shoved aside by junk like *Black Sheep* and *Happy Gilmore.*

Q. One of the burgeoning trends is the rise of the twenty-plus screen megaplex. By the end of 1997, there will be at least 120 screens in only five locations in Orange County. The big selling point is supposed to be that they can show the blockbusters and still have screens left over for the smaller artsy films. Of course, summer rolls around and of the twenty screens, five are showing *Independence Day,* four are showing *Mission: Impossible,* four are showing *The Nutty Professor* and, well, you get the picture. The twenty screens gives them extra seats for the big money makers and Merchant-Ivory be damned. I think they're reneging on their promise. (Paul McElligott, Lake Forest, Calif.)

A. Whenever any large corporate or civic organization announces a big project, they promise what they know they should be doing. Then they go right ahead and do exactly what they were doing before. We're told state lotteries raise money for education, gambling casinos increase local employment, and movie monsterplexes provide more screens for independent, art, and documentary films. That is why we have such fine schools, no unemployment, and so many challenging and intelligent movies.

Q. I am a theater owner. The reason Paramount keeps losing at the box office is because I put a curse on them because they refuse to license films in my theater. They concocted a flimsy excuse to shut me out so they could "exclusively" play at a cheapjack, mega-shoddy exhibitor in the area. I just thought you'd like to know why lately you have been forced to give terrible reviews to Paramount films like *Intersection* and *A Thing Called Love.* (Rusty Gordon, Nashville, Tenn.)

A. Now would you put a curse on Steven Seagal?

Q. I'm a reporter doing a story on movie-hopping, where a scofflaw buys a ticket at a multiplex for one movie, watches it, and then ducks into another auditorium for a free viewing. Is this ethically wrong? Is it ever justified? (I'm told by theater owners that the typical response when someone is caught is that they feel they are justified because of high ticket prices.) Did you ever do it? And what would be an appropriate punishment for those caught in the act? (Steve Pokin, Riverside, Calif.)

A. I never did it because when I was growing up there was only one movie per theater—but I did sometimes sit through them twice, which I think is a moviegoer's right, and I oppose the barbarous modern practice of emptying the auditorium after each screening. Is movie-hopping justified? Maybe you could make a case under situational ethics, but, in general—no, it's stealing. Punishment? Throw 'em out.

Q. Is this a trend? Usually, you get to see movies before I do, but that seems to be changing. They are being prereleased on cable. Then when you review 'em, it's déjà vu all over again. This started with *Red Rock West.* Then *The Last Seduction, Freeway,* and the latest, *Normal Life.* Is there a financial incentive to letting the cable companies have movies before their theatrical release? (Don Howard, San Jose, Calif.)

A. The story with all of these movies is the same. They were intended for theaters, were released to cable over the dead bodies of their directors, and then got limited theatrical releases as the distributions went through the motions of "giving them a chance." I reviewed them because I felt they deserved attention. In the cases of *The Last Seduction* and *Normal Life,* the straight-to-cable policy deprived their stars, Linda Fiorentino and Ashley Judd, of well-deserved Oscar consideration. All four of the titles mentioned are much better films than a lot of the junk that does get theatrical release (which may explain, sad to say, the doubts the distributors had about their prospects).

Doubles and Look-alikes

Q. I read that Jeanne Tripplehorn requested a body double to replace her in certain scenes in the movie *Waterworld.* I've wondered for a long time why they don't include the names of the body doubles in the end credits. Surely if they acknowledge people like caterers, first-aid nurses, truck drivers, etc., they should recognize the contribution of someone who actually appears on the screen. (Gary Currie, Montreal, Canada)

A. In an industry where even "trout wranglers" get mentioned in the end credits, the professional body double is the last anonymous artist. However, it could get tricky if body parts were supplied by more than one double; the credits would read like the contents of a package of chicken parts.

Q. Okay, was that you, or a highly-paid celeb look-alike in the movie premier scene of *Last Action Hero?* (Jim Deck)

A. If he had been highly-paid, it would have been me.

Q. Gene Hackman has an uncanny resemblance to author Elmore Leonard in *Get Shorty,* with the hair and the goatee. Coincidence or inside humor? (Eric M. Davitt, Toronto, Canada)

A. Not a coincidence, I suspect. I've met them both and was also struck by the similarity. For another inside joke, check out Alan Parker's *Angel Heart* (1987), where Robert De Niro, playing the devil, does a wicked impersonation of his friend Martin Scorsese.

Q. Regarding *It Takes Two,* with the Olsen twins playing two girls who look just alike: I had already decided to pass on this film as it strikes me as a last-ditch effort to exploit the Olsen sisters before they outgrow being cute. The identity-switching bit seems a part of our collective consciousness and will undoubtedly keep reappearing in movies for better or worse. At least no one has come up with triplets changing roles. Would that give us the good sister, the evil sister, and the mediocre sister? (Larry Jones, Ontario, Calif.)

A. Now there's an exercise for screenwriting class: Write a story in which there are identical triplets, and find a way for the audience to keep them straight. At least with twins we always know we're looking at this one and not the other one.

Q. At the end of the movie *Apollo 13*, Tom Hanks is seen shaking hands with the crew and officers of the recovery ship. The camera focuses on one officer in particular. I worked at NASA in the early 1970s and noticed the officer looks like the real-life Jim Lovell, the commander of *Apollo 13*. Ron Howard likes to put his family in his movies. Did he also put in Lovell? (Bruce Worthen, Salt Lake City)

A. That is the real Jim Lovell.

Q. I recently saw the movie *Tombstone,* and could have sworn I saw Mel Gibson in one of the scenes, in the background. He did not appear in any credits. Am I imagining this? (Christopher Voisey, Willowdale, Ontario, Canada)

A. Disney spokesman Jeff Marden says Gibson was not in the film.

Drive-in Theaters

Q. In 1958 there were 4,063 drive-in screens in the United States, and now there are less than nine hundred. Why do you think drive-ins are an endangered species? Do you think there's the slightest chance they will become popular again? (Alison L. Lundgren, Urbana, Ill.)

A. I'm amazed (and pleased) there are still nine hundred. Land values have gone up in desirable locations, where more money can be made with a shopping mall than a drive-in (and malls have theaters, too). With all the emphasis on "per-screen averages," drive-ins can only show a feature once at a convenient time on most nights, especially during their prime summer season, while indoor theaters can schedule two or three showings. I like the *idea* of drive-ins, as part of the American experience, but haven't attended one in years; I find the picture and sound better in a good conventional theater.

Dubbing, Subtitles, and Voice-overs

Q. Here in Germany they dub films, often changing the dialogue at the same time. Some I have noticed: In Kubrick's *Lolita*, Peter Sellers says to James Mason: "You're either Australian or a German refugee." The German version is "You're either a gangster or a tramp." In Woody Allen's *Bananas*, in the scene in the porn shop, he says, "I'm doing a sociological study on perversion. I'm up to advanced child-molesting." This has been changed to: "I'm up to sexual offense to mules." (Bernd Backhaus, Bochum, Germany)

A. And instead of "I'll be back," Arnold Schwarzenegger says, "I never left."

Q. Regarding your column about how certain details are changed when movies are dubbed into German, the reality in German theaters is *a lot worse!* In the German version of *Die Hard*, the German terrorists weren't Germans anymore but Brits—and Hans Gruber was changed to "Jack" Gruber, even though Bruce Willis was still seen writing the name Hans on his arm. In the German version of the Gene Hackman flick *Loose Cannons*, it was not German terrorists, 'cause that might imply to German audiences that Americans think all Germans are Nazis. Even when Hackman and Dan Aykroyd are standing in the German embassy and you see the German flag, in the German version they say they're in some South American embassy. Yeah, those people really look South American. (Wolfgang Karle, Karlsruhe, Germany)

A. Remember *Casablanca?* Bogie says, "Yeah, I remember Paris. The Uruguayans wore gray. You wore blue."

Q. For the past twenty years, my husband and I have been trying to identify the female off-screen narrator in *To Kill a Mockingbird*. Do you know who she is? (Julia Van Buskirk, Geneva, Ill.)

A. The great Kim Stanley. And check out her work in *The Goddess*, a 1958 film loosely inspired by the career of Marilyn Monroe. Bonus answer: The voice on the telephone in *Rosemary's Baby* is Tony Curtis.

Q. While watching *Il Postino (The Postman)*, I noticed a couple of times that Philippe Noiret's voice had been dubbed. Most people in North America probably wouldn't have noticed this because they were reading the subtitles as he spoke. Surely enough, listed in the credits was "The voice of Mr. Noiret." What is the reason for this? (Rob McKenzie Stratford, Ontario, Canada)

A. Noiret spoke in French and was dubbed into Italian.

Q. In a segment on TV showing the making of *Hunchback of Notre Dame*, Jason Alexander of *Seinfeld* was shown dubbing in the voice for the Hunchback. He was being interviewed about his role in the picture—but when I read the credits for that part, Tom Hulce was named as the voice. What became of Alexander? Did they decide to replace him in the middle of the picture, or didn't it ever get off the ground?" (Henrietta Friedman, Skokie, Ill.)

A. Disney spokesman Peter Dangerfield of Iltis Associates in Chicago says Jason Alexander is the voice of Hugo, one of the gargoyles. He was never contracted to do Quasimodo.

Q. I saw the French film *The Visitors* and enjoyed it a great deal. Much of the humor was based on the dialogue. It really isn't fair to critique a film (a two-star rating, no less) when one doesn't understand all the nuances of the language. (Eileen Blum, New York)

A. Then it isn't fair to sell $8 tickets to an audience and give them a subtitled film. Obviously, the film should have been shown only in French, and tickets sold only to French speakers. But since the majority of the people seeing this film in America are depending on the English subtitles, it wouldn't have been fair to review it any other way.

Q. Why are European movies not popular in the United States? I am originally from Russia (I'm twenty and I've lived here for three and a half years now) and even in the worst years we were able to watch many good French and Italian pictures. And I don't mean only Fellini or Truffaut; there were a lot of good action and comedy flicks. The reason that the American public doesn't like subtitles is not good enough, since in Russia they used to put a different voice over the original sound track. (Dmitri Pekker, Dallas)

A. Hollywood has a worldwide near-monopoly on commercial blockbusters, which is why even the French and the Italians go to more American movies than European films. In this country most subtitled films rarely venture beyond the largest cities, unless they're big hits such as *Like Water for Chocolate.* Yet the primary audience for foreign films here prefers subtitles, so they can hear the voices of the actual actors.

Dumb Audiences

Q. Ever notice that when characters in costume dramas use a term modern audiences aren't likely to understand, they immediately follow it with the definition? In *Rob Roy,* for example: "He's a vile Jacobite! A supporter of the exiled King James!" (Rich Elias, Delaware, Ohio)

A. This is just a precaution. Hollywood learned its lesson with titles like *Wrestling Ernest Hemingway* and *Searching for Bobby Fischer,* which bombed because nobody knew who Ernest Hemingway or Bobby Fischer were. On the other hand, *Beethoven's 2nd* was a hit because everyone knew Beethoven was a dog.

Q. In your review of *Hot Shots: Part Deux,* you said that many people would not know that "deux" means "two" in French. Why do members of the media believe the public is ignorant of all facts not found in the Sunday funnies? After a while it becomes irritating to constantly listen to media figures talk down to the public. We do have intelligence reaching above that of a trained seal. I am by no means a dummy. I even know that "trois" means "three." (Laura Elizabeth Durnell, Oak Lawn, Ill.)

A. And that's just for starters.

Q. Re your Answer Man item about people talking during movies. Many years ago, I was in a theater watching *A Man for All Seasons.* It reached the point when Sir Thomas More had been incarcerated, and, to indicate the passage of time, the camera showed a wall of the cell with a window on a winter scene that dissolved into a scene of spring. Up to that point, the people around me had been pretty quiet, but as that shot unfolded, a lady behind me said to her companion, "See? There are the seasons!" (Steve Kallis Jr., Tampa, Fla.)

A. Only winter and spring? I hope she asked for her money back.

This letter somehow reminded me of my long-ago viewing of King and Country *in a London theater. The whole plot hinges on the refusal of British soliders in a firing squad to execute one of their fellows. An overhead shot shows their rifle barrels swinging away from the target before the order to fire is given. Behind me, one Londoner said to another, "Crikey! And they say the Yanks are lousy shots!"*

Q. Re your low rating of *Striptease* and your high rating of heidi fleiss movie. Think it may be related to your feeling uncomfortable good lookig, beatiful bodied, talented women with brains. As well as a sad delight when viewing people with severe personality disorders i.e. the madam movie about Fleiss. Think about it. (Dr. Name Withheld, via CompuServe)

A. Frankly, I doubt you are Dr. Name Withheld, and I suspect you are Dr. Withheld's son, logging on to his CompuServe account while he is out saving lives. This message has all the earmarks of having been written by someone in junior high who still has a lot of work to do in the areas of spelling, grammar, and punctuation. In any event, I will simply tell you that my reviews are based on the quality of the films, not the quality of the bodies in them. One day when you are older you will understand. For analysis of the bodies, you can try the reviews of Joe Bob Briggs, whose work can be found right there on CompuServe. Keep an ear out for your dad.

Q. Recently, I attended a screening of *The Exorcist* at Radio City Music Hall. Although I enjoyed the film, I noticed that the intensity seemed to be lacking, thanks to the audience, which laughed and applauded at the most inopportune moments (i.e., the vomit scene and during the climactic exorcism itself). They even managed to giggle when X rays of Regan's brain flashed on the screen! Admittedly, there were a few lighter moments, but it seemed as though every ten minutes something tickled the audience. *The Exorcist* is not your run-of-the-mill horror flick; it borders on the spiritual at times and is hardly worthy of snickering. My guess is that films such as *Pulp Fiction* and *Trainspotting*, with their emphasis on using violence and shock for humor, have "dumbed down" most filmgoers to the point where they can't differentiate serious chills from purposely outrageous situations. (Rob Wolejsza, Astoria, N.Y.)

A. I heard that something similar happened in Boston last week at a screening of *Vertigo*. I don't think *Pulp Fiction* can be blamed (for one thing, it's not dumb). Two factors are at work: (1) laughter is a common reaction among those too touched or embarrassed to reveal true emotion, and (2) unsophisticated audiences consider any sign that a movie is dated (period dialogue, references, clothes) to be a laugh cue. I saw *The Exorcist* again a couple of years ago at the Hawaii Film Festival, while doing a shot-by-shot analysis with its cinematographer, Owen Roizman. The movie was as effective as ever. But of course the audience was probably more hip.

Q. Re your item from Cannes about how stupid people are for taking flash pictures of a movie screen. They can't be any more stupid than the people who take flash pictures at night games from two hundred feet up in the stands. Like the flash is going to illuminate the player way down on the field! (Andy Cappellano, Chicago)

A. They're related to the people who take flash pictures at rock concerts. I picture them eagerly opening their returned photos at the drugstore and saying, "Gee, I wonder why these didn't turn out!"

Edited Videos and TV

Q. Guess I've been living in a cave, but just recently I realized that what we see on video is not necessarily what we saw in theatrical release. Can you enlighten me as to why movies would be arbitrarily edited for video release? I've noticed this in some films but wonder if it's done as a matter of course and I just haven't been paying attention? I should mention, I see most films on video rather than in the theater, unfortunately. (Kathy Nickerson, Meadow Vista, Calif.)

A. In general, the video release represents the theatrical version. In the case of Blockbuster Video, however, the company has a policy against NC-17–rated material, and so much marketing clout that studios will sometimes edit offending material out of a movie in order to quality for Blockbuster distribution. On the other side of the coin, studios sometimes release "unrated" versions of movies that include steamy scenes originally cut out to qualify for the R rating. A third variation is the "director's cut," a version including scenes the studio wanted deleted but that the director now wants you to see.

Q. In a letter to you, Janice Hargrove complained that editing-for-TV made the plot of *Cabaret* meaningless by removing references to the homosexuality of Joel Gray's character. I can top that: I must have seen *Deliverance* on TV half a dozen times and never understood what happened because the rape scenes were completely excised. In fact, I've never seen the full movie, and can only surmise what happened from friends' accounts of the plot. (Joseph Holmes, Brooklyn, N.Y.)

A. It was about two guys banging each other over the head with banjos, right?

Q. After some searching, I found *The Sailor Who Fell from Grace with the Sea*, with Kris Kristofferson and Sarah Miles, on video. A steamy movie, as you may recall, but when I watched it at home, I found 95 percent of the erotic content deleted! There was nothing on the cover to indicate that the movie had been edited for video release. Is such a practice (sanitizing) common? (George Onstot, New Westminster, British Columbia, Canada)

A. Yes, as explained above. And unfair.

Q. While watching *Prince of Tides* on HBO, imagine my horror when I noticed that several scenes had been cut! Some of them pivotal to the story. Now, mind you, these scenes were not of a sexual nature so I was really surprised they had been cut. I'm really angry, since when you subscribe to a premium channel, such as HBO, one of their key advertising lines is that you get the uncut original, just as it appeared in theaters. (Annelise I. Pichardo, Rego Park, N.Y.)

A. HBO does indeed show movies in their original theatrical versions. And director Barbra Streisand has a no-cut provision in her contracts. Perhaps you are a victim of the Phantom Scene Syndrome, in which the imagination provides "memories" of scenes that were not actually in the film.

Q. A reader wrote and asked about several scenes from *Prince of Tides* which she felt were missing when she viewed it on HBO. You answered that HBO shows movies in their original theatrical versions, and accused the reader of being a victim of the Phantom Scene Syndrome, in which the imagination provides "memories" of scenes that were not actually in the film.

I beg to differ from this opinion. I have found many scenes missing from movies on Showtime. Not pivotal scenes or lines . . . but a camera pan here and there . . . lingering on a scene or subject a little less. In a few cases, I own the film on video, and have used a stopwatch to back up what I initially thought was my imagination (with *Dances With Wolves,* for example). They have time constraints and maybe want to squeeze in a promo of upcoming movies or keep the schedule from straying too far from the top of the hour. They should notify the viewer that any scene is cut and for what reason. They cannot just assume we are so stupid as not to notice that the picture is altered. (Matthew Miller)

A. The Phantom Scenes were apparently my own. Others wrote in with complaints similar to yours, adding that many local stations use "time compression" to squeeze movies into shorter running times. That's not news; local stations treat movies like sausages. On a premium cable channel like Showtime or HBO, however, what is the viewer paying for, if not the movie as actually made?

Q. Do you know that one national video store chain is renting *Bad Lieutenant* as an R-rated film, hacking out so much footage that it becomes ineffective as the psychotic, real-life horror story it is supposed to be? I rented the film thinking that it was the original theatrical release, and started wondering why it was so badly edited. I then noticed the box said, not "edited," but merely "Rated R Version." This is not only misleading, but a vile and sneaky form of censorship. If this were done to a book, people would be outraged; this is no less a slaughtering of art. (Joe Clarke, New York)

A. *Bad Lieutenant* was rated NC-17 in its theatrical release, and I agree with you that the cuts necessary to make it an "R" destroy the point of the film. That was the very reason the director, Abel Ferrara, refused to trim it for the R rating. Video stores should have the courage of their convictions, and not try to make money off of bowdlerized versions of films they will not handle in the NC-17 director's cut. This is one more example of the way the MPAA's rating system, allegedly designed only to advise parents, actually results in de facto censorship.

Q. Re your discussion of whether studios sometimes add adult dialogue to movies to get a PG-13 or R rating (fearing that moviegoers will think G or PG are too tame). I understand it is common practice to add a nude scene or dub language into made-for-TV "movies of the week" when they are released on home video, to get them an R rating. This makes them more attractive to renters. A few years back Drew Barrymore complained that they hired a body double for nude scenes added to her MOW about Amy Fisher. She would have done the nude scene herself, and was mad that the actress hired didn't resemble her enough (maybe there was a tattoo issue, here). (W.C. Martell, Studio City, Calif.)

A. Yet many video stores make much of their decision not to stock NC-17 films (not porno—but legit NC-17s like *Showgirls*). Let me see if I can follow this reasoning: They're encouraging spicy content for movies available to younger viewers, while forbidding it in videos available to adults.

Editing

Q. Would you agree that one of the biggest failings of recent blockbusters has been poor editing in terms of continuity and plot development? The latest *Die Hard* film seems extremely jumpy, and *Jurassic Park* needed another reel to tie up the loose ends. Has Hollywood decided that given enough stunts and special effects, the viewer won't notice that things don't make sense? (Larry E. Jones, Ontario, Calif.)

A. Basically, yes. Another problem is that blockbusters are rushed through editing in order to make crucial opening-date deadlines. And often their endings are reshot after "test screenings." In the case of *Die Hard III*, several endings were filmed, and the print arrived in theaters hardly dry from the lab.

Q. Why does Tim Robbins announce in the credits for *Dead Man Walking* that "this movie was edited on good old-fashioned editing machines"? Do you know if there's some advantage to editing them that way, as opposed to on an Avid system? (Michael E. Isbell, Oklahoma City)

A. Avid systems allow editors to quickly and inexpensively view many different cuts of a scene, without having to physically cut and reassemble the film, as in traditional methods. Some editors and directors are entering only reluctantly into this new computerized video system, preferring the hands-on approach of physically manipulating the film.

Q. I've heard many stories about how studios want "last-minute reshoots" to "clear up confusion," "add more dramatic punch," and other nonsense. *Die Hard With a Vengeance* did reshoots mere weeks before its premiere; *Star Trek Generations* went back to "more clearly define Kirk's death." If I'm not mistaken, the producers, actors, and directors should be taking extra care in trying to place these "reshot" endings or sequences into the finished product as seamlessly as possible. But now the reshoots are starting to clash with the actual movie, and I'm starting to get mad. In *Striptease*, the entire sequence at the end in the refinery must have been added late. Reason? Because, presumably seconds later, they're walking in broad daylight *near a cornfield*! While *Striptease* itself could have numbed the audience's mind to allow these details to slide, I'm hoping reshoots don't show their cut-and-paste edges so prominently in the future. What are your thoughts? (Paul Fuhr, Milan, Ohio)

A. I don't pretend to remember *Striptease* shot by shot, but wasn't that a sugar refinery? Was it connected to corn syrup and other corn by-products? Just asking, since there were so many corn by-products in the rest of the movie . . .

Eraser Rail Guns

Q. In your discussion of the weapons named rail guns in *Eraser,* you quote the director, who says, "They can pierce three-foot-thick cement walls and then knock a canary off a tin can with absolute accuracy." Shooting anything through a three-foot wall of cement wouldn't be that big a trick, cement being a fine, gray powder having little intrinsic strength. Mix cement, sand, gravel, and water, let it set up, and you have: concrete, which is considerably stronger. (Bruce Small, Tucson, Ariz.)

A. Hey, I just quote these Hollywood geniuses, I don't do their contracting for them.

Q. Re your doubts about the plausibility of the "rail guns" that shoot bullets at almost the speed of light, in Arnold Schwarzenegger's *Eraser.* My cousin was one of the developers of the rail gun at the University of Texas in the '80s. It actually, in theory, does fire at the speed of light, because a man-made lightning bolt propels the object. There is no recoil, because there is no explosion in your typical gunpowder fashion. It's being developed in a project called *Brilliant Pebbles,* as a *Star Wars*–type device that would actually shoot out numerous pieces of clay at this extremely high rate of speed into space to knock out incoming ballistic missiles. It's one of those secret projects the government is working on, which is not so secret. (Drew Deiches, Orlando, Fla.)

A. At least not as long as your cousin blabs everything to you.

Explanations

Q. Although I thought *The Piano* was well acted, especially by Holly Hunter as Ada, I was distracted by some inconsistencies in the plot. For example, early in the film Baines, the Keitel character, tells her he cannot read. Yet in the climactic scene she writes him a message on a piano key. Has she forgotten he is illiterate? (James Walton, Edmonton, Canada)

A. This is an excellent question. I referred it to Jan Chapman, who produced the film. Her response: "Ada sent the written key because she knew that Baines would somehow respond to it. At the time, she was feeling so much emotion she couldn't verbally express, that she couldn't help but write on the key."

Q. I have a couple questions about the movie *The Big Sleep*. (1) What was the point of the "cipher" that Bogart was trying to solve? It was never referred to again in the movie. (2) Did you find the movie as confusing as I did? It seemed like there were about a dozen minor characters who are thrown in along the way. (John Jensen, Wilbraham, Mass.)

A. One of the writers of the screenplay for *The Big Sleep* was the great novelist William Faulkner, who couldn't make sense of the story. According to a Hollywood legend, he called Raymond Chandler, author of the original novel, and asked him for an explanation. After Chandler provided it, Faulkner pointed out several loopholes and inconsistencies. "Then I'm as confused as you are," Chandler said.

Q. I just read your review of *Assassins*, where you talk about the characters' names, and I thought you might like to know that Elektra (spelled with a "k") is a comic book character in the DareDevil series (written by Frank Miller, the same guy who did "Dark Knight"). She is one of those assassin/ninja types . . . so maybe it makes sense??? (Joe Long, Redmond, Wash.)

A. So *that's* where they got the name! And here I thought it was a reference to the title character in plays by Sophocles and Euripides. In psychiatry, the Electra Complex reflects a young woman's attraction to her father and hostility to her mother, but there are, of course, no mothers in *Assassins*.

Extras

Q. I was an extra in the Julia Roberts film, *My Best Friend's Wedding*, shot in Chicago. We were filming at Buddy Guy's club. At the crew table, I noticed to my surprise that there was an abundance of grass for cast and crew. Not the kind you smoke, however. I'm talking about lawn-type grass, growing in plastic nursery containers. Next to the grass they put a pair of scissors to cut it with. People would grind it up and drink it. I learned that this was "wheat grass," and apparently it was good for the digestion. The extras were having a ball making jokes and stealing grass to eat. I had some and it was delicious. Not as good as in my backyard, but better than what I eat at the park. I'm going to have to add this to my health diet. (Rev. Steven L. Schuneman, Niles, Mich.)

A. Heh, heh. On every movie set since the dawn of time, the extras have complained that they're fed bologna on white bread while the cast dines on sirloin. Now the cast gets grass and the extras are still trying to sneak a bite. Did anyone eat one of the plastic nursery containers?

Q. I am a part-time film extra with twenty-five films since 1986, starting with *The Color of Money* and including *Rookie of the Year, Gladiator,* etc. I am now retired. My big question: What chance does a mostly unnoticed film extra, commonly known as "background actor with no lines," or stooge in crowd scenes, have as perhaps a bit actor with lines, name on credits, etc.? I love show business. "Background! Lights! Camera! Action! Roll 'em! Cut!" are music to my ears. But how does an extra get to be an actor? (Herbert Bussewitz, Chicago)

A. Can you act? If you can, there are two possibilities. (1) You might be given a line or a bit of business on the spur of the moment if a scene calls for it and you look the type. (2) You could offer your services free to film students and other filmmakers on small budgets. They have all the young volunteers they need but often need older characters in their movies. Post a notice on the bulletin boards of campus film departments. If one of those kids becomes the next Philip Kaufman, William Friedkin, Andrew Davis, or Robert Zemeckis (who all have humble Chicago filmmaking origins), they might remember you.

Fargo

Q. My only problem with *Fargo* was that the guy played by William H. Macy seems to have one more scam going than he needs. (Spoiler warning: Do not read further if you have not seen the movie.) He's scamming GM for $320,000, he's scamming his father-in-law for a million dollars, and on top of that he's trying to get him to loan him $750,000—and all of this is taking place simultaneously. The only way I think *Fargo* could have been improved is if we were told more about why he needed all that money. If he set up the kidnapping to get the dough he needed for the real-estate deal, then why not wait until after he knows the loan isn't gonna happen? And what did he do with the $320,000 he stole from GM? Any two of these three schemes make sense together, but the three are unnecessary unless he's just trying to get up as much cash as possible and then flee to Argentina or something. (Andy Ihnatko, Westwood, Mass.)

A. What I like the most about your question is that it inaugurates the inevitable *Pulp Fiction* phase of the *Fargo* phenomenon, where the plot is micro-analyzed. Does this movie have its own Web page yet? A matter of time. As to your question, I look forward to a review of the movie by an accountant, who may be able to explain where the money is supposed to be going, and why.

Q. *Fargo* is *not* based on a true story. The opening credits say that it is and the press notes make the same claim. However, reporters in Minneapolis (hometown of the Coens) did their homework and investigated police records and the Bureau of Crime Statistics. There was no case like this in Minnesota, nor anything close to it. And when "confronted," the Coen brothers were cheerfully evasive about it. They're famous for playing tricks and putting inside jokes in their work. For example, Roderick Jayne, the guy listed as the "editor" in *Fargo* and, I believe, *The Hudsucker Proxy*, doesn't exist. "He" is really the Coen brothers themselves. (Mary Jo Kaplan, New York)

A. The strange thing is, after seeing the movie I seemed to vaguely recall a true case it could have been based on, involving an auto dealer hiring a couple of guys to kidnap his wife. The film has such a down-home authenticity to it that it seems drawn from life, even if it isn't.

Q. I saw *Fargo* yesterday, really enjoyed it and definitely agree with your assessment, but I believe this film broke the Law of Economy of Character Development in *Ebert's Little Movie Glossary*, which states ". . . all characters in a movie are necessary to the story." Although the old high school friend contributed a scene of great humor and angst, he appeared to be extraneous to the plot. Any thoughts? (Bret Hayden, Thousand Oaks, Calif.)

A. He's a character out of left field with no purpose except to provide a wonderful interlude, almost like a free-standing short film within the body of the longer one. But that was okay with me.

Q. In the closing credits of *Fargo*, the actor who played the dead driver in the field isn't listed by name. Instead, there is a strange symbol in the credits. What does it mean? (Rich Leahy, Oakland, Calif.)

A. Seymour Uranowitz of the CompuServe ShowBiz Forum says Ethan Coen told *Premiere*: "That was our storyboard artist, who played the guy who drives by in the car with the red parka. He asked us if he could have that credit."

Ironically, the symbol in the cast credits has been misinterpreted by some viewers, leading to a rumor that the Singer Formerly Known as Prince plays the dead man. That's what you get for filming in Minneapolis.

Q. So why is *Fargo* named *Fargo* if, as *Time* magazine says, it "has not much at all to do with Fargo, North Dakota"? Why didn't they name it "Brainerd"? (J. Cole, Bismarck, N.Dak.)

A. Well, the unhappy husband *does* travel to Fargo to hire the kidnappers, which is sort of an answer. More to the point, the Coens said on the Charlie Rose show that it was a choice between "Fargo" and "Brainerd," and so they chose *Fargo*. Are we ready for a movie named "Brainerd"?

Q. Regarding the Answer Man question about the complex scams William H. Macy has going in *Fargo*, you responded, "I look forward to a review of the movie by an accountant, who may be able to explain where the money is supposed to be going." My wife had a thought. Perhaps the same accountants who figured out that *Forrest Gump* lost money (after a $300 million–plus gross on U.S. screens alone) would be the ones to contact. (Robert Haynes-Peterson, Boise, Id.)

A. If the Macy character in *Fargo* had been a Hollywood studio accountant, he would never have been caught.

Q. The movie *Fargo* has an actor named Peter Stormare in it, playing the kidnapper who hardly ever speaks. My husband thinks that he is a semi-well-known Swedish actor. I have never heard of the man, but I wanted to check on it. (Lisa Ahlstedt, Knoxville, Tenn.)

A. He is a semi-well-known Swedish actor who can also be seen, in quite a different role, in Louis Malle's *Damage* (1992).

Q. In my opinion *Fargo* is full of unnecessary scenes, such as the last one discussing the "duck stamp," the scene with the earthworms, the scene with the old classmate, the scene of the police chief calling an old friend, the scene of the two kidnappers having sex and later watching the *Tonight Show,* etc. (Mike Pollard, Ballwin, Mo.)

A. All scenes in all movies are unnecessary—unless they entertain or interest us. The notion that every single scene must advance the plot is responsible for many of the thin, untextured, big-budget action pictures that are dulling the imagination of the mass movie audience. One of the many charms of *Fargo* was the way it allowed the three-dimensional humanity of the characters to coexist with the kidnapping plot.

Fat and Thin

Q. I just read your review of *Angus* and I'm fuming. You had the nerve to say it's about time there was a movie where the fat kid finally gets the girl. What crap! When haven't you seen a movie where some fat slob didn't have a young, thin, beautiful wife or girlfriend?

Why is it perfectly okay for him to be fat and she has to be thin and pretty? You will *never* see a film where a fat, homely, dumpy-looking girl gets the handsome jock guy. (Rebecca McKay, Chicago)

A. I am drawing up a list of male fat slobs who are movie stars and get thin, beautiful women. Let's see. John Belushi, John Candy, John Goodman . . . but Candy usually played lonely guys, and Goodman, of course, became famous on TV by playing the husband of a fat, homely, dumpy-looking girl. I felt *Splash* would have been funnier if Darryl Hannah's mermaid, who had never seen human males before, chose the John Candy character to love, but noooo: She picked Tom Hanks. Hollywood's bias against fat is an equal opportunity prejudice.

Q. I am very concerned about the promos I'm seeing for *The Nutty Professor.* As an activist and advocate for large-size people, it seems to me that the kind of "jokes" I see played out on the screen perpetuate the myths about fat people that keep us from being given equal opportunities in society. Do you think this movie will be offensive to fat people, and if so, how you think we could best handle the situation? Should we picket movie theaters, do a letter-writing campaign, or complain to theater owners or studio heads? (Lynn McAfee, Mount Marion, N.Y.)

A. In the movie, Eddie Murphy plays a fat professor who takes a secret potion and becomes a thin person. As a fat person, he is genial, intelligent, attractive to the opposite sex, and completely lovable. As a thin person, he is an obnoxious womanizer and lounge lizard who goes berserk in nightclubs. The movie, in other words, is based on real life.

Q. I'm intrigued by actors who have either lost or gained a lot of weight during the filming of a movie—for example, De Niro in *Raging Bull,* and more recently, Matt Damon in *Courage Under Fire.* Both actors were fat and skinny in the *same movie.* I'd like to know whether they started filming fat and then fasted for a month, or whether they started filming skinny and then ate shakes all day to change their bodies. (Mark McSweeney, Indianapolis, Ind.)

A. Director Martin Scorsese shut down the production of *Rag-*

ing Bull for three months so that De Niro could go to Europe and pig out, putting on some sixty pounds.

According to Mike Nolan, assistant to Matt Damon's CAA agent Patrick Whitesell, "Matt dropped forty pounds during the filming of *Courage Under Fire* by going on a strict diet and undertaking an arduous workout schedule with a personal trainer. Toward the end of the film, he was so weak that he would faint nearly every day. After the film was completed and he tried to put the weight back on, Matt found that his weakness and dizziness continued. In fact, Matt's regimen had thrown off his blood sugar level to the degree that he had to go on medication. Now, Matt is back to his regular weight and back in perfect health. The perils of method acting!"

Film Critics

Q. Have the critics now explicitly joined the marketing conspiracy surrounding *The Crying Game?* I can't shake the image of film critics across the country tittering as they leaf through thesauri to perpetuate the film's secret. Has this movie blurred the line between critics and marketing agents in the same way it blurs so many other lines? I'm a great fan of Neil Jordan and of the film. Just, perhaps, excessively curious in a troublesome poststructural way. (Steve Solnick, Harvard University)

A. My feeling is that if I had revealed the secret in my review, readers would have been outraged. I assumed the Oscar nominations would essentially spoil the game, but they haven't as yet. Congratulations on getting into Harvard. At the University of Illinois, my alma mater, if we felt excessively curious in a troublesome poststructural way, we went to the chiropractor.

Q. A great majority of the time the movies that earn raves from the critics are seldom the movies which earn raves from the moviegoer at large. My question is how do you explain this? I assume that you review and recommend movies on the basis of your personal taste. Do you believe a case could be made for a critic to review and recommend movies on a basis of what the general public would like instead of the critic's personal taste? (J. David Mecham)

A. This solution would require a critic who is prepared to lie, by pretending that his opinion is the same as he perceives the public's opinion to be. There is no shortage of such critics. Send me a stamped, self-addressed envelope and I will be happy to supply you with a list.

Q. When a movie ends, do you get up as soon as the credits start to roll or do you watch all of the credits and see who was involved behind the scenes? (Noah W. Kadner, Albuquerque, N. Mex.)

A. Depends on (a) if I was interested in the movie's technical credits, (b) if I like the background music, and (c) whether it's one of those *Airplane!*-style movies with extra bonus gags to look forward to. If the answer to all three questions is "no," you'll find me, in the immortal words of *Variety,* "ankling for the exit."

Q. Help me settle something. If Writer A and Writer B both wrote their opinions on a film—both with diligence and pride in their work—what difference in the two pieces would identify Writer A as a film critic and Writer B as someone just offering an opinion? Take the weekly feature you see in some papers, where kids review films. At what point do they cross the line, and can be called critics as opposed to reviewers? Is there some sort of certification program, like taking the Sally Struthers correspondence course in gun repair? (Andy Ihnatko, Westwood, Mass.)

A. This is a fascinating question, not unrelated to, "at what point do we know Swift doesn't really intend for the starving Irish to eat their babies?" The noncritic reviewer will often betray himself by these mistakes: (1) Pretense of objectivity; (2) reluctance to introduce extraneous knowledge; (3) predictions of which audiences will or will not enjoy the film; (4) bashfulness about writing in the first person; (5) distancing self from actual experience of viewing the film; (7) an overwritten first paragraph. The genuine critic will write in such a way as to acknowledge that he had a subjective personal experience that he wants to share with you, and which reminded him of other films or other subjects. He will wear his knowledge lightly and never presume to speak for other than himself.

Q. Do you think that because you've reviewed so many movies, your opinions may not reflect that of the public? If you say the story line has been overused, does it mean it isn't a good movie to other people who haven't seen as many movies as you? Others may think it's an original story line and enjoy the movie. Is it possible to be an objective movie critic? (Andy Chin, San Diego)

A. I have no interest in being objective or in reflecting the public's opinion. A critic should not be a ventriloquist's dummy, sitting on the knee of the public and letting it put words into his mouth. The only critics of any use or worth are those who express their *own* opinions, which the readers are then free to use or ignore. Anyone who believes a critic must reflect the views of the public has not thought much about the purpose of criticism.

Q. I saw a documentary about David Lean in which he talked about an incident in which Pauline Kael said some mean-spirited things about his then current film *Ryan's Daughter.* Lean said that all of the negative reaction, culminating with Kael's remarks, led him to abandon directing for more than a decade. First, do you know anything more about the whole event? Perhaps it is unfair to blame Kael for losing a decade's worth of David Lean films, but I wonder, what purpose does this sort of attack criticism serve? (Michael Levy)

A. I have not heard about the incident you describe, although it is certainly true that *Ryan's Daughter* deserved negative criticism. If David Lean allowed Pauline Kael to influence him so much that he quit making films for ten years, then he was a fool. I can't imagine anyone with the temperament of a film director having such a fragile ego. But the "lost decade" is not Kael's fault. Actually, Lean lost many years in the 1980s preparing an ill-fated version of *Mutiny on the Bounty,* with producer Dino De Laurentiis pulling the plug shortly before filming was set to begin.

Q. What is your personal preference in seating within a theater? I have heard so many different opinions, I'd like yours. (Tom Jacobs, Vernon Hills, Ill.)

A. I follow two consistent rules: (1) Sit twice as far back as the screen is wide. (2) Sit on the "outboard" aisle seat—in other words, *across* the aisle from the center section. That way, there will be no one between you and the screen.

Q. When you review a movie and give it two and a half stars in the paper, is that a thumbs-up or thumbs-down on your TV program? (Mike D'Alessandro, Actor, Mass.)

A. Three stars means thumbs-up, anything less means thumbs-down. This is a firm rule with me. My colleague Gene Siskel on three occasions has given thumbs-up to 2.5-star movies—always, he assures me, after prudent consideration. What is obviously required here is a horizontal thumb.

Q. I'm curious. I occasionally tend to write in the first person in reviews. I saw in your book your feeling on that, and I tend to agree, but many people I've talked to believe that as a twenty-year-old college student, it's a bit of hubris on my part to use it in my reviews, since I'm not established like yourself. Advice? Comments? Suggestions? Recipes? (Will Leitch, *The Daily Illini*, Urbana, Ill.)

A. All reviews are tacitly written in the first person anyway, since they are the opinion of the person who is writing, and make no pretense of objectivity. So go ahead and write that way. And be thankful the "editorial we" has bitten the dust.

Q. Your *Little Movie Glossary* should include the "Left Is Right Principle of Movie Reviewing." This law, employed by many reviewers, is used faithfully by you. Simply stated, if the movie in question promotes an agenda that agrees with your politics, it will automatically get four stars (current examples: *Nixon, The American President*). You will point out a few examples of "left" films that you trashed, but for the most part, you tend to praise anything that believes like you do. (Dave Wilkie, Ozark, Mo.)

A. Here is the real test: Are *Nixon* and *The American President* good films? I say they are. I tried to explain why in my reviews. If you say they aren't, is it because they disagree with your politics?

You seem to feel the movies are bad primarily because of their political orientation. A critic who says a good film is bad, or a bad film is good, is a bad critic regardless of his politics.

Q. I was watching *Tonight Show* a few weeks ago and saw you on the same show with Dennis Miller. You and Gene were very complimentary to Miller (Gene at one point even suggesting that Dennis should be the Oscar host) and he seemed to return the favor. So I picked up a copy of Dennis's new book, *The Rants*, and I was surprised to read a rant in which he denounces criticism and critics in general, saying that they are useless and arrogant. At the end he basically says that the next time you give a review, the American public should tell you to go **** yourself. I was wondering, did you know of this particular section of his book that night on the *Tonight Show*, and if so, did you ever get a chance to discuss it with him? (Jeff McGinnis, Bowling Green, Ohio)

A. I had no idea that, or anything else, was in his book. Funny that he's so down on critics, since he kept interrupting during our segment with observations and suggestions, and during the commercial breaks kept shouting, "Hey, Jay, I got a great line you oughta use next!"

Q. If you were not a movie critic by profession, how many times a week would you go to the movies, and how often would you rent movies on video? (John Palino, Fremont, Calif.)

A. Before I became a movie critic, I went to the movies at least once or twice every week. Today, I think I'd watch movies much more often, because I've become interested in the careers of so many directors and actors, and because the invention of home video makes it easier to view almost any title. I would always prefer to attend movies in theaters, however, since light through celluloid onto a big screen is still by far the best way to exhibit a film.

Q. Did you happen to read the latest issue of *Entertainment Weekly*? Mel Brooks said: "There's a great quote: 'Critics are like eunuchs at an orgy—they just don't get it.' I ran into Roger Ebert. He didn't like *Dracula*. He made no bones about it—thumbs, pinkies, every digit that he had. And I said to him: 'Listen, you, I made twenty-one movies. I'm very talented. I'll live in history. I have a body of work. You only have a body.'" (Michael Hatch, North Kingstown, R.I.)

A. I was saddened by my encounter with Mel, because I have been a supporter of his work (when it deserved it) since *The Producers*, in 1967. I was one of the few critics who liked *Life Stinks*. I was surprised he didn't realize himself that *Dracula: Dead and Loving It* just didn't work. Yes, Brooks has put together a body of work and yes, a lot of it has made me laugh, but I would not be doing him a favor if I did not tell the truth. (The correct version of that quote, by the way, is by Brendan Behan, who said, "A critic at a performance is like a eunuch in a harem: He sees it performed nightly, but cannot do it himself.")

Q. I wasted $8.50 this weekend on *The Fan*. Why? Because you had not reviewed it and I had some free time. This was a major opening and many of us rely upon you. (Mark James, New York)

A. Like many movies that a studio has little faith in, *The Fan* was not previewed for critics before its opening. The obvious answer is to never attend a movie I have not reviewed.

Q. I watched the new CBS show *Early Edition* and found out that they use the *Chicago Sun-Times* as their one-day-ahead paper. When the paper was zoomed in, I could clearly see and read "Roger Ebert's Movie Review" on the paper. I was wondering if you have seen the show or not. (Min Woong Lee, Costa Mesa, Calif.)

A. I haven't yet seen the show, because I've been so busy with the flood of new movies to review. But you've given me an idea. If I could read the *Sun-Times two* days ahead, I could simply copy down my review and send it in to the paper, making it unnecessary for me to write it. This would save me a lot of work, and I could watch more TV.

In the Spring of 1997, I did a guest appearance on the show, consoling a little boy who was depressed that Bosco the Bunny had died.

Fireballs

Q. On a *Siskel & Ebert* program you showed Hollywood's frequent use of scenes where characters outrun shock waves from blasts. There was a true-life instance of this, the day Mt. St. Helens erupted, and trees were felled like matchsticks for miles around. At the moment of the blast there were two cars driving near each other and away from the volcano. One was a station wagon and the other a Jaguar (I think). When the volcano erupted the station wagon accelerated to about 80 mph and reached its limit. The Jaguar accelerated into the 100s. The station wagon was knocked off the road; the people in the Jaguar escaped. (David Shapiro, Libertyville, Ill.)

A. Call me a skeptic, but I don't believe even a Jaguar can outrun a shock wave. However, it might be able to get enough of a head start on an explosion at some distance that the shock wave would be safely dissipated by the time it reached the car. It's all a matter of physics.

Flops

Q. Whose responsibility is it when the art of the film fails? I had several criticisms of *Disclosure*, mostly on artistic grounds. These involved such parties as the screenwriter, the scorer, the cinematographer. Is this a group failure, or does the director have the artistic buck stop with him? (Jim Mork, Minneapolis)

A. The director must take ultimate responsibility. In the case of *Disclosure*, the entire plot hinges on the so-called sexual harassment scene between Demi Moore and Michael Douglas. The viewer has to pay close attention to figure out that she staged the scene, not out of lust, but because she *wanted* to file charges against Douglas in order to keep her assembly-line screw-up from being discovered. But in that case, why did she bother with the harassment at all? If lust was not her motivation, why was she willing to go all the way with a man she apparently hated? Why not just fabricate the charges? It would still be his word against hers. The answer is obvious: Because the movie needed the sex scene to sell tickets. As I explained in my review, the movie is essentially an inspiring shot of Demi Moore's cleavage, surrounded by goofiness. The sets are great, though.

Q. Whatever happened to the epic movie *Hurricane* that was supposed to be produced by Dino De Laurentiis? (O. Wallace, Chicago)

A. Questions like yours bring tears to the eyes of moviemakers. *Hurricane* was produced by Dino De Laurentiis at a cost of untold millions, was widely advertised, was released, was a critical and box office disaster, sank without a trace, and can now be found on video. And here you are still waiting for it. I actually spent a week in 1978 on the island of Bora Bora watching *Hurricane* being filmed, and attending the local Bastille Day celebration with Trevor Howard, who was on the wagon and thus not in the mood to celebrate much of anything. The production was doomed almost from the start by financial, logistical, script, and romantic complications, and the experience of being involved in it was documented in a book by Tim Zinnemann, who was an assistant producer.

Foley Artists

Q. During the credits of every movie, we see the "Foley Editors." Exactly what are these? And are there movies in which viewers can "really notice" them at work? (Randy Johnson, Newport Beach, Calif.)

A. According to Ephraim Katz's magnificent new *Film Encyclopedia*, Foley *artists* work on the sound track after production, specializing in sounds made by people (kisses, footsteps, etc.). If they do their jobs well, you do not notice them at all.

Q. When movies are dubbed for release in other countries, the spoken words are dubbed but not the noise from the background (cars, footsteps, etc.). How is this done? (Vincent Assmann, Heidelberg, Germany)

A. The incidental noises on a sound track are controlled by "Foley artists," so named after a movie sound veteran, who mix the dialogue tracks with sounds and effects that were recorded on location and others that are added in postproduction. While filming, sound men try to minimize the nondialogue sounds in a scene to make mixing easier. Often after a scene has been filmed, the sound man will ask for complete silence while a recording is made of the ambient background sound of a location, which can later be used while matching different takes of the scene.

Forrest Gump

Q. After seeing *Forrest Gump*, I got into a big argument with my friend Sarah about how they made Gary Sinise's legs disappear. She claimed he just tucked them under, but I contend that if you are going to involve special effects wizards extensively in a film, they are going to be more hi-tech. Which one of us is right? (Lydia Smith, Winnetka, Canada)

A. You are. Special effects expert Marc Wielage of the Compu-Serve Consumer Electronics Forum explains: "Three techniques were used to hide Lt. Dan's legs: (1) digital computer removal (very expensive and complicated); (2) an incredible "mirror" arrangement in the wheelchair, partially designed by magician Ricky Jay; and (3) holes in the bed, holes in the floor, and careful shooting. It's the best effect of its type I've ever seen, and I swear, I've seen 'em all. If this movie doesn't win the Oscar for Best Visual Effects, they should digitally remove the Motion Picture Academy's building on Wilshire Boulevard." And Paul Voisine, also from CE-Forum, adds: "Notice particularly the scenes in the hospital where the orderlies have to pick up Lt. Dan off the bed and you can clearly see there are no legs, and no room to hide them bent under him. But there's something a little 'wrong' that a sharp eye can see. My gut feeling is that it's the shadows and lighting on the bed under them, since they had to digitally erase the shadows of his existing legs."

It won for Best Visual Effects.

Q. I've seen *Forrest Gump* twice now, and I'm convinced the "computer-generated amputation" is a publicity stunt, and they really cut off Gary Sinese's legs. Proof? Why does he play the grounded astronaut in *Apollo 13? Because he has no legs!* This way he can sit in a chair at mission control. Also, why didn't he win the Best Supporting Oscar? Because they couldn't computer-graft legs onto him during a live broadcast! I hope this clears things up, and that Mr. Sinese was fairly compensated for the sacrifice for *F.G.*, (i.e., gross, not net profits). (Robert Haynes-Peterson, Boise, Id.)

A. But what about the scene in *Apollo 13* where he parks his car, gets out of it, walks around it, and looks wistfully at the rocket launching? How do you explain that? Never mind; I'm afraid to ask. Moving on to your statement that the "computer-generated animation" was a "publicity stunt"—hey, I'm no publicist, but my guess is, cutting off an actor's legs would get even more publicity.

Q. I sat through the endless credits of *Forrest Gump* to find out who the dialect coach was, just so I could find out if it was the same one responsible for Jodie Foster's disastrous attempt at an Appalachian accent in *Silence of the Lambs*. Yeah, I know she won an Oscar, and Tom Hanks will at least be nominated for *Forrest Gump*, but neither of them has an ear for dialect. I hereby demand that neither of them ever, ever make another movie that calls for a southern dialect. Ever. The coach is one Jessica Drake, and either she is an incompetent pretender or she just gave up with Tom: "Just do it any old way, dear, no one will notice! You're supposed to be stupid anyway." By the way, in the South, they say "Fah-rest," not "Fore-est," so everyone had that wrong, too. (Guenveur Burnell, Kent, Ohio)

A. Lawd-a-mercy, chile, you *do* speak yo' mind!

Q. Had Ms. Burnell watched a recent HBO special about the making of *Forrest Gump* then she would know that Tom Hanks learned to say 'Forrest' and other words from one Michael Humphreys, who played young Forrest in the film. Humphreys has lived his life in small-town Mississippi and certainly should be capable of speaking in a southern accent correctly. Or maybe Ms. Burnell imagines some uniform southern accent which is promoted in Kent, Ohio. (Chris Morton, Edwardsville, Ill.)

A. For you, bubba, that's "Kay-yent, Ohiyuh."

Q. My wife and I are trying to figure out where else we've heard that music that's used in the TV ads and promos for *Forrest Gump*. Very big, sweeping theme. It's got to come from some other movie, but we can't figure it out. Do you know? (Noel Boulanger, Medford, Mass.)

A. David Abrams of the CompuServe ShowBiz Forum replies: "The music is from *Dragon: The Bruce Lee Story*. I liked the theme so much, I bought the sound track!"

Q. I enjoyed *Forrest Gump*, but had it been a male seducing a mildly retarded female, instead of the other way around, it would have been a rape scene, even though there was consent. My question is, Have I been a social worker for too long? (Jim Sinsky, Milwaukee)

A. Not long enough, apparently, if you can still ask the question.

Q. Do you believe *Forrest Gump* represents a politically conservative fable? Is the movie making a statement about integrity, Christian values, self-reliance, and traditional family structures? Rush Limbaugh entertained these thoughts to his twenty million listeners. Most callers believed the popularity of the movie was, in part, due to this appeal to the conservative values in America. (Tim O'Connor, Cleveland, Ohio)

A. *Forrest Gump* can be read as liberal or conservative, depending on your personal prejudices, but it makes a point of avoiding political ideology. Limbaugh often tries to hijack nonpolitical but popular subjects in order to bask in their glow.

Q. How gracious of you to show my letter about *Forrest Gump* to Tom Hanks. He wrote me a letter of thanks and sent me $15 to take a friend with me to the movies and buy some popcorn. Thank God for people like you and Tom Hanks to take time out of your busy days to make an eighty-four-year-old feel important. (Marie Hangel, Chicago)

A. Your letter of praise for Hanks's performance struck me as so heartfelt that I really wanted Tom to see it. By the way, Mrs. Hangel, I received a separate letter, that you may not know about, from your friend Mindie Bright. She wrote: "Mr. Hanks sent her $15 for *one* movie with a friend and popcorn. Are you kidding? Marie will go to the Senior Citizen's ladies' showings for fifty cents or $1. She'll be at the movies all year around now!"

Four-letter Words

Q. I was having lunch today and the subject of profanity in films came up. I asked the following trivia question, "When was the first time the F-word was spoken in a major motion picture?" By a man? By a woman? None of us knew. Do you? (Fred Ostby, Kansas City, Mo.)

A. Elizabeth Barnes of the Motion Picture Association of America told me it has no record of the first time the F-word was used. However, when I posted your query in the CompuServe ShowBiz Forum James Curran wrote, "I don't know about the first use, but *The Front* and *All the President's Men* tied for being the first PG-rated movies to use the word." And Odell Henderson of Jersey City, N.J., added: "I was reading my Guinness film book and it told me the F-wording-est movie of all time was Martin Scorsese's *Goodfellas*, in which something like 275 variations of youknowwhat were uttered. That works out to once every twenty-eight seconds. The censored TV print's sound track must sound like the Emergency Broadcast System signal."

Q. I recently saw *The Client* on a United Airlines flight and noticed that the sound track had been dubbed to replace profanities with substitute words. I would assume that a bit of violence may also have been removed, for example during the suicide episode. My guess is that the resulting movie would be given a PG rating. There are many popular movies that I would love to rent for viewing with my family if only they were rated G or (maybe) PG. Cleaning up the language, removing the sex, and toning down any graphic violence would make very little difference to the entertainment value for many people of the movies I'm talking about. Are "airline edits" available anywhere for rental? Have studios ever considered issuing "family" and "mature" versions of the same movie? (Jon Bale, San Jose, Calif.)

A. Such versions are not available through ordinary rental and sale channels. Some directors are so disturbed by the "airline edits" of their films that they have their names removed (Robert Mulligan, for example, took his name off of *The Man in the Moon*). Their contracts usually include the studio's right to edit for in-flight and broadcast use, however. Most directors would violently oppose a similar edited version for commercial video channels. I am sure you are correct that a market for such films exists; I doubt that an R movie could easily be transformed into a PG, but it would be easier to tone down a PG-13. I believe, however, that films are works of art, not commodities, and that every film should be seen as the director intended.

Q. While in Puerto Rico recently I went to see *The Shawshank Redemption.* It featured subtitles in Spanish, and I know enough Spanish to tell that the profanity spoken in English was muted to the point of nonexistence in the subtitles. In fact, while the movie was rated R in English, it could easily have been downgraded to PG-13 in Spanish. Does this kind of language-cleansing happen commonly? (Dave Blanchard, Kent, Ohio)

A. "The common industry practice on subtitling," according to a source at Castle Rock Foreign Distribution, "is to use what is called 'neutral language,' intended to impart a 'sense' of the original dialogue while avoiding certain phrases that could prove more shocking when read than heard." And in answer to what would probably be your next question—Is the same process used when foreign films are subtitled in English?—the answer is "no," possibly because in America these days there are no phrases that prove more shocking when read than heard.

Q. I just don't get it. I just watched *Bridge on the River Kwai* again. It still holds up well. All of the right ingredients and no bad language or gratuitous violence. Contrast that with almost any big-budget, extravaganza today and all you hear is "f——— this" and "f——— that," sandwiched between overblown chases, set pieces, and unnecessary violence. Why have the standards changed so much? Don't misread me—I love the new movies as much as the next guy, but I do get weary at times of shock language and unrealistic violence thrown in for no real reason. Don't filmmakers today have any sense of the past? I guess one look at Quentin Tarantino would answer that, though. (Mike Murrow, Wichita, Kans.)

A. I was with you right up to your slam at Tarantino, whose films have opened doors for writers and directors with original approaches—and who does have a sense of the past. I don't object to the language in R-rated films, but what I hate are the PG movies like *Eddie* that throw in a few four-letter words as a deliberate ploy to qualify for PG-13, so that teenagers won't dismiss them as "kids' movies."

Frankenactors

Q. Computer science has reached the point where producing a synthetic, realistic, original full-length movie with stars like Gable, Astaire, Garland, Bogart, etc., is possible. These are not just lifts from old movies (such as in soda commercials), but full-action computer models, convincingly real in speech and visual appearance. I look forward with anticipation to these new synthetic movies because they combine old talents with new directors and writers. How about morphing the looks of a Clark Gable with the dancing skill of Astaire and the voice of Pavarotti? (Lloyd E. Clark, Millersville, Md.)

A. And the legs of Betty Grable? The use of Frankenactors is immoral—a violation of the rights of the dead to have the book closed on their own lives. What actor would relinquish to a computer his control over tone, nuance, and emotion? If we see new movies with a computerized Bogart, will those "performances" then affect our view of his actual work? Such appropriation of images is artistic theft. The people who make those TV commercials with ripped-off footage from old movies should be ashamed of themselves. As punishment, they should be forced to watch porno flicks starring their grandmothers.

Q. *Forrest Gump* has me wondering about something. When is it okay and when is it not okay to use computerized versions of real people, deceased, in a film? Is it okay to use historical figures such as past presidents, but not okay to use actors since it's a little too close to home, and the real actors might very well have performed quite differently? Was it okay to use Elvis in this way in the film? I'm trying to get a grasp on why this is fine, but putting Bogart in a Coke commercial seemed to lean more toward bad taste. (Barb Schroeder)

A. Hmmm. Now that computers edge us closer to the day when a movie "performance" can be totally manufactured, this is a question with fascinating aspects. I was offended by Bogart in the Coke commercial—it seemed to me they were ripping off his memory—but I enjoyed Forrest Gump's computerized encounters with Kennedy, Johnson, Nixon, Elvis, and so forth. Maybe art redeems what commerce exploits? To do something briefly as an effect is one thing; to materialize an entire performance is something else.

Q. I do some computer programming on the side and I have learned much about the machine's capabilities. Seems that it might be possible one day to produce a movie completely by computer without the need for actors, props, sets, or human music. Would the public accept this? How about yourself? I doubt if I would like a Clint Eastwood movie with no Eastwood—just computer art and sound. How far should Hollywood go? Could everything become like that Holodeck on the new *Star Trek*? (Mike Jordan, Snow Camp, N.C.)

A. It will definitely be possible to produce a movie that looks "real" but is entirely the product of a computer. Already, a special effects company in the Silicon Valley is said to have a Marilyn Monroe program that can create a cyber-performance by MM. My guess, however, is that such programming will create images that don't have soul. To paraphrase Mark Twain, actors cloned by computer will know the words, but not the music.

Fruit Carts

Q. I had a great time at *The Rock*, and thought that the director, Michael Bay, winked at film lovers more than once, especially in the car chase that threw in every cliché in the chase book, including heroes who jump into cool vehicles that just happen to be waiting for them, the San Francisco hill ramping, the parking meters getting wiped out, guys in wheelchairs, a little old lady crossing the street with a shopping cart, the hero taking a shortcut through a building, a truck carrying water tanks crossing the street just in time to get slammed into, etc. I was waiting for a fruit cart to get hit or two guys to be carrying a plate-glass window across the street but I guess that would've been too much. (David Hunt, Springdale, Ark.)

A. But there *was* a Fruit Cart scene, complete with fruit flying through the air. Of all the entries in *Ebert's Little Movie Glossary*, that's the one that has achieved the most notoriety, so how could Bay leave it out? I agree that the chase scene, in addition to working on its own level, also functioned as a sly anthology of obligatory shots from every other chase scene.

The Fugitive

Q. What was in that bag that Tommy Lee Jones gave Harrison Ford at the end of *The Fugitive*? (Peter Sherman, Monroe, La.)

A. "An ice pack for his swollen hands," director Andrew Davis replies.

Q. In *The Fugitive*, why was a U.S. marshal involved in the search for an escaped convict in Illinois? Kimball was convicted of a state offense in Cook County Circuit Court and was on his way to a state prison, yet a marshal entered the investigation almost immediately, before there was any evidence he committed a federal offense. (Robert J. Smith)

A. Back to Andy Davis again: "It is little known, even within the law enforcement community, that U.S. marshals have long been primarily responsible for fugitives from the law. It was implied in our movie that a joint operation of federal, state, and local authorities was set up to investigate the train wreck, and that the governor of Illinois had personally asked the U.S. marshal to see to the matter downstate. If Richard Kimble had crossed state lines, the case would definitely have been handled by the FBI."

Goofy

Q. This may seem like a goofy question, but is Goofy a dog? My daughter says he doesn't have a species, he's just a cartoon character. Now wait, I argued. Donald is a duck, Mickey is a mouse, and Pluto is most definitely a dog. Goofy has what appear to be canine teeth, lop ears, a snout, and a blank nose. Is he a dog or not? (Vic Sussman, Washington, D.C.)

A. My rule is this: If they walk upright, they're cartoon characters. If they walk on all fours, they're dogs. Maybe it would help you to think of Goofy as a little further up the evolutionary ladder than Pluto.

Q. Regarding your review of *A Goofy Movie*, and your musing over whether Goofy is a dog or not: If I have my Disney history right, Goofy first appeared as a character named "Dippy Dawg." I imagine this answers the question, unless Dippy underwent some crash-evolution on the way to being Goofy. (Chris Rowland, Ocean, N.J.)

A. No dog would be worried sick about his teenage son going out on a date.

Q. Re your earlier discussion of Goofy as a single parent: As most of us with children know (having been subjected to a billion hours of the *Disney Afternoon*), Goofy did not go through a custody battle to gain his single-parent status. Max was adopted prior to the beginning of *Goof Troop* on television. Just thought I'd let you know. My wife Annetta, however, has expressed an interest in Goofy in the past, so there are women out there who would be glad to have him. (Neil Moody)

A. Gorsh!

Hair

Q. I'm a bit puzzled by your comments about Brad Pitt's hairstyle on this week's *Siskel & Ebert* program. In your review of *Legends of the Fall* you said you liked the film but thought Pitt needed a haircut. I was wondering, if his hair were cut for the more conservative look, would the film have been better? What difference does it make if Marlon Brando is fat or skinny or if Patrick Stewart has a full head of hair, just as long as they give a good performance? (Herman Chang, Hacienda Heights, Calif.)

A. I think Brad Pitt is very talented, and would have had no problem with his hair length in another story. But I felt a man living at the time of World War I would not be likely to wear his hair in a ponytail below his shoulders unless his name was Buffalo Bill.

For a look at men's hairstyles of the time, see any photograph of Woodrow Wilson.

Q. I am experiencing a crisis with a friend who insists on lowering some of my favorite films to the common denominator of "Hair Movies." I really liked *Last of the Mohicans,* as there have never been enough decent Revolutionary era films. My friend says the film was a failure because nobody had access to cream rinse in those days, as "Hawkeye" must have, since his hair was too perfect. Now when I think of this film, I can only see Daniel Day-Lewis in curlers on the way to the set. It happened again with *Legends of the Fall,* where Brad Pitt's hair (according to my friend) had an unnatural luster that could not have been achieved without cream rinse.

Now it has gone too far. I am a history buff, Mel Gibson fan, and Scotsman by descent. I am eagerly awaiting *Braveheart,* but my friend mischievously commented the other day "Oh, another Hair Movie, eh?" I have now lodged in my consciousness a picture of Sir William Wallace looking like Fabio on a paperback cover, replete with wind machines and unbuttoned shirt. All period movies now look like *Dr. Quinn, Medicine Woman* to me. What do you think about this, and do you have any remedial suggestions? (James T. Cook, Corpus Christi, Tex.)

A. As a corrective, I suggest you rent *Roadie,* and study Meat Loaf's hair carefully to see what the heroes of the movies you love would have looked like without modern advances in hair care.

Q. I wish whoever is dyeing all those people's hair red would find a new profession. I've never seen so much bad hair as there is in movies lately. Look into it. (Guenveur Burnell, Kent, Ohio)

A. I'm on the case.

Q. Why do movie directors feel compelled to change Jim Carrey's hair? In *Earth Girls Are Easy* it was dyed blond, in *Ace Ventura* it was a '50s Elvis pompadour, *Dumb and Dumber* I don't even like to think about, *The Mask* altered it for obvious reasons, and the preview of *Batman Forever* has him as the Riddler with a blond buzz-cut. What gives? The man's normal hair is wonderful. (Carolyn Hurwitz, Owings Mills, Md.)

A. Maybe he is saving it for the day when he plays his first normal character.

Q. Do actors and actresses get paid extra to cut or shave their hair for a movie? (Murray James-Bosch, Scarborough, Ontario, Canada)

A. No. They get paid plenty to begin with, and make whatever alterations to their appearance they think will add to their performance. Extras and bit players, however, get paid extra if they have to cut their hair.

Footnote: When you see a star who has hair and a shaved head in different scenes of the same movie (De Niro's Mohawk cut in Taxi Driver, *for example) the bald effect is almost always some sort of makeup technique, such as a skull cap. That's because if retakes of "hair" scenes were necessary, it would take too long for the hair to grow back.*

Q. Do you think Burt Reynolds learned something from his hairpiece in *Striptease*? I thought it looked good on him. "Mr. Reynolds," his assistant should have said one day on the set, "look carefully in the mirror. Notice that the wig you're now wearing (a) is colored to realistically jibe with your age, (b) is sized to fit your scalp, and most important, (c) is *not* intended to give you the hairline and thickness of Van Cliburn at age eighteen. And though it did require over half an hour to apply it to your scalp, at least it doesn't look as though it came with a chin strap. In conclusion, sir, I hope that you bear these things in mind when you shop for your new hairpiece." (Andy Ihnatko, Westwood, Mass.)

A. I am wondering if there is something seriously wrong with a man who attends *Striptease* and spends his time evaluating Burt Reynolds's hairpiece.

Hard-to-Find Videos

Q. Here in Kansas City, there is only one video store I have found that has a copy of *The War Room*. Because *it* only has one copy, I have not had a chance to see it since it was released. Blockbuster seems to stock many other videos that would be commercially less viable than this one, including some documentaries. They wouldn't make the decision not to carry it because they don't like Clinton, would they? It's all about money, right? (Jonathan Plummer, Kansas City, Mo.)

A. Right. *The War Room* is a behind-the-scenes documentary about the Clinton advance team during the 1992 campaign. Documentaries traditionally do poorly at the box office and in rentals, and many video chains have grown hit-oriented, ordering multiple copies of box office successes but few copies of "marginal" films. Many film buffs use mail order to find obscure titles. Two of the most comprehensive outlets are Facets Multimedia (800-331-6197 or, in Illinois, 312-281-9075) and Movies Unlimited (800-466-8437).

Q. In one of the reports about the death of Lillian Gish, it said few of her silent films are available on home video. Is this so? (Ashley St. Ives, Chicago)

A. No. Splendid new restorations of *Birth of a Nation, Broken Blossoms*, and *Orphans of the Storm* have recently been released on laserdisc. On tape, a lot of her work is available, including *Way Down East, Hearts of the World, True Heart Susie*, and many of the early D.W. Griffith shorts starring Miss Gish, as well as *The Wind* (1928), considered her finest silent performance. Once again, I recommend Facets Multimedia and Movies Unlimited. You didn't ask, but, yes, I met Miss Gish once. It was on the set of Robert Altman's *A Wedding* (1978). A photographer knelt down to get a low-angle shot of Miss Gish, who snapped, "Young man, get up from there! If God had meant you to photograph me from that angle, he would have given you a camera in your navel."

Q. As you know, Alexander Jodorowsky's 1971 classic *El Topo* has long been unavailable on video in the United States, except in imported Japanese videos. In my search for a copy, I was informed that about two weeks ago all American resellers of the Japanese release of the film were recently served with legal papers from Jodorowsky's lawyers. These papers reassert Jodorowsky's right as owner to control the distribution of *El Topo*. (Eric Geilker, Charlottesville, Va.)

A. Until recently, rights to the film were controlled by Allen Klein, who for reasons of his own did not wish to release it in the United States. When I interviewed Jodorowsky at the 1989 Cannes Film Festival (where his *Santa Sangre* played), he said Klein would not talk to him or release the film. If Jodorowsky indeed has control of it again, that means a new generation of moviegoers can see one of the most remarkable films ever made.

Hats

Q. In one of your comments on *Mulholland Falls*, you asked why those four cops driving around in the Buick Skylark convertible are somehow "funny-looking." I can tell you why. It's because they're driving in a convertible at 100 mph with hats on—and the hats *don't fly off.* I wear a hat like theirs and it isn't easy to keep it on my head when the wind blows. My guess is that the art director fastened the hats on with a twelve-penny nail hammered firmly through the crown and right into the actors' heads. This would explain quite a lot about *Mulholland Falls.* (Rich Elias, Delaware, Ohio)

A. In my review, I said "the Hat Squad in their shiny Buick look like male action dolls out for a spin in *Toy Story.*" But I found this and other stylistic touches part of the movie's appeal. I gather that you disagree.

Q. Having seen the movie *Mulholland Falls*, which is surely intended as a parody of the old *Dick Tracy* comic strips, I'm moved to ask: Why can't modern actors get the hang of wearing fedoras? They look so awkward and self-conscious. They're subliminally ill at ease wearing hats, and it comes through. Men of the 1990s just can't wear hats with any kind of panache. Even soldiers wearing army hats or caps can't get them right. They look like I remember recruits looking the first few weeks after being drafted. In a month or so, they lose that "green" look and get the hang of wearing their caps—jaunty and casual. Maybe if today's actors wore a hat regularly for a break-in period they'd overcome that obvious greenhorn look. (G.P. Lucchetti, Oak Park, Ill.)

A. This may also be related to the fact that the movie stars of the

1940s looked older in their twenties than today's movie stars look in their forties. Robert Mitchum never looked young. Robert Redford never looks old.

Hidden Details

Q. Regarding all the controversy over the secret of *The Crying Game*: There was an interesting article in the *Pittsburgh Post-Gazette* saying that in Richard Corliss's original review of the movie in *Time* magazine, he revealed the secret very sneakily. If you read just the first letter of each paragraph of the review, it tells the secret! (Michael Leger, Pittsburgh)

A. I ran into Corliss and he confirmed this story. He used a sentence like "Initially, the secret is not obvious," as a clue to look for the initials, which (read no further if you don't want to know, etc.,) spelled out, "He is a she."

Q. In watching *The Silence of the Lambs* the other night, my wife Sara came across another hidden tidbit. After Lecter has been transferred to Memphis, and Clarice is asking him how to catch Buffalo Bill, he tells her: "First principles, Clarice. Simplicity." Well, "Simplicity" is the name of a type of dress pattern, and dressmaking is the favorite pastime of the serial killer, Buffalo Bill. An interesting aside: we have two cats—Hannibal the Cannibal, and Clarice. You wouldn't believe the weird looks we get from people when they ask what our cats are named. (Dan Buchan, Dickinson College, Carlisle, Pa.)

A. You missed the detail that while the FBI is on its wild-goose chase in Calumet City, Illinois, Clarice approaches the house of the real killer—and on the lawn is a little windmill using the same Indian that is depicted on boxes of *Calumet* brand baking soda!

Q. Now that Altman's *The Player* is out on video, it is possible to detect a subtle device on the sound track that increases the atmosphere of paranoia running through the film. The hero, Griffin Mill (Tim Robbins), commits a murder and is afraid he will be caught. His name is constantly repeated in the dialogue. One character will say, "Griffin! Griffin!" Or one says, "Griffin," and another echoes it,

"Griffin." Thomas Newman, who wrote the music for the film, uses the same motif subliminally in the music when Griffin arrives at the hotel where he bumps into Malcolm McDowell. You'll need a good sound system to identify it, but every two bars throughout this music, the words "Griffin-Griffin" are audible in time to the music. McDowell's opening line of the scene that follows is, "Griffin? Griffin Mill?" (Paul Chapman, London, England)

A. I listened to my laserdisc, and you are correct. This sort of detail may be why some movies seem to work on us in almost inexplicable ways. Certainly during *The Player* I identified with Griffin's growing fear of exposure.

Hitchcock's Cameos

Q. I am curious about when Alfred Hitchcock first started doing cameos in his films. My father has recently given me videos of the first ten Hitchcock films, such as *The Lady Vanishes*, *The Thirty-Nine Steps*, and *Juno and the Paycock*. Do you know when he first started making his brief appearances? (Ann Alquist, Butzbach, Germany)

A. Hitchcock's first cameo was in *The Lodger* (1927), and his walk-ons subsequently became famous. When he filmed *Lifeboat* (1944), it appeared he had outsmarted himself—how could he do a cameo appearance in a movie set entirely at sea? Walk on the water? His solution: You can see him in a "before and after" ad for a diet cure, in a newspaper being read on board.

Home Video

Q. I teach marketing at Concordia College. I understand that Viacom plans to use the fifty million customer base of Blockbuster Video, where two million transactions are recorded every day, to "reverse engineer" movies. In other words, scripts and stars will be determined by data gathered from marketing surveys. What do you think about this? (Craig C. Lien, St. Paul, Minn.)

A. If it were not absolute goofiness, I would be alarmed. Viacom is likely to lose millions on "reverse engineered" movies, because one of the problems in entertainment marketing is that people don't know what they want until they see it. *Star Wars* tested so horribly that Fox considered recycling the footage into a Saturday morning kiddie show. It doesn't take a genius (or a marketing survey) to know Tom Cruise or Whoopi Goldberg sell tickets, or that a Schwarzenegger science fiction film will probably do well. Beyond that, though, the marketers are likely to find people "want" movies similar to those they just enjoyed. This is the wisdom that gave us *Honey, I Blew Up the Kids.* Marketing works for soap and fast food. But in a volatile area like popular entertainment, it provides obvious answers at great cost, while counseling against original proposals because the survey audience cannot relate to them. How well do you think *Pulp Fiction, Silence of the Lambs, Forrest Gump, Schindler's List* or *Quiz Show* would have tested, as compared to such sure-fire backward-engineered projects as *Wagons East, On Deadly Ground, City Slickers II,* or *Highlander III?* Viacom and Blockbuster specialize in selling what others have created, and they are good at that. They will discover it is much trickier to create what others will sell.

Q. One of my favorite films is *The Cook, the Thief, His Wife and Her Lover.* It totally disgusted me and throughout the entire movie I had my thumb on the stop button, yet never pushed it. (Gus Koerner, Utah State University, Logan, Utah)

A. This certainly qualifies as one test of a great movie.

Q. While watching the "thriller" *Trespass* (what can I say?—it was on free TV), one thing caught my eye. Why do modern movie directors think that if a character is using a video camera, we need to be reminded of this by the putting the word "REC" in one corner of the screen? Are we all this dumb? (Thomas A. Heald, Rapid City, S.Dak.)

A. Perhaps the director wants to be sure you do not confuse the home movie with the real one.

Q. Can you tell me why the date of every movie appears in roman numerals? (Jean M. Dunne, Riverside, Ill.)

A. Copyrights are in roman numerals on movies to make it harder to instantly determine the date, thus extending their shelf lives.

Hoop Dreams

Q. We saw *Hoop Dreams* and agree with you it is one of the best movies ever made. But . . . what happened since the movie was made? How are William Gates and Arthur Agee faring in their basketball careers and lives? (Harris Allsworth, Chicago)

A. You're referring to the two young men whose lives are chronicled for six years in the film, from grade school to college, as they pursue the dream of pro basketball stardom. According to Chicago film executive John Iltis, who helped distribute the film, Agee is currently a starter at Arkansas State, and is also a disc jockey on the campus radio station. Gates dropped off the Marquette team last season to concentrate on his studies, but is back in uniform this season, with a 3.0 grade average. According to *Sports Illustrated,* a *San Francisco Chronicle* poll of forty film critics placed the film first among the year's releases, ahead of *Pulp Fiction* and *Quiz Show;* it headed my own Best Ten list.

Q. Just a note to let you know how wonderful my family (including three boys of seventeen to twenty-three) found *Hoop Dreams* and yet how disappointed we are that there are only three theaters showing that film in *all* of southern California! We have observed that the local theater chain regularly ignores films like *Do the Right Thing,* to say nothing of *Roger & Me.* We cannot believe that such a well-made and well-received film as *Hoop Dreams* is unavailable to most viewers. Why is this film getting so little exposure? (Paul Evans, Newport Beach, Calif.)

A. Actually, for a documentary, *Hoop Dreams* is doing quite well, and will be one of the top-grossing docs of recent years. But you are quite right that many theater chains write off large segments of their market as suitable only for action and mainstream product. More ambitious or challenging films (documentary, art, foreign, independent) are red-lined into a few big cities and college towns, and the rest of the country is considered dumb or dumber, I guess. Try calling the booker of your local chain, for all the good it will do.

Q. When I walked out of *Hoop Dreams,* I said to my date it was the best movie I had seen in years. After talking endlessly about it to anyone who would listen to me, I have convinced myself that it was one of the top three movies I have ever seen. The fact that it was not nominated for an Oscar tells me the Academy is a political backscratching organization that doesn't have a clue. I cannot express how disappointed I am. (Kevin Brouillette, Kansas City, Mo.)

A. The bizarre oversights of the Academy's documentary committee have been a scandal for years. One good thing may result from their egregious snub of *Hoop Dreams:* The resulting stink has been too big for the Academy to overlook, and its president, Arthur Hiller, has promised an investigation. The Academy has been able to ignore protests in past years from critics, documentary filmmakers, and other "outsiders," but this year, I understand, there was an outraged outcry from many Academy members themselves, including some members of its board of directors.

Q. Whatever happened to the investigation regarding the *Hoop Dreams* nonnomination incident? Is it still in progress or has it been resolved? (Gary Currie, Montreal, Canada)

A. Although the Motion Picture Academy has reformed the rules for the documentary category for next year, no rerun of the 1995 race is planned, despite the *Entertainment Weekly* article suggesting that some members of the nominating committee may have deliberately acted to skewer the chances of *Hoop Dreams.* It's some consolation for the filmmakers that many millions of viewers were able to see the film recently when it played on PBS.

IMAX, Omnimax, AND 70mm

Q. On your recommendation we went to see *Wings of Courage,* the 3-D IMAX movie. You were right! The 3-D effect was sensational—far better than we had ever seen before. The glasses are more like science fiction headsets, and we were wondering how they work? Are they responsible for the realistic effect? (Harris Allsworth, Chicago)

A. The IMAX 3-D headsets are a vast improvement on the old red-and-green cardboard glasses we used to wear at 3-D movies, according to Seymour Uranowitz of the CompuServe ShowBiz Forum. He tells me: "There are infrared transmitters in the front of the theater that send a signal to sensors in the headsets. The signals are synchronized with the frames of film so that for some frames, the left LCD lens in the headset is blacked out, and for other frames the right LCD frame is blacked out. This system produces a superior 3D effect because the left/right blocking is more complete for each eye, and the glass is a higher quality medium through which to see the film, compared to plastic."

Q. I am a fan of 70mm movies, and would like to see more of them in theaters. It's a shame that *Baraka* and the Tom Cruise movie *Far and Away,* both from 1992, seem to have been the last shot in this great format, since they didn't evoke enough interest in Hollywood or the public. I wish I could see *Lawrence of Arabia* in 70mm. I've had little success in asking theaters to bring it in, including the IMAX theater, which has the perfect-size screen for 70mm. I have received short responses from Spielberg's and Lucas's secretaries, which is somewhat encouraging. (Scott Pickering, Vancouver, British Columbia, Canada)

A. The prints for 70mm movies offer four times more surface area for the light to shine through than traditional 35mm, and as a result the picture quality is much better. However, the prints are very expensive, and can only be shown in theaters equipped with costly and seldom-used 70mm projectors. The current emphasis is on massive opening-day grosses, with movies booked onto 1,500 screens or more. Because of its smaller number of screens, a new movie in 70mm would *seem* to have low grosses (it wouldn't crack the Top Ten). Given the herd mentality of moviegoers and their obsession with box office "winners," it would be handicapped by its more limited launch.

Q. Enjoyed your recent article about Ridefilm, the process that, as you wrote, "encloses you in a space with about eighteen other people. It shows you a high-quality movie image on a wraparound screen. And it straps you to a seat and a platform that makes more than two hundred movements a second, creating the illusion that you are participating in the action on the screen." Do you have any idea why Sony-IMAX doesn't combine their 3-D headsets with their Ridefilm? It seems to me that, combined, it would top either experience alone. Maybe they're afraid the expensive headset will fly off and break, eh? . . . But hey, this is exactly the kind of situation that Gulliver Q. Chinstrap invented his famous headgear accessory for! (Steven D. Souza, Honolulu, Hawaii)

A. One little technical problem with the giant-screen processes, Omnimax and IMAX, is that the illusion is so real that quick cutting can cause motion sickness, vertigo, and even nausea in the audience. That's why they usually use slow dissolves between long shots of largely static natural scenes. Combining the "max" process with a "Ridefilm" would require the inventions not just of Gulliver Q. Chinstrap but also of Ichabod Z. Barfbag.

Independence Day

Q. In your review of *Independence Day*, referring to the gigantic alien spacecraft, you write: "an object that size in near-Earth orbit might be expected to cause tidal waves." Tidal waves, or tsunamis, are caused by sudden earth movement, not extraterrestrial objects. However, a craft one-fourth the mass of the Moon, if at the same distance as the Moon, would result in tides (not tidal waves) approximately 25 percent above normal—not fun but tolerable. If the mother ship were located one-half the distance of the Moon, tidal influence of the ship would be equal to that of the Moon. *But,* its orbital speed would be substantially faster, resulting in wild tides. The closer the object, the worse the effect. If the object were in close Earth orbit, it wouldn't need "death rays" to destroy cities; since most major cities are seaports, they would be ravaged by wild tides. I suspect this is what you meant and it is an excellent point. (Richard George, San Jacinto, Calif.)

A. That is what I meant and it is an excellent point.

Q. I have to disagree with you on your review of *Independence Day.* Here is a wonderful, exciting summer experience for the entire populace of the United States that does not cause people to go out and riot in the streets, etc., but instead gives us collectively a prescription for unity, national pride, and an elevated appreciation for how much we all need each other. (Sue Guss, Corvallis, Oreg.)

A. Hey, I said the movie was "silly summer fun, and on that level I kind of liked it." But I only gave it two and a half stars because I thought the characters and dialogue were corny and the special effects were only competent (the mother ship looked like a vast burnt waffle in the sky). As for that prescription for unity, national pride, etc., I guess I missed it, unless it was "nuke the aliens."

Q. Why is *Independence Day* such a hit? Is it just a result of media hype (covers of *Time* and *Newsweek*, etc.)? Although I contributed to the opening weekend receipts, I wasn't all that impressed. The effects weren't that impressive and the story was predictable, although I did like Jeff Goldblum and Will Smith. As far as alien action movies, this one doesn't touch my fave, *Aliens*. (Laurie Sullivan, San Francisco)

A. It was the right movie at the right time. It grabbed the coveted Fourth of July weekend and scared away the competition; millions of Americans with time on their hands were convinced by a brilliant advertising and marketing campaign that this was an event. So they went. Many of the members of an audience that huge are infrequent moviegoers, and so perhaps did not realize how unoriginal the story was.

Q. In your review of *Independence Day*, questioning the digital read-out on Jeff Goldblum's computer, you asked, "Why are the aliens using hours and minutes? Does their home planet have exactly the same length of day and year as ours?" It was my understanding that Goldblum recognized the signal and *calculated* the time in hours and minutes. (George Burkhart, Honolulu, Hawaii)

A. You are right. I am wrong. I am still a little dubious, however, about another detail: We're told the aliens needed to use Earth's satellite system because the Moon blocked their transmissions. Huh?

Q. This may sound paranoid, but I believe the makers of *Independence Day* have been paying people to post anonymous messages on America Online that shill for the movie. After reading the message boards over there, I've become convinced that there are three or four people who just don't sound like "civilian" moviegoers but rather more like people working for the studio. I was simply wondering whether this is a practice among the studios these days. I suppose they have the right, but it would bug me a little to realize some messages are fake. (Robert Mason, Cleveland, Ohio)

A. Here's a movie that is grossing hundreds of millions, and the studio is sneaking on-line to propagandize maybe a couple hundred AOL members? I don't buy it. It may be a studio employee doing it on his own time, but it's very unlikely to be an actual Twentieth Century Fox marketing tactic.

Q. Is it safe to predict, as 1996 edges toward a close, that the future holds a movie titled something like *Independence Day 2?* If you know anyone foolish enough to bet otherwise, please send them my way. (Chris Foreman, Takoma Park, Md.)

A. My contact at Twentieth Century Fox says there will "definitely" be a sequel to *Independence Day* but no story has been settled on, and *ID4* makers Roland Emerick and Dean Devlin haven't committed to it.

Indoor Plumbing

Q. In your review of *Dragonheart*, you placed the time of the movie somewhere between the time of King Arthur and the "invention of indoor plumbing." Archaeology has confirmed that the historical Arthur reigned in the fifth century. Since the Romans invented indoor plumbing long before this, I suppose that you're placing the action as contemporaneous with the Council of Nicea or thereabouts? (Steve Kallis Jr., Tampa, Fla.)

A. My mistake. I should have placed it between the time of King Arthur and Albert Giblin's invention of the flushable toilet in 1819.

Q. In your Answer Man column, you placed the time of *Dragonheart* as being "between the time of King Arthur and Albert Giblin's invention of the flushable toilet in 1819." Albert Giblin was born in 1869, and was granted a cistern patent in 1898. This historically insignificant patent is usually wrongly attributed to Thomas Crapper. Actually, neither he nor Giblin invented the modern flush toilet. This is weird because the only time I have seen "1819" in connection with Albert Giblin was in an article I was one of the sources for, Heather McCune's "Thomas Crapper: Myth and Reality," in the June 1993 *Plumbing & Mechanical* magazine. In a phone conversation with Ms. McCune I told her that British Patent 4990 was issued in 1898 to Giblin for his product, "Crapper's Silent Valveless Water Waste Preventer." Because we were on a bad line or I was slurring my words, 1898 became 1819. Unless you are a reader of *Plumbing & Mechanical* magazine (and I trust you are not!), I wonder, what is your source? (Ken Grabowski, Chicago)

A. My source is indeed that troublesome June 1993 issue of *Plumbing & Mechanical* magazine, of which I am a faithful reader. There you are identified as the author of a forthcoming book on Thomas Crapper's life. Your research indicates Crapper was issued nine patents, "four for improvements to drains, three for water closets, one for manhole covers, and the last for pipe joints," but none for a flushable toilet. Albert Giblin's invention allowed a toilet to flush effectively when the cistern was only half full, which still leaves unanswered the question of who invented the flush toilet in the first place. After examining all the evidence, I have rewritten my review of *Dragonheart* to read, "the movie takes place between the time of King Arthur and Albert Giblin's invention of the Silent Valveless Water Waste Preventer in 1898." Interested readers can investigate further on the Web (http://www.theplumber.com/crapper.html).

Injuries

Q. I have noticed that in Teri Garr's recent appearances she seems to have a limp. What happened? Was she in an accident? (Denise Marks, Chicago)

A. Garr, a former dancer, has said she is rehabilitating from a degenerative back injury. As the consistently funniest guest on the Letterman program, she would be a natural as a talk show hostess.

Q. I noticed in *While You Were Sleeping* that Sandra Bullock has a large scar over her left eye. It's even more evident in *The Net.* Know how she got it? Just curious. (Mark Blanchard, Norwalk, Conn.)

A. It's not *that* large! When asked this question during an America Online chat session, Bullock said she got the scar at the age of ten, while crossing a river with her father. She hit her head on a rock, which she named Bob. (Thanks to Douglas C. Thompson of Anchorage for this information.)

Q. I recently saw *The Island of Dr. Moreau,* and noticed that Val Kilmer wore a blue brace on his left elbow. In the movie *Heat,* there's a scene where Kilmer and De Niro have a conversation at a beachhouse. Kilmer's elbow seems to be inflamed. Is this a coincidence? Did Kilmer have elbow surgery? (Rob Dybas, Chicago)

A. Val Kilmer replies: "It is a coincidence."

Interactive Movies

Q. Re the "interactive" movie *Mr. Payback.* The whole idea of interactive cinema makes me itch. I mean, in the good old days, the only way your fellow audience members could ruin the movie for you was to talk and throw food. Do we really want to give these lugnuts the power to skeezix the *story,* too? Now I'll have to arrive at the theater an hour earlier—not to get the best seat, but to stand by the entrance and screen the audience before I commit to using my ticket. Perhaps some sort of written exam should be implemented. (Andy Ihnatko, Westwood, Mass.)

A. In the film intro to *Mr. Payback,* the announcer encourages audience members to "shout, scream, whistle, offer advice, and in general act like you were born in a barn." There comes a time in everyone's life when he begins to believe that civilization as we know it is going to hell. Call me a cockeyed optimist, but that moment didn't come for me until I heard this announcement.

Jim Carrey

Q. Please Roger, say it ain't so—are you beginning to like Jim Carrey? What audience is this man aiming at? Ten-year-olds? Beavis & Butthead wannabes? What I find most upsetting about the phenomenon is that it exists at all. Why do people watch his work? Is it funny, or are people just so embarrassed that they laugh to relieve their tension? (Mel Heillman, Shawnee Mission, Kans.)

A. I've given a favorable review to only one of his three films (*The Mask*), but I did laugh a lot during *Dumb and Dumber.* The guy is sort of growing on me, and if there is not a place in this world for pure goofiness, count me out.

I also liked his Liar, Liar *in March 1997.*

Q. Does Jim Carrey star in the Dirty Harry film *The Dead Pool?* I saw the film and thought I recognized Jim Carrey as the drug-addicted rock star who is murdered at the beginning. I watched the credits and saw the name of the actor as being James Carrey. Is this the same man? (Ian Turnbull, Richmond-upon-Thames, England)

A. It is. Before he became the $20 Million Man, Carrey starred in *Once Bitten, Earth Girls Are Easy,* and *The Dead Pool.*

Q. Will we ever again be able to look down on the French for idolizing Jerry Lewis when multimillions are paid to such as Jim Carrey and, heaven help us, the very unfunny Chris Farley? (Hank Oettinger, Chicago)

A. I personally find Carrey funnier than Jerry Lewis, but I have attended screenings of Jerry Lewis comedies in France and can promise you the French really do love him—maybe because he makes Americans look like idiots.

Q. In your review of *The Cable Guy,* you wrote: "We want to like Jim Carrey. A movie that makes us dislike him is a strategic mistake." Maybe the problem with *The Cable Guy* isn't Lou Holtz Jr.'s screenplay; maybe the problem is Ben Stiller's direction. I've only seen ten minutes of the *Ben Stiller Show,* but in that ten minutes Stiller made very unfunny, vicious fun of Amish people. Janeane

Garafalo (star of *The Truth About Cats and Dogs*) was in the skit and afterward, in a taped segment showing her and Stiller walking down the street talking to each other, she notes her skepticism about just how funny a vicious attack on gentle, peace-loving people can be. Stiller's face seems to register not a single sign he's got a clue what she's saying. (Michael Brant, San Rafael, Calif.)

A. The story of how Columbia paid Carrey to star in a $20 million bomb that trashes his own image is becoming the stuff of Hollywood legend. My sources say Holtz's original script was a lighthearted buddy comedy, originally set to star Chris Elliott and then Chris Farley. When Farley dropped out because of a contract conflict, it fell into the hands of Jim Carrey, who brought in writer Judd Apatow. Carrey ordered a third act like *War of the Roses*, where the two characters kill each other. Apatow rewrote the script and was a link to director Stiller, whose TV show he had written for. Their early drafts were even darker than the final version, and Columbia executives protested they didn't want such a grim movie. But even after rewrites, *The Cable Guy* is a sour, unpleasant turn-off. Amazing. You'd think that Carrey, who was collecting the biggest single acting paycheck in movie history, would have done everything possible to make a popular, accessible movie.

John Grisham

Q. I take issue with your assessment of *The Pelican Brief* as "apolitical." This movie was made by the same *Washington Post*–loving, liberal Nazi that brought us the "I hate Republicans" movie *All the President's Men*. The president is portrayed in a typical leftish Hollywood dunderhead "Obviously Republican" uncaring nitwit role. Throughout the movie we are lambasted with political correctness of unbridled proportions in showing a female student who's obviously smarter than the professor who is twice her age. The ending is an obvious allusion to the racial barriers that exist in society when our heroine finds herself in love with Denzel Washington, but it just can't be because of the invisible barrier which we in society have placed before her. It's our fault! (Norman T. Corts, Arlington, Va.)

A. Aside from racial barriers, I can think of another reason why

Julia Roberts and Denzel Washington do not fall in love. Her lover is blown to bits in a car explosion at the beginning of the film, and the subsequent action takes only two weeks, hardly time to get over her grief even if she is only a typical leftish Hollywood dunderhead uncaring nitwit smarter than a man twice her age.

Q. My wife and I were watching *The Firm* and noticed an inconsistency in the scene where the private investigator is shot by the two hitmen. The girlfriend (Holly Hunter) crawls under the desk in a hurry, and never looks out from underneath the desk until after the hitmen leave. Yet later she describes both of them with great detail and says one got shot in the leg and would be easy to identify. How did she see them? (Douglas Pearn, Windsor, Ontario, Canada)

A. Jeffrey Graebner of Los Angeles replies: "When the PI shoots the guy in the leg, he shoots right through the desk. In a later shot, you see that the shot left a great big hole in the front of the desk. The girlfriend could very easily have seen the hitmen through that hole."

Q. John Grisham has recently attacked Oliver Stone's *Natural Born Killers* because of its possible influence on copycat killers. Stone replied that Grisham has become a rich man by making movies about violence. Your reaction? (Ronnie Barzell, Los Angeles)

A. My feeling is that no one can easily be influenced to do anything that is against their moral grain and outside their sphere of potential action. Grisham's forthcoming film, *A Time to Kill*, portrays the Ku Klux Klan in a way that might be misconstrued as attractive to anyone bent in that direction. Of course he will reply that the movie is anti-Klan, just as Oliver Stone saw *NBK* as a satire aimed at the way the media glamorizes violence. Grisham should look to be sure he is not living in a glass house.

Q. In your review of *A Time to Kill*, you wrote that it was "a skillfully-constructed morality play that pushes all the right buttons and arrives at all the right conclusions." Okay, close your eyes. Now imagine the two rapists were killed by three hundred white men with a rope. Now imagine the two rapists were black. Does it still arrive at all the right conclusions? (John Lampkins, Los Angeles)

A. The movie is about two redneck rapists killed by the father of the young black girl they have raped. I intended a shade of irony in my comment, but you make a strong point. It is always wrong to take the law into one's own hands, something that *A Time to Kill* obscures by stacking the emotional deck. We understand why the Samuel Jackson character did what he did, and we sympathize with his feelings, but he did kill those men. When the crowd is cheering the "innocent" verdict at the end of the film, anyone with respect for the law should feel a little queasy; the movie can be seen as a "politically correct" defense of revenge.

Kane and Welles

Q. Regarding your comment that any well-informed adult should have seen *Citizen Kane,* I did an informal poll among people in my office. Of ten people, six had not seen *Citizen Kane*! Several of them remarked that they don't bother with movies made before they were born, unless they are "cool like James Bond." My office, incidentally, is a bunch of computer analysts, all college educated, but I have noticed before that you can't really talk to them about books either. (Diana MacDonald. Columbia, Mo.)

A. What sets man apart from the beasts is our interest in things that took place before we were born, or will take place after we die. Do any of your office mates moo?

Q. How come I can't buy one of those little glass balls with water and imitation snowflakes and a vintage house with a sled out in front that says "Rosebud"? I can buy cels from *The Lion King,* a replica of the Maltese Falcon, and probably one of Mae West's bustles, but not this. America's memorabilia industry is letting us down. (Win Smith, Chicago)

A. There has never been a *Citizen Kane* collectable paperweight, according to Lisa Kentala of Chicago's Metro Golden Memories. So you should obviously manufacture them. Put me down for one.

Q. The one thing I disliked about *Ed Wood* was the movie's cheap shot at Charlton Heston, in the scene with "Orson Welles," who is shown complaining that the studio wants him to use Heston in *Touch of Evil.* Heston was one of the true friends and supporters of

Welles, and without his clout Welles would never have been able to make that film. (Tim Ennis, Chatham Township, N.J.)

A. Scott Alexander, one of the writers of *Ed Wood*, has been quoted as saying that the scene with Welles is the only one in the movie that's completely fictional.

Kubrick

Q. There's a restored version of Stanley Kubrick's *Dr. Strangelove* out on video. I was disappointed that he did not include the pie-fight ending he had originally planned. (Petronella Danforth, Chicago)

A. Film buffs have known for years that Kubrick planned a pie-fight sequence, and indeed a table full of pies can be glimpsed as part of the buffet spread in the war room. But he decided his eventual ending—Slim Pickens riding a nuclear bomb down to an apocalyptic explosion—was more effective. Although many filmmakers bring out a "director's cut" of their movies for home video, Kubrick's restored *Strangelove* wisely avoids any temptation to put the pie fight back in. Quite likely, the original footage no longer exists. The master negative of *Strangelove* was so shoddily preserved by Columbia Pictures that it was almost lost—the same fate narrowly escaped by *Strangelove*'s near contemporary, *Lawrence of Arabia*.

Q. I am a huge Stanley Kubrick fan and am wondering if you have any information on his new movie, called *A.I. (Artificial Intelligence)*. When is it coming out and what's it about? (Scott Clements, Etobicoke, Ontario, Canada)

A. I went Web-surfing to the Kubrick page in search of information, and found that *A.I.* is about a computer that becomes aware of its own existence. Kubrick is maintaining secrecy, but rumors abound. The most intriguing is that he's been filming for two months every five years, to allow his young star actor to grow up onscreen. One industry source says the film was nearly finished when Kubrick saw *Jurassic Park* and decided his special effects weren't state of the art; as he was reshooting, the story began to evolve, making even more production necessary. Of course all of this is hearsay.

Kubrick shelved A.I. to work on Eyes Wide Shut *with Tom Cruise.*

Q. I am a mathematician by training, a computer nerd by profession, and a sci-fi nut from way back. After recently seeing the latest big-budget sci-fi flick *Independence Day*, my taste for "real" sci-fi was still unquenched, so I watched—for at least the tenth time—Stanley Kubrick's masterpiece *2001: A Space Odyssey*, and this time I picked up on a little tidbit that may interest you. The third segment, entitled "Jupiter Mission/18 Months Later," begins fifty-two minutes into the film. About five minutes into this segment, crewman Frank Poole, played by Gary Lockwood, is engrossed in a game of chess with Hal, *Discovery 1*'s on-board computer/villain/genius. Frank is playing White. The chess position reached is shown on a computer screen, reproduced here:

WQ	—	—	—	—	BR	BK	—
—	—	BP	—	BB	BP	BP	BP
BP	—	—	—	—	—	—	—
—	WN	—	—	BN	—	—	—
—	—	—	—	—	BN	—	—
—	—	WP	BQ	—	—	—	BB
WP	WP	—	WP	—	WP	WP	WP
WR	WN	WB	WB	—	WR	WK	—

The script goes as follows:

> Frank: Anyway, Queen takes Pawn. Uhh . . . okay.
> Hal: Bishop takes Knight's Pawn.
> Frank: What a lovely move. Uhh . . . Rook to King one.
> Hal: I'm sorry, Frank. I think you missed it.
> Queen to Bishop three, Bishop takes Queen, Knight takes Bishop mate.
> Frank: Uhh . . . yeh. It looks like you're right. I resign.
> Hal: Thank you for a very enjoyable game.
> Frank: Yeah, thank you.

There is something wrong here. Although this is a chess position that could very well arise in a game (it looks like a typical Amateur vs. Paul Morphy game) and Black does, indeed, have an overwhelming attack, Hal's explanation of the winning line of play is flawed. He should have said "Queen to Bishop *six*," not three.

Since a properly functioning computer would never make this

type of mistake—a mistake in reporting a positional move—there are only two possibilities:

1. This is an inadvertent flaw in the film.
2. This is a deliberate hint, albeit a very subtle one, that something is wrong with Hal.

As *2001* is my all-time favorite film, I would like to think the second of these is correct, but perhaps only Stanley Kubrick and Arthur C. Clarke know for certain. (Clay Waldrop Jr., Garland, Tex.)

A. Kubrick is as usual incommunicado, so I took your query to Arthur C. Clarke, via e-mail to Sri Lanka. He replies: "Meaningless to me—I deliberately avoided learning even the basic moves of chess when I was a boy—afraid I'd be engulfed. How glad I was— *2001* would never have been made! Arthur."

Q. I write this in response to the question about Hal's mistake in *2001*. Some have said that Hal is testing the pilots for their reaction and ability to acknowledge mistakes. I am certain that the chess miss was not an error on Kubrick's part. He is by far one of the most anal directors working. Not that this is a bad thing by any means. He is also a huge chess player. He loves the game and has been seen playing the game with different actors and technical crew on the sets of his films. (Karsten Lundquist, Mankato, Minn.)

A. Kubrick of course is incommunicado. I admire his anal qualities while observing the perfectionism of his movies, but at times like these I wish he had a few oral aspects, too.

Leaving Las Vegas

Q. I saw *Leaving Las Vegas* and thought Nicolas Cage was "chewing the furniture" throughout the entire film. (Fred McGrath Jr., Minneapolis, Minn.)

A. Cage told me his intent was to position himself as far as possible from realistic or naturalistic acting, because, as the movie is essentially operatic, it needed larger emotions than realism would supply. Even so, I don't agree he was chewing the furniture (or the scenery, for that matter). He plays a drunk in every scene, and yet succeeds in finding a great many gradations to the performance, which builds toward its final epiphany.

Q. The one (and only) flaw with *Leaving Las Vegas* was that Elisabeth Shue's character wasn't very realistic. She was way too good-looking to be a street hooker, don't you think? I know this is Hollywood and we have to allow things to be a bit more beautiful than reality, and often this is a good thing. But not in this particular film, I didn't think. (Robert Mason, Shaker Heights, Ohio)

A. Was Paul Newman too good-looking to be a pool hustler? Was Richard Gere too good-looking to be a gigolo? Was Demi Moore too good-looking to be a business tycoon? Was Babe too good-looking to be a pig?

Q. During Cage and Shue's desert retreat in *Leaving Las Vegas*, *The Third Man* plays on a pool-side television set. Did you glean any metaphorical significance from this? (Michael Green, Tempe, Ariz.)

A. My guess: The director, Mike Figgis, loves *film noir* (his *Stormy Monday* is a homage to the genre) and *The Third Man* is one of the greatest. No other significance, except that in both movies a good woman persists in loving a self-destructive man.

Letterboxing

Q. When *Schindler's List* came out on video, there was an article in the local paper about the fact that Blockbuster Video had established a policy against stocking the letterboxed version of a film if there is also a nonletterboxed version available. The reason was that they had received too many complaints about *Last of the Mohicans*, and they didn't feel that their clerks should have to be "bothered" by trying to explain letterboxing. What do you think about this? (Jeffrey Graebner, Los Angeles)

A. I think it is short-sighted, since so many people insist on letterboxing and do not like to be short-changed by the "pan and scan" versions that eliminate from 20 to 55 percent of the total picture. Video stores that forsake that audience are suggesting that they consider the movies only as a product, not as an art they care about. Call me a dreamer, but I think video store clerks exist to be bothered.

Q. I hate what I call the Letterbox Bait and Switch Tactic. On video, this is the annoying practice of letterboxing a film's opening credits and then switching to pan and scan for the rest of the movie. This allows the viewers to see exactly how much of the frame they will miss for the next two hours. (Charles W. Strader, Baton Rouge, La.)

A. Yeah, if they're going to cut out 50 percent of the movie, they don't have to rub our noses in it. Another reason why all knowledgeable video viewers insist on the letterboxed version.

Q. Disney has said they will release a letterboxed version of *Pulp Fiction*, due to consumer demand. I work part-time at Blockbuster Video and am trying to convince the store to purchase a few copies. I am sure that there are many others who, like me, would much rather see the 2.35:1 width rather than the square television image. We have received a panned-and-scanned demo copy of *PF*, and it is revolting. My problem is that the average video consumer is so ignorant of the filmmaking process that he has no idea that there is any difference between the two versions. When I try to explain about aspect ratios, etc., the customers have either refused to listen or angrily told me that they will not pay for "half a picture"! My reply was, "You already are." My question is: What is a good, concise way to explain the concept of letterboxing to the average Blockbuster customer? (Yancey Martin, Huntsville, Ala.)

A. In the case of *Pulp Fiction*, which has such fanatic fans, I'm surprised your store wouldn't leap to stock the letterboxed version, since no one who loves the movie could possibly view the cropped version without anguish. Just ask customers this question: "Would you rather see the whole movie, or this version we have that is missing one-third of the movie?" When they say "the whole movie," explain that movie screens are not the same shape as TV screens (this will come as news to some people), and that letterboxing is the only way the entire picture area can be seen on a TV screen. If a little social pressure seems called for, quietly add, "People who don't demand letterboxing are revealing that they don't know or care much about movies."

Q. Will Blockbuster Video be offering *Pulp Fiction* in the letterbox version on VHS tape? I checked and it's not mentioned as being available in their computer. I can't believe a film like this would be offered only in the "pan-and-scan" version by the largest video chain in the country. (Mike Barnett, Riverview, Mich.)

A. There was a firestorm on the Internet over this very issue last week, as disgruntled Blockbuster employees logged on to report that the chain did not plan to make the letterboxed version available on tape (although it would be available on laserdisc).

A letterboxed version of a film shows the complete, original widescreen image by stretching it across the center of a TV screen, with black bands at top and bottom. There was once a time when dim-witted video renters thought this meant their TV was broken. Anyone who hasn't caught on by now is seriously behind the curve.

In the case of *Pulp Fiction*, the original movie was shot in the screen ratio of 1-to-2.35. That means it was 2.35 feet wide for every foot in height. A 1-to-1.40 pan-and-scan version of such an image would eliminate *at least 40 percent of the entire picture!* For *Pulp Fiction* fans, who scrutinize the entire frame for clues, this would of course be unacceptable.

I contacted Blockbuster to get an answer to your question, Mike. I spoke first to an official Blockbuster spokesman, Wally Knief, who told me the letterboxed version would be carried by the chain "on laserdisc only—not on VHS tape."

I contacted the filmmakers to discover what they thought about this. Director Quentin Tarantino was on vacation in Ireland and unreachable, but Roger Avary, who coauthored the film with him, was forthright: "It won't matter to me," he said. "I'll buy my copy from one of their competitors. I'd sooner drink battery acid and stab a fork in my eye than walk into a Blockbuster."

The next day, Wally Knief called back. There was a "correction" to his earlier statement, he said. Blockbuster would indeed carry the letterboxed tape version "in major cities." Which cities? I asked.

"New York, Los Angeles, and the strong possibility of Chicago," he said.

I called Miramax, the film's distributor, and talked with Erica Steinberg, who said she understood that Blockbuster would not be carrying the letterboxed version because the chain believes "consumers get confused if they have the option. They're doing the laserdiscs letterboxed, because laser users are technophiles and know the difference."

She suggested I speak with Dennis Rice, senior vice president of Buena Vista Home Video, which is distributing the tape. "I was just talking today with Gerry Geddis, president of Blockbuster," Rice said. "Often with letterboxing we get a backlash because there are a whole bunch of consumers out there who think their TV set is broken. But for a movie as significant as *Pulp Fiction*, we have been working closely to represent it as it was meant to be seen. Of course Blockbuster will make it available in letterbox."

Not according to their spokesman, I told him. "That's strange," Rice said. "This will be one of the biggest titles this year."

The next day, I got a fax from the office of Gerry Geddis himself, asking me to call, because there had been a misunderstanding of Blockbuster's policy. I called, and talked with Sue Ehrenberg, his assistant, who told me Geddis was in a meeting, but wanted me to know the letterboxed version "would be available."

Then why, I asked, was it not listed in its computerized catalog of available titles, and why had a Blockbuster spokesman said the chain would not carry it?

Ms. Ehrenberg said she would check with Geddis and call me back. She did. "Buena Vista did not inform Blockbuster that there would be a letterbox VHS tape made available, in addition to the pan-and-scan version," she said.

Now that you know this, I said, will you make a letterbox version available in every one of your stores? She said she would check.

I called Dennis Rice of Buena Vista and told him Blockbuster said that his organization had not informed them a letterbox version would be available. "That's strange," he said. "Certainly Tower and Wherehouse knew a letterbox version was available, because they've ordered it in quantity."

Sue Ehrenberg called back. "Gerry Geddis says the letterboxed version will be available on tape in all of Blockbuster's stores," she said.

So the answer to your question, Mike, is—yes, Blockbuster *will* be offering *Pulp Fiction* in letterbox in the VHS tape version. I don't know where you got the idea they wouldn't be.

Q. We have two Blockbuster Video stores. I just called both stores, and they said they would not carry the letterboxed version of *Pulp Fiction* for rent or purchase. This really upsets me. I love *Pulp Fiction,* and the thought of watching the movie cropped gives me chills. Do you think there's any way I could get a copy? (Andre Mallette, Wilmington, N.C.)

A. I am shocked—shocked!—to hear this news. Admittedly, Blockbuster is not a fan of letterboxing, believing it "confuses" customers. But as reported, I was assured by Blockbuster president Gerry Geddis that all Blockbuster stores would carry the letterboxed version of *Pulp Fiction* on VHS tape. I sure hope the store managers in Wilmington don't get in trouble for violating company policy!

Q. Finding my economics class canceled today, I rushed to my local video store to purchase a copy of *Pulp Fiction.* To my shock and amazement, it was selling for $100! I haven't gotten my degree yet, but I can't imagine more than a microscopic segment of the potential market shelling out that kind of cash. Are they stupid? But what truly got my goat is that the letterbox version was not available for renting. What amazes me is that Quentin Tarantino even let his movie be released in "pan and scan." If anybody should know what is lost it's Tarantino, and you'd think he would have the clout. They should have gotten Tarantino to give a brief lecture at the beginning of the tape extolling the virtues of the letterbox format. (Carter Young, Orlando, Fla.)

A. The $100 price tag is typical of a hot movie in its original video release. Consumers are expected to rent it, not buy it. When the rental action tapers off, the movie is rereleased at a "sell-through" price in the vicinity of $24.95, probably with extra bells and whistles provided by Tarantino, such as outtakes. It would be a big mistake to buy it at $100.

Speaking of Tarantino, I ran into him at the Toronto Film Festival, and he deplored the lack of letterboxed versions of *PF* in many video stores. His estimate: "With the pan-and-scan version, you miss almost 50 percent of the original picture. Instead of *Thelma and Louise.* you get *Thelma or Louise.*"

To make the best of the situation, he said, he personally supervised the pan-and-scan version of *PF.* Some scenes were real challenges. "In the scene in the kids' apartment," he said, "when Samuel Jackson is talking to one guy and shoots the other guy who is on the couch, in pan-and-scan the shooting would happen out of sight. To prevent that, as the director I felt free to do something a video transfer guy would have been afraid to do. I put in a real fast swish-pan from one side of the screen to the other."

I'm sure Tarantino did his best, but let's face it: That scene works *because* it's in one static shot. Jackson doesn't budge as he coldly pulls the trigger. The quick camera movement is not the same thing, and viewers of the pan-and-scan version will not be experiencing the same impact.

Meanwhile, from far and wide I'm getting complaints that the nation's video stores (not just Blockbuster) are not stocking the season's hottest video title in the letterboxed format—which means viewers of the pan-and-scan version are missing half the viewing area of the original widescreen picture. A sampling:

— Not only is my local Blockbuster not carrying *Pulp Fiction* in the letterbox format—but the manager *doesn't know what letterboxing is!* I swear to God! (J. Walker, Nashville, Tenn.)

— My local West Coast Video didn't get the letterbox version. Another outlet even told me that there was no letterbox version. As a last resort, I called Blockbuster (I had given up my Blockbuster membership years ago because of their NC-17 policy). That's right, neither Blockbuster near me had the letterbox version. One clerk even said there was "really no difference" between P&S and LBX! (Alan Tignanelli, North Versailles, Pa.)

— I live in the home of Texas A&M University. We apparently do not qualify as one of the "major" cities (as defined by Blockbuster) that will get the letterbox version. According to the salesclerk, they will have thirty-four pan-and-scan copies and one letterbox version. If only Quentin Tarantino still worked at video stores. (Mark Bendiksen, College Station, Tex.)

— Blockbuster had eighty copies of the pan-and-scan version but only *one* copy of the letterbox version. Video Warehouse had two hundred copies but *none* were letterboxed. The clerk said the last time they got a movie that was letterboxed, customers thought their televisions were broken. I tried to explain the benefits of letterboxing, but she didn't take me seriously. I think there needs to be some kind of education for people who work in video stores. (Joe Carlson, Savannah, Ga.)

Q. Let me tell you what a local video store does to educate the public about the letterbox format. They have two screens side by side playing the same movie. One is letterboxed, one is not. It's a good way to show the average viewer just how much they sacrifice for pan-and-scan. (Derrick Calcote, Memphis, Tenn.)

A. Another method: Cut out two pieces of paper. Make one piece 1 inch high and 1.33 inches wide. Make the other 1 inch high and 2.35 inches wide. Place the smaller on top of the larger, and the parts that stick out show how much of the picture you're missing with the pan-and-scan version.

Q. I read that we miss 43 percent of a widescreen movie when we see it on TV, but this never takes into account that TV "overscans" the picture. Six percent of the image is lost around the edges of the tube. That means viewers miss 56 percent of a scope picture. It gets worse. The TV engineer's alignment chart shows the "safe title area"—the center part of the picture that must contain all text, to be sure it's readable. Recalculating with this chart shows that as much as 66 percent of a widescreen movie may be cut away! (Scott Marshall, East Windsor, N.J.)

A. Yeah, but what's left can be terrific. Just last week I was enjoying Charlton Heston in *Ben*, Omar Sharif in *Doctor*, and Kubrick's great sci-fi picture *20*.

Q. I recently moved here from Los Angeles to manage the Fox theater in Watsonville, and I stopped into the local Blockbuster to order the letterboxed version of *Jaws* coming out later this month. The manager did a check on their computer and told me that they could not order it for me, as they will not be carrying it. (Ed Havens, Santa Cruz, Calif.)

A. Blockbuster appears to avoid the letterboxed versions of movies, even though true movie buffs dislike "pan and scan." Earlier this year, the chain first said it would not carry the letterboxed version of *Pulp Fiction*, then reversed itself. With *Jaws*, they are back to ground zero, despite director Steven Spielberg's long and loud support of letterboxing.

Q. I saw the closing moments of a couple of movies on TV last week. The movies were presented in the pan-and-scan format, yet the closing credits were shown in widescreen format. Any reason this is done? (Gary Currie, Montreal, Quebec, Canada)

A. Yes. Many of the words in the credits would be invisible if slice-and-dice method were used for the credits (and the opening titles). So the credits serve as a dramatic example of how much of the total picture area you're losing when you view a pan-and-scan movie. True movie lovers refuse to rent videos or view movies on TV that have been vandalized in this way.

Lion King

Q. Is it possible that Disney took *The Lion King* into the shop for a little retooling between its first and second release? I thought the best sight gag in the movie was when Timon and Pumbaa staged their mini-luau to lure away the hyenas. There's a hilarious contrast between carefree Timon, doing his manic little hula, and poor, pragmatic Pumbaa, stuck motionless on a plate, agony in his eyes and sweat literally spouting out of every pore. So, a few weeks back, I take the kids to the rerelease and wait patiently for my favorite scene and . . . lo and behold! No sweat! No agony! Pumbaa's lying on the plate, big smile on his face, apparently having the time of his life! At first, I think I'm suffering from MAMLS (Middle-Age

Memory Loss Syndrome), but my eleven-year old daughter, who re-
members *everything*, backs me up on it. (Chuck Mathias, Tacoma, Wash.)

A. But Don Hahn, who produced *The Lion King* for Disney, does
not. "There are very definitely *not* two versions out there," he told
me. "Before we animated, we had contemplated Pumbaa being really nervous. But finally we settled on just two of them having a
great time doing the hula. The movie has not changed. Pumbaa is
enjoying himself, an apple in his mouth, not sweaty or nervous."

After I talked with Hahn, I got e-mail from no less than David
Pruiksma, the artist who animated all the Pumbaas in the luau sequence, who wrote: "I can assure you that only one version of the
scene exists. The sequence was done in about three weeks and there
was no time for monkeying around with alternate 'takes' of any
scenes."

Q. There was no reason for *The Lion King* to deal with murder. I
am not a shrinking violet; I have worked as a reporter, police
officer, and now a government prosecutor. I have dealt with death
many times, although I have reached the age where I am totally
burned out by tragedy, particularly senseless random killings. What
we as parents expect from Disney is a "safe harbor." We would hope
for Disney to provide warm "G" movies for children and give them
a chance to escape the horrors of our society. Kids need opportunities to be kids. To feel safe and secure. We're bummed out because
our ten-year-old dog died suddenly today and I have a five-year-old
daughter who we're trying to help though this when we can barely
get through it ourselves. Maybe Disney can rationalize this movie.
I'm sure they can. But that's not the point. If parents and kids can't
turn to Disney, what's left? (Dick Ginkowski, Kenosha, Wisc.)

A. I mentioned in my review that *The Lion King* was probably
too intense for younger children, and several letters have confirmed
this. I think Disney is essentially reaching for a mass audience of
all ages by including themes that are more mature than small children are capable of handling.

Q. In your review of *The Lion King* you say the friend of the
warthog is a "meerkat." I cannot find this animal in dict. or ency.

Was this a misprint or a made-up name by Disney? (Wayne Wendels-dorf, Louisville, Ky.)

A. Funny, it's in both my dict. *and* ency.

Locations

Q. You made a comment on *Letterman* concerning the Madonna movie. It went something like, "Even in Portland, Oregon, they'd notice her nude on the houseboat." In case you care, most of the houseboats in the Portland area *are* secluded, and she could very well have not been seen. There's not much river traffic around the areas the houseboats are in, particularly at night. Even if Port-landers could have seen her, they very likely didn't care. During filming, a contest was run by a local paper for Madonna photos, and they got two entries. Big deal! Not a very good movie, but Port-land looked great, I thought. (Julie Kidd, Portland, Oreg.)

A. It *did* look great, didn't it? Especially with that houseboat in the foreground with the naked woman standing in the window.

Q. In your review of *Needful Things,* you wrote: "The story takes place in one of those peaceable little Stephen King towns where everybody knows each other and they're mostly all doomed. The town is named Castle Rock, after the name of the company that is releasing the film (ho, ho)." I guess you are not a reader of Stephen King's books, because many of them, from *'Salem's Lot* on, have been set in his fictional town of Castle Rock, which is much like Bangor, Maine (King's home for many years). I think that Castle Rock Productions was started by Rob Reiner when he made the film *Stand By Me* from one of King's novellas, also set in that town. (Reid Powell, Guelph, Ontario, Canada)

A. You were the first of about four dozen people to correct my mistake about Castle Rock. Any ideas why there's no company named Guelph Productions?

Q. There was a lot of publicity when a helicopter crashed into an active volcano in the Hawaiian Islands while filming for the movie *Sliver.* The cameraman and crew were saved only after much danger. When I went to see the movie, there were no shots of a volcano in it. What happened? (Ronnie Barzell, Chicago)

A. The volcano footage was planned for the film's original ending, which was subsequently changed, making it unnecessary. The thoughts of the men who nearly died to get the footage can only be imagined. Maybe they can sell their story to the movies.

Q. In your review of *A Perfect World* you mentioned a restaurant named the "Squat and Gobble." Near Canyon Lake, between San Antonio and Austin, there is a little barbecue place named "The Squat and Gobble" where you eat your food off of a wooden utility wire spool and sit on old tractor seats. Really cool. My husband and I went there on our honeymoon four years ago. (Tracy Standley, Austin)

A. They're all over the place. The "Squat and Gobble" in Bluffton, S.C., even sent me a T-shirt. As I said in my review, "Squat and Gobble" is the best restaurant name I have ever seen in a movie.

Q. I was delighted to read your review of *I.Q.*, which was also favorably noticed by Janet Maslin in the *New York Times.* I was lucky enough to be an extra in the film, which premiered here in Princeton to mixed reviews (a friend pronounced it the "worst film I've ever seen"). The problem is, Princeton people are very protective of Einstein, whom they think they "know." Even though locals loved Matthau as a person while he was filming here, they worry whether Einstein himself would have approved. I'm glad non-Princetonians are enjoying the film; around here, they're too busy noticing the scenery ("Hey, I think I saw my house!"). (Bob Brown, Princeton, N.J.)

A. It was the great French director François Truffaut who once said no one could appreciate even the greatest film if it was shot in their own house, because they would always be looking at the wallpaper.

Q. I was glad to see your favorable review of *Nell.* In your review you said it was hard to believe people could live so isolated as Nell and her mother did. Until September of this year I lived twenty miles south of Robbinsville, N.C. (where the movie was filmed), and some people in that area of the country do indeed live in almost total seclusion. Some take great pride in the fact that they only come off of their mountain once or twice a year for supplies. Most probably collect some type of government handout but there are many who grow, make, and hunt for items they need and for items to barter with. They chose a perfect town in which to film *Nell*—a case of "art imitating life" and vice versa. (Roxanne Diesel, Simi Valley, Calif.)

A. I related to the movie more as a fable than as something that could literally be true, but you're correct that the director, Michael Apted, found a location that was so evocative it added mood to the whole story.

Q. I was visiting New York City and was trying to cross 6th Avenue. But there was a film being shot, with a number of self-important PAs running around with walkie-talkies, none of whom would allow anyone to cross the street. As I walked on, I noticed that the lettering on the storefronts was in reverse image. I went into a theater to see *The Lion King,* and while inside heard a massive explosion. When I came out, 6th Avenue looked like Beirut. They had blown out a block's worth of storefronts for *Die Hard With a Vengeance.* My question is: What was the purpose of the reverse lettering? Did they film the scene with mirrors? (Peter Contarino, Chapel Hill, N.C.)

A. According to Michael Tadross, a producer on *Die Hard III,* they flipped the signs so that after shooting the scene, they could flip the film so traffic would seem to be going the right way. This leads to the obvious question: If you look real close, can you see that all the steering wheels are on the wrong sides of the cars?

Q. Does anyone besides me wonder where, in the Tidewater area of Virginia, all those spectacular cliffs and waterfalls in *Pocahontas* came from? I have just returned from a trip to that area, visiting the actual site of Jamestown. It's pretty darn flat and marshy, with clouds of biting flies and mosquitoes. They sell three different kinds of bug repellent at the gift shop. There are vast swamps all around the area with charming names like "Pitch and Tar Swamp." There are no soaring cliffs and mountains there. I wanted my kids to see where the *real* Captain Smith and Pocahontas lived and to learn about her *real* history, before plunging into the Disney fantasy. (Leslie Scalfano, Decatur, Ala.)

A. Judging by the movie, the original soaring cliffs and mountains must have all been leveled by the evil Governor Ratcliffe, the original mall developer.

Q. A small point. You referred to the power station used in *Richard III* as being the "Bankside Power Station" and noted its "single towering chimney." Any Londoner knows this building as the Battersea Power Station—it has four chimneys and is visible for miles—and, until recently, was being redeveloped into a theme park. (Oliver Moor, North Lauderdale, Fla.)

A. Bankside Power Station has one central chimney. Battersea Power Station has four. It looked to me as if the power station in *Richard III* had one chimney. I stand by my review.

Q. I'd like to know the name and location of the coffee shop/restaurant that's in every other movie I've seen lately. It was where the restaurant scenes were shot for *Pulp Fiction*. It was where Ike Turner smacked Tina Turner in *What's Love Got to Do With It*. It was where Buck Henry and Fred Ward had breakfast (and where Lily Tomlin's character worked) in *Short Cuts*. And I saw it most recently in *Heat*. It's where the De Niro gang debriefed after the armored-car job. I wonder if directors think people don't notice stuff like this. I do. (Nancy Nall, Fort Wayne, Ind.)

A. Coffee shops are so generic that they can look the same without being the same. The location for *What's Love* is Johnny's Broiler at 7447 Firestone Boulevard, Downey, California, which is now out of business. For *Heat*, it's Bob's Big Boy, 4211 Riverside Drive, Toluca Lake, California. I have queried Fine Line and Miramax about the *Short Cuts* and *Pulp Fiction* coffee shops, but tracking down this info does not seem to be high on their list of priorities.

Q. This is a film industry question you might be able to shed some light on. I started working on a production called *Stepping in the Dogwater* for Miramax, directed by David Schwimmer of *Friends*.

Now, here's the thing: Everyone I've talked to has told me that they heard it's a mess, it ran into all kinds of problems on the set in Chicago, and David doesn't know what he's doing. I saw the rough cut and it looks good—I would even recommend it to my friends. And from what I heard and could see, the production went just fine under David. How does bad buzz spread? Is it just one well-placed rumor? Is someone trying to sabotage the project? Or is it some kind of accident? A consensus spread by people who want to believe they're in the know? (Name withheld by request)

A. Bad news is sexy, and gossip is one of the most powerful engines in society. A lot of toes are stepped on during the production of any film, and those whose feelings are hurt are happy to spread negative vibes. Most film shoots are a state of semi-controlled chaos, a carnival of last-minute rewrites, late production schedules, star egos, budget problems, interfering producers, agents with demands, location hassles, injuries, and illness. I've visited a lot of movie locations, and the odd thing is, the shoots that are happiest and most trouble-free often produce the worst movies.

Logos

Q. Columbia Pictures has changed their logo within the past year. It's still a lady with a torch, but as the camera pulls back from the torch bearer, I notice she looks uncannily like Annette Bening. Was she the model for the new logo? (Daniel E. Tienes, St. Louis, Mo.)

A. "It's not her," according to John Moore, a Columbia spokesman in Chicago. "The figure is a computer-generated image. But many people have asked the same question."

Q. It's almost the twenty-first century. What does Twentieth Century Fox do then? (Harris Allsworth, Chicago)

A. The name stays the same, according to Nancy Meyer of Fox's Chicago office. My own hunch, however, is that the word "Fox" will be emphasized—just as it currently is on the TV network—and "Twentieth Century" will appear mainly on letterheads and contracts.

Q. What does it say around the lion's head on the MGM trademark? (Ronnie Barzell, Chicago)

A. *Ars gratia artis,* Latin for "art for art's sake," a motto the studio of course has scrupulously observed over the years.

Makeup

Q. Why must films these days *overkill* with modern makeup techniques? Billy Crystal and Julie Warner aren't convincing as old people in *Mr. Saturday Night.* It just looks like bad makeup. This irks me even more with bios, such as *Chaplin.* In the early scenes Robert Downey looks like Chaplin, because he acts like Chaplin. At film's end, however, the attempt to exactly duplicate Chaplin's appearance is grotesque. Paul Muni didn't need to look like his screen bio subjects to act like them. (David F. Stein)

A. You have not even mentioned the final scene of *For the Boys,* with Bette Midler and James Caan made up to resemble Geriatric Mutant Ninja Turtles.

Matthews

Q. I notice that the inmate played by Sean Penn in *Dead Man Walking* is named Matthew Poncelet. Have you ever noticed how many Matthews there are in TV and the movies these days? I was nearly sixteen years old before *I ever met* another person with the same first name as me, "Matthew." Now it seems to be as common as "John" used to be. And Hollywood has really picked up on it. There's Matthew Broderick *(War Games)* (okay, he's about the same age as me, so I guess I can't accuse him of stealing *my name*), Matthew Garber *(Gnome-Mobile),* Matthew Betz *(The Wedding March),* Matthew Groom, Matt Dillon *(Tex),* Matthew Modine *(Wind),* Matthew Penn *(Delta Force III),* Matthew Laborteaux *(Shattered Spirits),* Matthew Lawrence *(Eddie & the Cruisers II),* Matthew Marsh *(An Affair in Mind),* Matthew Perry *(Dance 'Til Dawn),* Matthew Faison *(Puppet Master 3),* Matt Schwimer, and more among the "brat pack" of TV sitcoms and movie newcomers. Either the name of the character is Matthew or the name of the actor is Matthew. They're going to *use it up!* (Matthew J.W. Ratcliff, Villa Ridge, Mo.)

A. Quit bellyaching. A database search of *Microsoft Cinemania* reveals only 433 actors or characters named "Matthew," as compared to 1,314 "Rogers."

Minnesotans and Mississippians

Q. We Minnesotans are chuckling about a glaring inaccuracy in *Grumpy Old Men*. A fish placed in the backseat of a car here wouldn't rot during one of our frigid winters. It would take at least a week or two of operating the vehicle day in and day out, using the heater, to get a fish to rot. (Terry McKinley, Minneapolis)

A. How did you find that out?

Q. Re: Richard Corliss's review in *Time*, where he accused the Coen brothers of making fun of Minnesotans in their movie *Fargo*. As a twenty-three-year resident of the Coen brothers' hometown, it was crystal-clear to me that their portrayal of Minnesota culture was derived from their love of it, not to make fun of it. Not that it wasn't hilarious. When Marge was standing out in the field saying "this execution-type thing" probably wasn't committed by "anyone from Brainerd," the nine hundred people who packed the Uptown Theater in Minneapolis for last Saturday's 4:30 P.M. show laughed longer and louder than I'd ever heard from a movie audience in this state. Maybe Corliss should stop making judgments about who's making fun of whom when he has no clue about the sense of humor he's critiquing. (Seymour Uranowitz, St. Louis Park, Minn.)

A. Hey, like I always say, you can't make an omelette without breaking a few Minnesotans.

Q. Re the debate about whether *Fargo* ridicules Minnesotans: I have a theory about poking fun at ethnic groups. I think there is nothing inherently bad or malicious about doing so. It only (but, sadly, often) becomes so when there is an undercurrent of hate or oppressiveness associated with it. But Minnesotans? Come on. Nobody has ever hated Minnesotans. Nobody has ever oppressed Minnesotans. Poking fun at Minnesotans is completely innocent and good-hearted. I say this as a person of Scandinavian descent, myself. (Eric Isaacson, Bloomington, Ind.)

A. I personally thought *Fargo* loved Minnesotans, and that Frances McDormand's pregnant police chief from "up Brainerd" was one of the most affectionate portraits imaginable. When you say no one has ever hated Minnesotans, however, I gather you are excluding Big Ten fans.

Q. As a student at the University of Mississippi, I was very upset by your incorrect spelling of the nickname for my school in your review of *A Time to Kill*. The university is affectionately referred to as *Ole Miss*, not "Old" Miss. As Chancellor Alfred Hume said, "Gentlemen, you may move the University of Mississippi. You may move it to Jackson or anywhere else. You may uproot it from the hallowed ground on which it has stood for eighty years. You may take it from these surroundings which have become dear to the thousands who have gone from its doors. But gentlemen, don't call it Ole Miss!" I can only hope that Yankee ignorance was behind the error. (Kathy Vick, Oxford, Miss.)

A. Hey! A mistake like that can happen to anybody. For example, in your quote from Chancellor Hume, did you by any chance intend to type "old" instead of "ole"?

Mission: Impossible

Q. The plot of *Mission: Impossible,* which you said was confusing, could have been worse. Martin Landau recently said that the original *M:I* television cast was contacted to appear in the first ten minutes of the movie so that they could get killed off. (Steven Bailey, Jacksonville Beach, Fla.)

A. "Your mission, should you choose to accept it, is to join in a group suicide . . . "

Q. I am incredulous that though you picked up on all the major problems with *Mission: Impossible,* you nonetheless award it three stars. Granted, there is a nice visual flair to the movie, but since when is that enough to overcome a plot that not only fails to make sense on a logical level, but is wholly unintelligible as a story from the get-go? When critics begin urging audiences to see films that offer nothing more than eye candy, they run the risk of rewarding sloppy filmmakers who more and more these days assume their audience is too stupid to follow a well-thought-out plot. (Joseph Grove, Louisville, Ky.)

A. *Mission: Impossible* is a smart movie—but on a visual and visceral level, not a narrative one. It requires intelligent audiences to enjoy its sophisticated style and jazzlike riffs on other films. Not all intelligence needs be expressed in a linear way. When a movie botches the plot and has nothing else, *that's* sloppy filmmaking. Example: The European version of *The Vanishing* was a masterpiece of plot and style. The American remake (by the same director) dumbed down the plot and was a wretched movie.

Mistakes and Oversights

Q. I enjoy your reviews, but I think you have trouble sorting out relationships. You did this in your review of *Clueless* when you referred to Cher's "stepbrother" Paul when (if he was her father's son by a previous marriage) he was actually her *half*-brother. (Lorna Churchill, Davis, Calif.)

A. Josh (Paul Rudd) is in fact Cher's stepbrother because he is the stepson of her father (the son of a previous husband of his former wife). If he was her half-brother we would be getting into incest territory.

Q The movie *Courage Under Fire* says the Meg Ryan character is supposed to be the first woman ever nominated for the Medal of Honor. This is erroneous. Dr. Mary Walker received the medal from the Civil War. Such wrong information devalues women. (Jim Balser, Director of Veterans, City of Chicago)

A. According to a checklist of Medal of Honor winners compiled by Commander David L. Riley of the Center of Military History, Mary Walker, a contract surgeon attached to the U.S. Army, was awarded the medal by presidential fiat in 1865. It was rescinded in 1917, along with 910 others, but restored by President Carter in 1977. However, the Meg Ryan character in *Courage Under Fire* is said to be the first woman who would win the medal for conduct *in combat*.

Q. I thought *Escape From L.A.* was a pretty good movie. But after thinking about it, I realized something that few if any of the reviews even touched on. (If you use this in the Answer Man, please say *spoiler* so people who haven't seen it won't learn the ending.) Anyway, do you realize that if Snake truly did shut off the planetary energy source in the last scene, he killed more people in one instant than any war, and became the biggest mass murderer in history? By shutting off the power, he caused all airplanes to crash, countless cars to have wrecks because of dead traffic lights, all computers and all of their functions to stop dead, all hospital emergency power to shut off, etc. The movie ends without dealing with the fact that Snake has killed probably more than half a billion people. (Andre R. Mallette, Wilmington, N.C.)

A. I did write in my review, "the implications of his final scene are breath-taking." But I saw his act more as a defiant gesture against the mega-state. Your more logical approach is chilling. Interesting, how in special effects and science fiction movies the hero becomes so overwhelmingly important that when he makes a grand defiant gesture, it is somehow justified even though, as you point out, half a billion people might die to satisfy his ego. I guess we should not be surprised that this did not occur to Snake.

Q. We were just reading your book of movie reviews, and about *The Verdict* you wrote: ". . . It has a lot of truth in it, right down to a great final scene in which Newman, still drinking, finds that if you wash it down with booze, victory tastes a lot like defeat." We agree it's a great final scene. But the only problem is, Newman isn't still drinking. He's sitting in his office drinking coffee." (Paul Kornacki, Cheektowaga, N.Y.)

A. What's in the coffee cup? Booze, or java? Now we have the final word, from Paul Newman himself, who told me: "Coffee. Otherwise, what would the point of the movie be?" I could write an essay on why I thought it was booze, but let's just say I was wrong.

Q. In your review of *Basquiat*, you wrote: "His work is good (when you see it in the movie, you can feel why people liked it so much)." I understand the paintings in the film attributed to Basquiat were actually done by Julian Schnabel! So, Schnabel created not only the paintings for Gary Oldman's character, as you noted, but also the strikingly different ones that were putatively Basquiat's. (Bradley B. Miller, Dallas, Tex.)

A. Zounds! You're right. Basquiat's father would not allow the original paintings to be shown in the movie. Well, the work is good, anyway, even if Schnabel did it. In *Surviving Picasso*, by the way, permission was denied to use Picasso's work, so the filmmakers created fake Picassos. This leads to a rather strange scene in which two women roll on the floor fighting for Picasso's love, while he paints *Guernica*, which is not seen.

Movie Endings

Q. Just saw *When a Man Loves a Woman* with my wife, and agree that it's a four-star film. But the *ending . . .* aaargh!!! I read your review before I saw it, but that still didn't prepare me for seeing this very real, believable, and moving film going so completely off the wall so suddenly with a completely clueless and inappropriate ending. *How does this happen* to so many good films?? *Who* is responsible for perpetrating this kind of cinematic assault? The front office people? The marketing pukes? Surely not the director? Who? And whoever they are, *why* do they believe we moviegoers are all such *brainless dweebs* that this is the kind of dreck we always want to see at the end of movies that try to deal honestly with the human condition? (Bill VanAlstyne, Aptos, Calif.)

A. I guess the theory was that the movie needed an "upbeat," happy ending—as if the triumph of the heroine's recovery from alcoholism was not upbeat enough. So we got that silly Andy Garcia speech and the big kiss with Meg Ryan in the middle of an AA meeting. As I mentioned in my review, the movie should have ended one speech sooner, with her remarks. It never stepped wrong until then. So why was the idiotic final speech put in? Frankly, Bill, because they believe you moviegoers are *brainless dweebs*.

Q. I recently bought *Clerks* on laserdisc, and was shocked at the original ending, which was included among the bonus outtakes. The movie continues after the ending of the theatrical release. Dante is behind the counter, doing the day's books, when a robber enters the store, surprises him, pulls out a gun, and without a word, blows him away. After the assailant empties the register and leaves, the film ends with a couple of long shots of Dante's bloody body crumpled behind the counter. During the credits, instead of music, all we hear is the very faint beep of the cash register. How would this film have been received had Kevin Smith not made the cut, and where would his movie career be today? (Dominic Armato, Burbank, Calif.)

A. I checked out the scene myself. It's as you described it. On the laserdisc's parallel sound track, Smith credits one of the movie's producers with talking him out of the fatal ending, and says that was probably the right thing to do. I agree. The death would have been gratuitous, and in violation of the tone of the rest the movie. And Kevin Smith would still be clerking.

Q. You didn't like *The Usual Suspects* because of the ending. I liked the ending, the dark atmosphere director Bryan Singer created, the acting (especially by Gabriel Byrne, Kevin Spacey, and Chazz Palminteri), and the movie as a whole. The last time I had this much fun at the movies was at *Pulp Fiction.* Maybe you should ask random people from the audience, because you could be the only one who didn't like the trick ending. (Mike D'Alessandro, Acton, Mass.)

A. I'm a critic, not a pollster, and I think a lot of mischief is done to the movies these days because the studios poll sneak preview audiences, and then re-edit movies based on their reactions. In the case of *The Usual Suspects*, I am certainly in the minority. This is the most-debated film since *Pulp Fiction,* and I have received countless communications from its fans. The ending left me feeling let down and manipulated. There is a difference between the chronological trickery in *Pulp Fiction,* which plays fair, and the narrative trick in

The Usual Suspects, which strikes me as arbitrary. You're right about the acting, though; in this movie and *Seven,* Kevin Spacey develops a very particular screen presence—also seen in *Glengarry Glen Ross* and *Swimming With Sharks.*

Movie Math

Q. Read your review of *Quick and the Dead,* and I have some advice for you: Stay off the riverboats. You mention the contestants must be crazy to enter a contest where the odds are ten-to-one in favor of their being killed. You are way off on the odds. Assuming an even-money bet in each of the shoot-outs (one chance in two), the chance of a contestant winning ten successive even-money shoot-outs are 1,023 to 1. (Tony Licata, Chicago)

A. You are right about riverboat math. Now let's figure the odds the Hollywood way. Assuming a contest involving twelve supporting actors, plus Gene Hackman, Sharon Stone, and Leonardo Di Caprio as The Kid, what do you think the odds are that Hackman will kill The Kid in order to face Stone in the final round?

It was a year later that I had a twinge of déjà vu while reading Darwin's Dangerous Idea, by Daniel C. Dennett, in which he explains that you can always produce a person who wins ten coin-tosses in a row, simply by starting with 1,024 contestants and pairing them off in a series of tosses. The winner of the toss between the last two contestants has, by definition, won ten times in a row.

Movie Titles

Q. I read some time ago that the novel *The Dork of Cork* was being made into a film, but I can't find it listed among the upcoming releases. Do you have a progress report? (John McHugh, Three Oaks, Mich.)

A. The movie was released as *Frankie Starlight.* It's the story of a dwarf born to a French mother and an American father and raised in Ireland, where he becomes a local legend. I would love to sit down and have a cup of Irish tea and a friendly chat with the marketing genius who thought a nebulous title like *Frankie Starlight* would sell more tickets than *The Dork of Cork,* a title that almost compels you to seek out the movie.

Q. Heard a delicious rumor that *The Madness of King George* was originally named *The Madness of George III,* but they changed the title for the American release because they were afraid everyone would think this was a sequel! Is this true? (Molly Ivins, Austin, Tex.)

A. Absolutely true. And then there was the Hollywood producer who asked his partner, "Have you seen *Henry the Fifth?*" And the partner replied, "Hell, I haven't even seen the first four."

MPAA Ratings

Q. I understand Warner Bros. was forced to suspend plans for the release of a new 70mm print of the restored "director's cut" of Sam Peckinpah's *The Wild Bunch* after the MPAA rated the film NC-17. I would very much like to hear Jack Valenti explain why *The Wild Bunch* gets an NC-17 when even more violent films like *Total Recall* get an R. Violence is okay only so long as it occurs among cardboard characters in a cartoon script? (Robert Lauriston, San Francisco)

A. In a tragedy crossed with a travesty, *The Wild Bunch* has been outgunned by the MPAA's Code and Rating Administration. The movie was rated R when it was released in 1967. That version reflected some seventeen minutes of cuts made by Peckinpah after the film's world premiere. The original cut was thought for years to be lost, but then Warner Bros. rediscovered it, and made plans to rerelease Peckinpah's version in theaters in Chicago, New York, Los Angeles, San Francisco, Boston, and Houston.

Imagine their surprise when the MPAA slapped the movie with an NC-17 rating. The studio is caught in a catch-22. Because 85 percent of American theaters will not play an NC-17 film and many media outlets will not accept advertising for one, the movie cannot be released with the rating. But if the studio makes any cuts to get an R rating, the film, of course, will no longer be the "director's cut."

I spoke to Warner's executives over the recent Oscar weekend. They were livid. I spoke to Robert Rehme, president of the Academy of Motion Picture Arts and Sciences. He said the MPAA board had made "a terrible mistake." I think this is yet another proof of the need for a workable "A" rating, that would fall between "R" and hard-core porno. The movie industry resists this change for one reason: Greed. Their worst nightmares involve turning away anyone with the price of admission.

The restored version was eventually released with an "R" rating.

Q. I just returned from seeing *A Far Off Place* with my eight- and ten-year-old daughters. This is a Disney children's movie. Yet with an audience full of little children, men are machine-gunning elephants, then chainsawing off their tusks! That is followed by the massacres of the parents in the bedroom, the burning of the farm, and men actually firing on children from helicopters. All, yes, amid a sweet and otherwise well-done story. Is our society now that callous and brazen and violent . . . or is it just me? (Jon Albert, Carmel, Calif.)

A. The movie was rated PG (suitable for all ages; parental guidance suggested) by the MPAA. I would like to know what sort of parental guidance you provided your daughters about why elephants had to be shot down and their tusks sawed off. One good thing about the parents being killed—at least the movie didn't dwell on it by having the kids weep and mourn a whole lot.

Q. This weekend, my friend and I were planning to see *Kids.* We're both under seventeen, and we were shocked to find out that the only theater showing *Kids* was treating it as an NC-17 film. Larry Clark, the film's director, was quoted as saying, "We want kids to see this film. It could save lives." Is this hypocrisy or what? (David K. Austin, Atlanta)

A. This is a tough call. *Kids* is a harsh, cruel, shocking movie that is not for most kids, certainly not younger ones. Yet it reflects a reality of teenage sex and drugs that for some kids could be a lifesaving wake-up call. The MPAA rated it NC-17, and the distributors responded by releasing it unrated. Some theaters are treating it as adults only. Larry Clark thinks it should have been an R—with those under seventeen being firmly required to bring a parent or guardian along. However, this might be an embarrassing movie to see with your parents. The answer may be: Wait for the video.

Q. Who are the bozos that rate movies? I took my two-year-old son to see *Free Willy 2* today, and I noticed that it was rated PG. I also noticed that the *Power Rangers* movie was rated G. *What is up???* The previews *alone* from *Power Rangers* upset me with their violent nature. *Free Willy 2*, on the other hand, left me with a nice, calm, back-to-nature (except for the oil spill) feeling. Who's to blame? (Juan Delgado, Philadelphia)

A. My guess is they gave *Mighty Morphin Power Rangers* the G because it had no sex, drugs, or social problems (except, of course, for monsters attacking cities). *Free Willy 2* contained the material about the boy's wayward mother, and that was considered a more mature theme. The MPAA probably thinks children might not understand why the mother left and what happened to her. Given today's divorce statistics, maybe they should explain to kids what it means when there's a movie where Mommy and Daddy live together happily.

Q. Agreed with your comment on the MPAA ratings of *Showgirls* (NC-17) and *Seven* (R). I think it was Shelley Winters who said, "If a man cuts off a woman's breast, it's rated R. If he kisses it, it's an X." (Steven Bailey, Jacksonville Beach, Fla.)

A. *Seven* has a man forced to choke on his own vomit, another who dies after being forced to cut off a pound of his own flesh, another who is chained to a bed for a year, and a fashion model who is given the choice of calling for help or killing herself, after her nose is cut off. But at least it doesn't have bare breasts, or any of that awful lap dancing.

Q. I note that director Paul Verhoeven has cut four minutes out of *Showgirls* to make a tamer video release, and this version has received an R rating. Blockbuster has announced that they will carry that version. Of course, the film will also be available in the NC-17 version in other stores. (Jeffrey Graebner, Los Angeles)

A. Funny, that's just what I was thinking while I watched the movie: Take out four minutes, and it's a highly moral story.

Q. Does complexity ever play a role in how a film gets rated? Some films may not be appropriate for young children, not because of offensive content, but because they won't understand. It's difficult in some cases to understand why a film has a PG-13 rating unless complexity is a factor. It would seem to make sense, but I've never heard that complexity was a consideration. My family had a long discussion on this recently. (Ellen White, Madison, Wisc.)

A. The MPAA's rating board works from a checklist of elements, such as language, nudity, violence, and "adult themes," and if a film lacks those, it's rated as okay for younger audiences whether or not it's appropriate for them. Example: *Sense and Sensibility* got a PG, not a PG-13, although it is probably incomprehensible to many grade-schoolers.

Q. Though I don't really look for extra sex or violence in a movie drama, I tend to think that any film rated lower than R is likely to be either aimed at a younger audience or not a serious piece of work. I wonder if this is a common reaction, and if studios make sure that most dramas have R-ratable content in order to market or "position" them for adult audiences, even if such content is not intrinsically necessary to the film. (David Bateman, Chattanooga, Tenn.)

A. Audience surveys have shown that teenagers tend to stay away from G- and PG-rated material because they think it's for "kids," and there are anecdotal reports that some filmmakers have slipped in a few four-letter words just be to be sure they get a PG-13. On the other hand, R-rated movies face a potential loss of business from moviegoers under seventeen, so there is no good box office reason to try for an R when it's not necessary.

Mrs. Carlson's Class

You said you would answer some questions from our second-grade class. Here they are! (Karri Dosmann, for Mrs. Carlson's class, Tremont School, Columbus, Ohio)

Q. What is your favorite movie of all time?

A. *Citizen Kane*, the story of a man who becomes so rich and famous that it seems he has everything he wants, but he lacks one thing—happiness. The movie shows that no matter how many possessions you have, unless you like yourself and can be proud of yourself, they do not matter.

Q. Do you like music? I do. What is your favorite song from a movie?

A. My favorite musical scene is in *Singin' in the Rain*, where Gene Kelly plays a man who has just discovered he is in love, and he thinks she may love him, too. It's raining, but he doesn't care. He sings and dances his way through the rain, swinging from lampposts and stamping his feet in puddles, singing, "What a glorious feeling! I'm happy again!" Then a policeman sees him, so he calms down and walks quietly away, because his girl might not like him so much if he gets picked up for disturbing the peace.

Q. How many movies do you watch in a day?

A. I have seen as many as five or six, but on a usual moviegoing day the total is more like two, or maybe three. Movie critics look at a lot of their films in small screening rooms that seat fewer than one hundred people, and we take a lot of notes, because when we write our reviews we don't want Mrs. Carlson to point out our mistakes.

Q. Would you like another job?

A. Not really. I have been doing this one a long time, and have come to love it. My career advice to you would be, take your time and figure out what you really enjoy doing, and then try to make that your job without thinking a whole lot about things like salary and status, because you will be working for a long time and it will help if you look forward to it in the morning.

Q. I hope I can have your job when I grow up.

A. Would Gene Siskel's job be okay?

Q. It must be fun going to movies all the time. You are lucky to have a job like this.

A. It is fun going to good movies, but not so much fun going to bad movies. Remember, I have to see them all. The consolation with the bad movies is that I usually get in free, and get to write about how bad they are in the paper.

Q. Did you like *Aladdin* or *The Lion King* better?
A. *The Lion King.* But of all the recent Disney musicals, the best one is *Beauty and the Beast.* Have you ever wondered why in almost all of these films, the little heroes lose their parents? I know it's sad, but I think it's because with a lot of grown-ups around, they wouldn't be able to be the stars.

Q. What is your job like?
A. Like going to the movies and then writing a letter to friends about what I thought while I was watching the film, and whether they should go. Try it yourself!

Q. I would love to get paid for watching movies.
A. I would go even if they didn't pay me. If I were not a movie critic I would still watch lots of movies every week. They're not just for entertainment, but are a way to share the lives of people all over the world, and learn how they live and how they feel. If a movie doesn't make you want to talk about it after you leave, it hasn't done its job.

Q. What do you do when you are off work?
A. Well, of course there are lots of family events and activities, and talking over everything with my wife, and doing stuff around the house, and then I like to read, travel, draw, cook, and mess around with my computer. They say the one thing you never outgrow is your curiosity, but I don't believe that, because I've met a lot of grown-ups who don't seem curious about anything, as if all of the returns are in. Keep wondering why, and you'll never get bored.

Q. Do you think you are getting paid enough?
A. Yes, but my agent doesn't. That's why it's always important to have a good agent, children.

Music and Sound Tracks

Q. In *Scent of a Woman*, toward the end the musical score picks up Charlie Chaplin's hauntingly beautiful melody from *City Lights*. Since both movies deal with blindness, it seemed significant, yet I saw no mention of *City Lights* or Chaplin in the credits. (Barry G. Silverman, Phoenix, Ariz.)

A. David J. Wally, the film's associate producer, tells me that although Director Martin Brest is such a lover of Chaplin that he named his company City Lights Films, the use of the song is coincidental. The song from *City Lights* is "La Violetera," written by Jose Padilla, not Chaplin. When Brest was researching music for the movie, he came across several recordings by the Tango Project, which he decided to use. One of them was "La Violetera." Both Padilla and the Tango Project did receive credit in the end titles.

Q. How is it that music companies can sell movie sound tracks that don't include all of the music selections from the movie? I purchased the sound track for *When a Man Loves a Woman* for a particular song. I didn't know the title, so couldn't check the list of contents. Nowhere on the CD did it say "some of" the sound track, but my song wasn't there. I wrote to Buena Vista Productions and told them of my disappointment, but received no answer. I'm fed up! (Mary Carrino, Berwyn, Ill.)

A. "In some cases copyright permission for certain songs is granted only for use in the movie and not on the sound track album," according to Buena Vista's Chicago spokesman, Jeff Marden. "In the case of *When a Man Loves a Woman*, both the Rickie Lee Jones song and an REM song ('Everybody Hurts') were not available on the sound track for this reason." To be on the safe side, he says, check out the end titles, when all songs are listed. ("I know this is difficult at best," he adds.)

Q. Why is it that in the movies whenever the radio plays "Moonlight Serenade" by Glenn Miller, the next thing that happens is the Japanese attack Pearl Harbor? (Dana L. Marek, Pasadena, Tex.)

A. What goes around, comes around. Every time you hear The Doors, we attack Vietnam.

Q. I recently bought a new laserdisc of *Slap Shot* to replace a flawed one from the early '80s, and I noticed that the music in the movie has been changed. I liked the original music much better and this new music changes the "feel" of the movie for me. Why would the music have been changed, and has this been done in other movies? (Brad Grube, Bowie, Md.)

A. David Wise of the CompuServe ShowBiz Forum writes, "The music was changed in *Slap Shot* because the film was made before the advent of home video, and thus the studio failed to obtain the home video rights for use of the songs. Renegotiating such rights (especially with heavy hitters like Elton John and Fleetwood Mac) would devour the profits of the film's home video release, and therefore 'soundalikes' were used. An earlier home video release of the film was done before the studio was even *aware* that it didn't own the home video-use rights! It took a few lawsuits (on other films) before MCA wised up to the problem."

Q. I just have to say something about that much-lauded flick *The Piano.* Of course, it is a fine movie, *but* I couldn't help thinking, as I was watching all that overwrought, inchoate lust: "Where are Sid Caesar and Imogene Coca when we need them?" I could imagine their parody so clearly that I spent most of the movie stifling giggles when I should have been overwhelmed by the passion of it all. Think about it: This guy under the piano, fingering a hole in her stocking, and she writing a note: "Get yer grimy claws offa my leg, buster! Geez, what are you, some kind of prevert?" And the music! Did the person who composed the score study with Yanni? The only real music, the Chopin prelude, was banged out to show her anger and the rest of the time it's "Twiddling from Wyndham Hill," that music that people who believe in unicorns and meditation listen to all the time. (Guenveur Burnell, Kent, Ohio)

A. Thanks for your note, which can serve as my answer to all the people who wrote in asking why the score for *The Piano* was overlooked in the Oscar nominations.

Q. How much of the music on *Mr. Holland's Opus* was performed by an actual high school band and how much was done using professional stunt musicians on a scoring stage? (Bill Hammond, Nashua, N.H.)

A. Jeffrey Graebner of Los Angeles says most of it was performed by the Seattle Symphony. Even the "bad" performances were by pros. And they were pretty bad, all right, since at one point I failed to recognize the first four notes of Beethoven's Fifth Symphony.

Q. I just saw *Grace of My Heart* and it was wonderful. What a fun, sweet, terrific movie. Great date bait. Then I bought the "original sound track album" and it wasn't. Same music, different artists. Kinda disappointing. What's the deal with that? (Luigio Salmo, New York)

A. Jeffrey Graebner, movie sound track expert from Los Angeles, has good news for you: "You may have a collector's item. Apparently a mistake was made causing a number of *Grace of My Heart* sound track CDs to be shipped using a cover version of at least one song instead of the version actually used in the film. The CDs were recalled and replacements with the correct recording have been shipped. Supposedly, the incorrect CDs are already being sought by collectors."

Nudity

Q. Why do some actresses insist on keeping it secret when they use a double for a nude scene? If they are too modest to do their own scenes, wouldn't they want to credit the double so the public would know they hadn't seen the star's body? (Francis T. Kennedy, Oakville, Conn.)

A. This assumes that modesty is the motivation for using a double. More frequently, it is vanity. The actress uses the best-looking double in town and wants you to think it's her. Some actors do the same thing, although Mel Gibson and Michael Douglas are so proud of doing their own work that they seem to include a bare-bums scene in almost every one of their movies.

Q. Why is there a double standard regarding male versus female nudity in the movies? Why are women seen naked so much more often than men? Do you suppose, as directors keep pushing at the taboo envelope, we'll have more full frontals in our future? Is the small-but-growing number of female directors changing this equation at all? (Martha Barnette, Louisville, Ky.)

A. Genitals, of either sex, reduce any scene to a documentary. Nudity below the waist is fatal to the dramatic impact of any scene, drawing attention away from the characters, dialogue, and situation. W.C. Fields felt uneasy sharing the screen with a baby or an animal, because he felt attention would be drawn away from him. If he had lived a little longer, I feel sure he would have added genitals to his list.

Okay for Kids?

Q. Despite your review saying it was too scary for younger kids, I just took my two children (ages four and seven) to *Jumanji*, prepared to yank them out of the theater at the first sign of terror. They loved it. The dangerous animals were animated in a somewhat cartoonish style that took out most of the sting. Certainly nothing worse than the scorpion scene in *Honey, I Shrunk the Kids*. Comparing this movie to, say, *Jurassic Park* (which every kid in America probably owns on video), I'd say it was fairly tame.

I really think you were too concerned about the child-in-danger plot. However, certain rules must be followed: Everything must work out okay in the end, nobody dies, and the kids must triumph over the monsters. I'm not claiming this was Great Cinema, and it's not as good as the book, but it hardly qualifies as an evil attempt at terrifying the unsuspecting children of the world. (Leslie Scalfanò, Decatur, Ala.)

A. I noticed that a lot of the reviews shared my concern; the movie would have been too intense for me as a kid. But then, I hadn't trained by seeing *Jurassic Park*. Thanks for the feedback: All parents should be so observant about what will, and won't, upset their children.

Q. Regarding the mean kid next door in *Toy Story*, who takes his toys apart and puts them together in strange ways: It might interest you to know that bashing commercial toys and making new toys out of the pieces is actually a very popular hobby with the kids today. The toy companies don't make action figures for some of the more obscure comics and movie characters, so these people build 'em themselves by cannibalizing the parts they need from existing action figures and then repainting and in some cases entirely re-sculpting. Many of the results are actually far better than com-mercial quality. A bunch of comix magazines I read run photos of readers' homemade figures, two or three pages' worth, every month. It's a cool hobby and I wish I had the time to take a crack at it myself. (Andy Ihnatko, Westwood, Mass.)

A. It is so heartening, in this modern age, to learn that kids still make their own toys. Here you go, Junior: Batman, Robin, and a hammer!

Q. My ten-year-old son and I took off half a day so we could see *Jack,* our favorite actor's "sweet little movie," as Robin Williams de-scribed it on Leno. I was stunned by the highly sexualized depiction of boys in the fifth grade. Since we have one, I can assure you that *Penthouse* magazine is really not part of the picture at this develop-mental stage. My greatest concern was the conduct between Fran Drescher and Robin Williams. None of the little boys were laugh-ing or even connecting with the weird scene of Williams pawing his friend's mother. The french kiss was offensive, and proved that somehow Hollywood felt it had to even the score by showing that boys can be exploited by women. What was the point? This was hardly intended for the same audience as *The Graduate* or *Summer of '42.* My son's reaction was confusion and disgust as he tried to figure out why this was in the movie. My reaction was, the movie was a colossal betrayal by Mr. Williams. FYI, I am a lawyer and have spent much of my professional career involved in the repre-sentation of children and the creation and implementation of laws related to child abuse and neglect. Please consider the content of the movie as people need to at least be aware that it is hardly the benign little story it is cracked up to be! (Myra Werrin Sacks, Harris-burg, Pa.)

A. I am in substantial agreement. I felt that the one sequence that did work involved the teacher (Jennifer Lopez) tactfully but firmly explaining to Jack why she couldn't go to the prom with him. (He had asked her because she was the only person his size.) The scenes with Drescher, especially the one in the bar, were filmed by and for adults who had long since forgotten what it was like to be in fifth grade. Maybe I have, too; rereading this, I asked myself— do they *have* proms in the fifth grade these days? I thought school dances didn't start until about seventh grade. In fifth grade we would rather have done arithmetic than dance with a girl.

Oscar Complaints

Q. We agree that Linda Fiorentino's work in *The Last Seduction* is one of the most amazing performances of the year. But since the movie played briefly on cable, does that mean she is not eligible for an Academy Award nomination? (Harris and Petronella Allsworth, Chicago)

A. I'm afraid that's exactly what it means. The movie played on HBO before being "rediscovered" in England and winning a theatrical release in the United States. Too bad, since no other female performance in 1994 is likely to be quite as memorable.

Q. The makers of *The Last Seduction* plan to sue the Academy of Motion Picture Arts and Sciences for not listing the movie on Oscar ballots. The Academy says the movie is not eligible for Oscar consideration because it played last July on cable TV before opening in theaters in November. As a big supporter of Linda Fiorentino's performance in the movie, where do you stand? (Harold Gasper, Chicago)

A. With the Academy. Fiorentino's performance was, in my opinion, the best of the year—but the Academy rules are very clear in their definition of how films can qualify. The distributors should have had more faith in *The Last Seduction* instead of selling it to HBO before a theatrical run. The same director, John Dahl, had the same thing happen to his previous film, *Red Rock West*, which played on Showtime before opening in theaters. Maybe sooner or later distributors will figure out that Dahl is ready for the first team. If *The Last Seduction* is eligible for an Oscar, then every other made-for-TV should be eligible, too.

Q. This year (1995) several actors seem to be potential Oscar nominees for more than one film, including Anthony Hopkins, Daniel Day-Lewis, Debra Winger, Tommy Lee Jones, Denzel Washington, Clint Eastwood, and Emma Thompson. What happens if they split their votes between two movies? For example, could Hopkins get enough total votes for *Shadowlands* and *Remains of the Day* to be nominated, but get shut out because they are divided? (Ronnie Barzell, Chicago)

A. I called Bob Werden, the Academy's legendary spokesman, for the answer, and found that your scenario is at least theoretically possible.

"They use a preferential accounting procedure," he said, "in which at a certain point in the vote-counting, if one movie is ahead, then they just go ahead and count only the votes for that movie."

In other words, I said, if at a certain point Hopkins has more votes for *Shadowlands* than for *Remains*, they count all of his remaining votes as if they were for *Shadowlands*?

"No. They stop counting the *Remains* votes altogether, and *only* count the *Shadowlands* votes."

But, I said, what if you counted *all* of the votes, and found out that *Remains* had a late surge and actually ended up with more votes?

"It is kind of a strange system," Werden said.

Let me get this straight, I said. If, for example, Hopkins has more votes for *Shadowlands* early on, but eventually not enough to get nominated, he would not be nominated—even if it turned out he had enough votes to be nominated for *Remains*? Or even if his total votes for the two movies would qualify him?

"That's right," said Werden. "I don't understand it, but the accountants say it works."

Q. Why wasn't *Like Water for Chocolate* nominated for Best Foreign Language Film in the Oscars? Was it ineligible for some reason, or were the other selections that much superior? (Alex Fallis, Ormond Beach, Fla.)

A. It wasn't this year's film (1993). It was submitted by Mexico for last year's Oscars, but not nominated, perhaps because it was then about forty minutes longer and did not play as well.

Q. The Actors' Branch of the Motion Picture Academy has denied Rodney Dangerfield's membership application, on the grounds that he has not made a sufficient artistic contribution to deserve it. So he cannot vote in the Oscars. What do you think about this? (Fred Rowley, Wilmette, Oreg.)

A. This is absolutely shameful. The rules require an applicant to submit two important credits, and be nominated and seconded. Dangerfield more than qualifies. He has been top-billed in five features, two of them grossing more than $100 million, and last year had an acclaimed supporting role in *Natural Born Killers*. But his bid for Academy membership was turned down. "I got a letter from Roddy McDowall, the head of the actor's branch," Dangerfield told me. "He wrote that I should 'improve my craft,' and apply again later. Hey, I'm seventy-three years old. What am I gonna do? Apply again when I'm 104?"

Q. Why was Samuel L. Jackson nominated for supporting actor in *Pulp Fiction* while John Travolta was nominated for lead actor? From what I can remember, their parts were either equal, or Jackson may have had more dialogue. I am not one to scream racism every time a black person is snubbed for something, but in this case it seems to me a plausible explanation. (Sharon Gordon, Skokie, Ill.)

A. Actually, Travolta was in a good deal more of the movie than Jackson—for example, in the "date from hell" sequence with Uma Thurman. He had more screen time than any other single character.

Q. Why was John Candy not acknowledged in the memorial section of the 1995 Academy Awards program? (Art Gorman, Chicago)

A. Many viewers asked the same question, according to Cheryl Behnke of the Academy, who told me: "Since Candy died on March 4, 1994, there was time for us to edit highlights of his career into the necrology which appeared on last year's telecast."

Q. I'd like to hear why you think the Academy continues to perpetuate categories like "Best Animated Short Subject" when most theaters these days find it more profitable to run ads, trailers, or snack bar promos in their place. And the cartoons that actually do get shown in theaters (including such recent Warner Bros. releases as Chuck Jones's *Chariots of Fur,* which was released at the head of *Richie Rich*) don't merit any Academy consideration at all. (Dave Mackey, Toms River, N.J.)

A. I think the Academy would be happy to emulate theater owners and drop several of those categories except that (a) there would be an uproar, and (b) if the Oscarcast runs longer, that means more commercials.

Q. Of all the films we saw last year, my favorite was *The Postman,* from Italy. Now I heard something about how it isn't eligible for the Academy Award as Best Foreign Film. Surely this is a major miscarriage of justice? (Susan Lake, Urbana, Ill.)

A. Foreign film nominations are made by each individual country, and the Italian committee passed over *The Postman* because its director—Michael Radford—is British. This despite the fact that one of the guiding spirits behind the film was an Italian, Massimo Troisi, who cowrote the script and starred as the postman. Troisi delayed heart surgery to complete the film, and died the day after shooting was finished. There's a campaign under way to win *The Postman* nominations in other categories, according to Harvey Weinstein, president of Miramax. "It's eligible in every category *except* foreign film," he told me.

Q. I was surprised to learn that the producers of *The Postman (Il Postino)* sent videocassettes to members of the Academy in order to get them to vote for the film. Is it considered acceptable to lobby members of the Academy for a particular film? (Bruce Worthen, Salt Lake City)

A. Absolutely. Oscar season is like Christmas for Academy members, whose mailboxes are stuffed with dozens of free cassettes— sometimes of movies that will not be released on video to the general public for months. There are also free screenings in Los Angeles, New York, and even Chicago and Toronto theaters for Academy members. And the trade papers are filled with ads touting the possible winners and urging voters to view the cassettes.

Q. In the Best Visual Effects category, instead of having five nominees like other categories, the 1996 Academy nominations indicate that only two pictures, *Babe* and *Apollo 13*, are even worthy of being nominated. This is just plain flat-out *wrong*. (Jeff Levin, Rochester, N.Y.)

A. So it would seem. I learn from Jeffrey Graebner of Los Angeles, the Answer Man's Man in Hollywood, that the way the nominees are chosen in this category is Byzantine, to say the least. He informs me: "The nomination process is rather goofy. There is now a visual effects branch of the category and they initially narrowed the list down to seven titles via submitted ballots. The titles that made the cut were *Babe*, *Apollo 13*, *Casper*, *Jumanji*, *Waterworld*, *Batman Forever*, and *The Indian in the Cupboard*. The makers of each of the nominated films were then required to put together a demo reel showing off the best of their effects. A special screening of the demo reels was held and the final nominees were chosen by those in attendance. For each reel, the attendees were asked to give a rating from 1 to 10. To get a nomination, the average score had to be 8 or above. If no films had received a high enough score, the Best Visual Effects category would have been skipped. If only one film had received an 8 or above, then it would have won automatically (this has happened a few times, including *Star Wars*, *The Empire Strikes Back*, and *Total Recall*). The implication seemed to be that there could have been anywhere from zero to seven nominated films in that category. Apparently, *City of Lost Children* was eliminated from the competition very early. My guess is that not enough people saw it (or had even heard of it) for it to make the first cut."

Q. I noticed that when the "Best Actor" nominees were shown on the 1996 Oscarcast, they only had a still photo of Sean Penn. Was he too stuck-up to attend the ceremony? (Ashley St. Ives, Chicago)

A. Not at all. Penn had every intention of attending, but was called to the hospital when his companion Robin Wright had to have emergency surgery. Penn attended the Independent Spirit Awards the previous Saturday in Santa Monica, and when he was announced as Best Actor for *Dead Man Walking*, he took Sally Field's famous acceptance speech as his motto. "You tolerate me!" he said. "You really tolerate me!"

Q. Nothing ticked me off so much this year as the "banning" of independent publicists from the Oscars. It is the biggest global media night of the year. I wouldn't want my client placed in the hands of some twenty-two-year-old "studio publicist" who's never even met my client, and wouldn't know a tabloid from a TV crew. (Elaine Johnson, Burbank, Calif.)

A. Warner Bros. publicity chief Rob Friedman tells me the reason for the ban was that the indee publicists were following *their* clients all the way through the process, instead of staying in position and moving *all* the stars along in an orderly fashion. The publicists are there to service all the stars, not just their clients.

Oscars

Q. Is there any movement to get the Pulitzer Prize committee to present an award for film, since they already do books, theater, and photography? (Gary Tellalian, Los Angeles)

A. None that I know of, but I think it's a good idea.

Q. What did you think about Tom Hanks's emotional acceptance speech on the Oscar telecast (1994)? (Harris Allsworth, Chicago)

A. It was great drama, but not strong on continuity. The transcript makes confusing reading. I am reminded of the speech Sir Laurence Olivier gave after winning his honorary Oscar. Like Hanks's, it was delivered in a tremendously dramatic manner. In a reaction shot of the audience, you could read Jon Voight's lips as he said, "God!" The next day, Olivier called up his pal Michael Caine and asked what he thought of the speech. "Wonderfully said," Caine replied, "but I didn't quite understand what you were getting at." "Exactly!" said Olivier. "I didn't have a clue what to say, so I just fell back on that old *We're off to Salisbury!* business that one uses when one wants to sound like Shakespeare but can't remember the words."

Q. I wasn't surprised that Tom Hanks won the Best Actor Oscar (1994)—because he is the only actor who portrayed a character with some illness or disability. This seems to be a guarantee of Oscar success. In the last six years we've had Al Pacino (blind), Anthony Hopkins (insane), Daniel Day-Lewis (only one working foot), and Dustin Hoffman (autistic), and now Hanks. Only Jeremy Irons in *Reversal of Fortune* goes against the trend. (Eric Polino, Cranford, N.J.)

A. Yeah, he only maybe murdered his wife.

Q. I was wondering how you felt about the young girl, Anna Paquin, winning for Best Supporting Actress? (Mike Chelucci, New Castle, Del.)

A. She gave an extraordinary performance in the film. That cannot be denied. But how did I feel? A little like when a tourist from out of state comes in and buys one ticket and wins the lottery.

Q. I recently saw the film *The Greatest Show on Earth*, which was 1952's Oscar winner for Best Picture. While I did not think it was a terrible movie, it might be one of the less deserving Oscar winners. I have to admit that I fell asleep before it was over. Just wondering what are some of your other "least favorite" Oscar winners? (James Hinkle, Boston)

A. I've always thought *All the King's Men* was overrated. *Around the World in 80 Days* was more spectacle than cinema. *Mrs. Miniver* and *Oliver!* seem weak today. And how could the Academy have selected *How Green Was My Valley* (admittedly a good movie) over *Citizen Kane*?

Q. Ah, the British press. What would we do without their legendary dedication to clarity and fair thinking? The AP reported that "the British press sulked about being snubbed at this year's Oscars." Said the *Daily Express:* "We don't want to appear bad losers, but we can't help wondering if someone like Mr. Gump was in charge of the judging." Christopher Tookey in the *Daily Mail* described Gump as "a menace to society. The man is so stupid that he just might make it as far as the White House." And the *Independent*'s Bryan Appleyard wrote: "The Oscars are not really about talent. If they were, then dozens of other British actors would be winners." (Andy Ihnatko, Westwood, Mass.)

A. Whatta bunch of crybabies! Brits won the Best Actor Award three years in a row (Day-Lewis in 1989, Irons in 1990, Hopkins in

1991). Emma Thompson won for best actress in 1992. In 1993, three of the five best actor nominees were British, and in 1983, for cryin' out loud, four of the five were. The French *invented* cinema, and they hardly ever get nominated, but do you hear them complaining? Mais non!

Q. What mystifies me is why the Academy of Motion Picture Arts and Sciences, of all organizations, still insists on using panned and scanned film clips on their awards programs. The Academy should be in the forefront of organizations educating the public on the benefits of letterboxing. (Gordon Meyer, North Hollywood, Calif.)

A. Excellent point. Clips on the Oscarcast which fill up the entire TV screen do so by eliminating the parts of the widescreen image that do not fit inside the narrower TV ratio. Directors should insist that their nominated films be shown in the letterbox format, displaying the full width of their original compositions. While they're at it, they might provide the Academy with *new* scenes from their films, instead of using the same tired old overexposed scenes that have been telecast repeatedly for months.

Q. How may one attend (in any capacity) the Academy Awards? It has been my wife's life-long dream to at least stand in line to see the stars arrive. I would like to give her that as a present at the 1997 Awards. (Steve Gomes, Streator, Ill.)

A. If you arrive at Dorothy Chandler Pavilion early in the morning, you can probably grab a seat in the bleachers, and see the stars walk in. To get a ticket to the actual ceremony, however, you'll need to find a concierge with very good connections, and be prepared to pay startling scalper's fees.

Q. What's the Oscar made out of? (Susan Lake, Urbana, Ill.)

A. Gold-plated pewter alloy, according to Owen R. Siegel, founder and president of R.S. Owen, Inc., in Chicago, which manufactures the famous statuette. "Starting in 1991, we greatly increased the amount of gold plating," he told me. "We were getting a lot of statuettes back for refinishing because the gold had worn through, and they thought, they spend millions on the Oscar ceremony, so why not a little more on the award?" Despite the extra gold (24 carat), there is no percentage in melting down an Oscar, since on the rare occasions when one has been sold, collectors have paid $50,000 and up. The Oscar weighs a little over eight pounds, he said, including its brass base. Because the Academy has no way of knowing how many Oscar winners there will be, the annual order varies between fifty and sixty-five.

Pirated Movies

Q. I have a love for laserdiscs because they are letterboxed (most of the time), but rarely is a tape that way. The only way for me to see them is to have a friend of mine use his laserdisc player and copy the movie for me so I can watch it in its widescreen splendor. Do I have a potential problem with the FBI? (David Ingersoll, Philadelphia)

A. You've read the warning, David, and you know that your crime is punishable with a fine of up to $10,000. Of course, no individual has ever been nabbed by the FBI for copying a video for personal use. So, by signing your name to your letter, you may become the first.

Q. Many videos are labeled with the information that they are closed-captioned, but when you get them home, they are not. I attended a meeting of my local deafened persons association recently, and I found out what seems to be the problem. Apparently a lot of video stores may be using pirated copies. These copies do not copy the captions. (Jerry Krueger, Canada)

A. And you know who would *love* to hear about a store selling or renting you such a tape? The studio that released the original film. They're eager to catch pirates.

Q. I have seen videos of relatively recent movies for sale at a price of $16. When I have seen the same movies at video rental stores the price was $80 or more. Please tell me the reason for the drastic price reduction. (Miles Loegering, Credit River, Minn.)

A. Were the $16 videos by any chance being sold by jumpy guys on street corners, and did the video box cover art look slightly photocopied? Often you can buy videos of movies that are still in theaters, but beware: You're probably paying for a shoddy pirate tape. I once bought a copy of a *Jurassic Park* video from a flea market vendor, brought it home, and found that somebody had simply bought a ticket to the movie and filmed it off the screen with his home video camera. The sound track included the audience laughter, and occasionally somebody would get up to go to the refreshment stand, and walk in front of the camera.

Q. I have a friend visiting from Moscow this month who says that cable TV over there has already broadcast videos of *Independence Day*. How is that possible, when it hasn't even been released to video in the United States? We make a stink about China pirating, but what about our good friends in Russia? (Sarah Frazier, Memphis)

A. Daphne Gronich, an attorney with Twentieth Century Fox in Los Angeles, says the studio takes all reports of piracy "very seriously." If *ID4* played on Moscow cable, it was an illegal broadcast, and they are looking into it.

Q. I rented a copy of John Wayne's *The High and the Mighty* at my local video store, and I was unpleasantly surprised to discover the quality of the tape was terrible! Is anyone aware of this obviously unauthorized (I hope) video? When I rented it, I was hoping that it was a new authorized version (like John Wayne's *McLintock*), but I was sadly mistaken. I watched the whole thing because I was so looking forward to seeing this classic again after so long, but it was really b-a-a-d! It looks like a fourth-generation copy of something taped off of TV. The sound is as poor as the picture. The opening credits (only) are in widescreen with yellow. (Hyde Flippo, Reno, Nev.)

A. The John Wayne estate, which brought out a restored version of *McLintock*, has not authorized a video version of *The High and the Mighty*, and major video catalogs such as Facets and Movies Unlimited do not list it.

Political Correctness

Q. What is your opinion on making movie classics Politically Correct? I bought the *Fantasia* video. The box said it was the "complete, restored" version, yet a sequence was missing: In the Greek mythology part, when a female centaur is getting ready for a date, a small black centaur is polishing her hooves. This part was missing. I detest stereotypes as much as anyone, but we are discussing a classic here: a period piece. Should we do the same to *Gone With the Wind* or *Birth of a Nation*? Should we cut out the "Beulah, peel me a grape" scene from the Mae West film? (Alexander Braun)

A. This query appeared in the ShowBiz Forum of CompuServe, where Sam Wass replied: "I have a near perfect memory of this sequence: The little 'black' attendant had big, exaggerated lips and a curly 'fro' with pink ribbons, and did a shuck and jive exclamation—shaking the head rapidly side to side and smiling, mugging with wide-open mouth, 'Lawsy! I do declare those hooves are shiny!' I remember, as a child, seeing the movie for the first time, hearing laughter from the audience around me and shrinking down in my seat embarrassed—and I'm white! But I was thankfully taught by my parents that these things aren't funny, just ignorant. I understand your concern about 'classic' film, but maybe there are some things better left on the cutting room floor."

To Wass's comment, I can add that while the original film should, of course, be preserved for historical purposes, there is no need for the general release version to perpetuate racist stereotypes in a film designed primarily for children. *GWTW* and *Birth of a Nation* are seen primarily by adults capable of understanding their historical context. As for Mae West's line, I've never found it objectionable, since its real comic target is Miss West herself, not her maid.

Q. There was no dialogue in *Fantasia*, except between musical selections. Why would Disney have ruined the effect of Beethoven's 6th Symphony with cheap racial humor? (Robert Forman, San Francisco)

A. David R. Smith, who is the archivist for the Disney company, tells me: "There was originally a black centaurette in *Fantasia* which was helping one of the other centaurettes with her toilette. In later years, the character was edited out of the film. What was acceptable in the 1940s is not 'politically correct' in the 1990s. There was no dialogue in the scene, as there is none in any of the *Fantasia* segments."

Q. Whilst reading your review of *Hear My Song*, I found myself appalled at something you said about "Appalachian Hillbillies" and talk shows. Are you suggesting these "hillbillies" are too backward to converse with talk-show pundits? People who live in the Appalachians are not "hillbillies," an offensive term that suggests inbred ignorance. I am sure a man of your "political correctness" could find a better way to describe Irish secretiveness. (Thomas W. Shipp Jr., Dublin, Ohio)

A. My exact wording was, "The locals in Ireland are so secretive they make Appalachian hillbillies look like talk-show guests." This is not great literature, perhaps, but read it carefully, and you will find it favorably compares taciturn Appalachians to blabbing talk-show guests. No opinion is expressed about the ability of Appalachians to hold their own on talk shows, nor do I imply that all Appalachians are hillbillies, although a current movie, *The Beverly Hillbillies*, believes that some are. Speaking of Political Correctness, I am rather offended, now that I think of it, by your phrase "Irish secretiveness." I was referring only to certain Irish locals, while you attribute this quality to an entire nation. Surely you do not mean to imply, etc., etc. . . .

Q. Have you seen the trailer Disney is running for its animated feature, *Pocahontas*? The lyrics are about the Amerind way of seeing the world: the spirits of the land, the trees, the animals. And about how the white settlers' idea of claiming the land as theirs was wrong, and as long as they thought that way they would never see the true beauty of the world. Seems like a lot of people are attacking the song in the trailer as being "too PC." Call me foolish or naive, but I just don't understand why. The only way these complaints make any sense is to assume that "politically correct" has been redefined by Swamp Newt, Rush Limbaugh, and their zombie followers as "anything to the left of them." Did that happen while I wasn't watching? (Jon Woolf, Beavercreek, Ohio)

A. Now, now. Disney could hardly have made the movie by reinforcing old stereotypes, in which the settlers brought "civilization" to the "savages." The drift of the trailer is basically proecology, in which we learn that we do not own the land, but are merely its custodians for future generations. This isn't controversial. Right?

Q. Just saw *Ace Ventura: When Nature Calls* movie last night. I'm a thirty-two-year-old white male, and a number of things bothered me (besides the fact that it was not very funny, but it cost $1 so what the heck), including:

— the black tribes worshiped a white bat
— the black virgin sought sex with the white Ace Ventura
— the white Brits manipulated the black tribesmen
— the sole black figure in "official" power, the game warden, sold out to the white Brits

Contrast this to the scenes with the Tibetan monks, who handled themselves with dignity and strove to rid themselves of Ace, even to the point of giving up the valuable medallion. Also, the monks were shown as having a "higher purpose," while the tribes simply worshiped a bat that had a name that sounded like another word for feces. This apparent belittling of the tribesmen bothered me. I'm not Mr. PC, but it seemed so . . . needless. I wondered what your opinion is? (Scott McCarty, Muncie, Ind.)

A. It was the kind of imagery you'd expect in one of those wheezy 1930s comedies with cannibals dancing around a pot. *Needless* is a good word. I can think of another.

Q. I am extremely disquieted by the blatant feminist slant of *Jurassic Park*. Three examples: 1. At one point, Ellie Sattler (Laura Dern) states: "Man creates dinosaurs. Dinosaurs eat man. Woman inherits the earth." This was *not in the book*. 2. As the Dern character is about to venture outside to restore power to the compound, the Attenborough character suggests he go, since he is a man. Sattler's response: "Cut the crap." *Again, not in the book*. 3. In the movie, it is the young girl who restores the computer, which saves the remnant. *Not in the book!* In the book, it is a male character. P-U-L-E-E-E-Z-E!! I am beginning to believe the most prescient person on film today is indeed Michael Medved, who says it is rare to find a film that does not have a liberal agenda. (Wayne Steadham)

A. Are we all agreed that portraying competent female characters is a liberal trait?

Q. Has any critic noted the weightist bias in *Jurassic Park?* At the beginning of the movie a plump kid is made to seem obnoxious while asking questions about the velociraptors. When Sam Neill's character objects to the idea of having kids, Laura Dern's says something like, "Well, not like that one." Then the only other heavy person in the movie turns out to be the principal villain, resentful, willing to kill everybody else off, and worst of all, incautious around dinosaurs. (Joseph Kaufman, Hollywood, Calif.)

A. *Not in the book!!* Get me Medved!

Politics

Q. Did you notice that there wasn't a vice president character in *The American President?* I've seen the movie five times already (I'm in love with the film!) and I never really thought about it before. I think maybe another character would have cluttered the movie. (Christi Scheirer, Rockledge, Fla.)

A. Funny, but no, I didn't notice. I wonder if Al Gore did.

Q. Re the suggestion by Newt Gingrich that his critics study *Boys' Town* to understand how orphanages work. I was surprised that he didn't also cite the 1959 Mamie Van Doren/Paul Anka/Mel Tormé classic, *Girls' Town.* (Jeff Levin, Rochester, N.Y.)

A. The movie was later retitled *Innocent and the Damned,* which might reflect Newt's view of himself and his critics.

Q. Concerning *The American President,* I agree with your high rating, but take exception to your saying it took courage to portray a president as a liberal. I cannot remember any recent movie that shows any high-ranking political figure as both clearly conservative and a "good guy." What would have been courageous would have been for Rob Reiner, a liberal, to make the president a conservative who's cast in a good light. I didn't expect to see that happen, and guess what? I was right. The left wing of Hollywood would never let a conservative political figure be shown as anything other than a greedy, uncaring fiend. (Steve Graham, Jackson, Miss.)

A. What I wrote was that it took "nerve" to portray the president as having any politics at all, rather than taking the safe route and making him an amorphous, apolitical slug. It's not so much that there's a liberal conspiracy in Hollywood, as that most artistic, creative types tend to be liberal, just as most business, investment and military types are more likely conservative. There are exceptions, of course. The conservatives in Hollywood with real clout (Willis, Stallone, Schwarzenegger), despite being able to get movies made, have been notably absent from the ranks of films with political themes.

Q. You go ballistic when a Washington politician chides Hollywood about the garbage it is producing, but are happy to have those Washington politicians dictate what each of the fifty states' speed limit laws should be. As a genetically-impaired leftist you are incapable of seeing a paradox there. (Alex R. Thomas, San Antonio, Tex.)

A. Actually, I would be against both national speed limits and movie censorship. But my argument was more precise. What I said was that when a popular target (Hollywood) is available, politicians go for votes by attacking it on the grounds that a movie may have inspired a murder. But when the target is unpopular (speed limits), politicians can happily live with thousands of deaths. This, I think you will agree, is hypocrisy. I would also like to query some of Washington's movie critics about their support of tobacco subsidies.

Q. What is your opinion of Senator Robert Dole's attack on the movie *Money Train* and how it might have inspired the subway firebombing in New York City? (Harris Allsworth, Chicago)

A. It is a relief to me that movies apparently have such a small influence on behavior. This year more than one billion movie tickets will be sold in the United States, and yet only a few incidents have been linked to the supposed influence of movies. On the other hand, an estimated ten thousand people will die annually if Dole and his colleagues in both parties successfully raise the national speed limit. Apparently they are prepared to risk more lives in the cause of faster driving than to the idea of free speech.

Q. Michael Medved said on Rush Limbaugh that when Siskel & Ebert put *Nixon* and *The American President* on your Top Ten lists you were reviewing the films as "self-conscious political liberals." Should we care what a critic's political views are? Or only if the reviewer liked the movie and would recommend it to others? (Thomas Heald, Rapid City, S.Dak.)

A. Medved did not study my list very carefully, since *The American President* was not on it, but never mind: I did give the movie a four-star rating, noting that it was a warm and funny romance, while noting twice in my review that it was made from a liberal perspective. There is nothing wrong with a critic having political views—indeed, it is impossible to imagine an intelligent person without them—but the views should not blind him to good filmmaking.

Q. In your article about Bob Dole and his attacks on Hollywood violence I felt you did not mention a couple of things about the movies he praised. *Schindler's List* is a great film but very violent. And in the same vein, with *Independence Day*, something like a billion people die. That is what I call violent, even if you cannot see it happen on screen. (John J. McIntyre, Saginaw, Mich.)

A. I don't think Dole is against "violence" itself, but uses it as a code word for "violence depicting the kinds of people and actions that I do not approve of or find appealing." In other words, he is really reacting according to a movie's context, but doesn't make that clear. I agree with former governor Jim Thompson (R.-Ill.), who said in an interview with the *Chicago Sun-Times* that the American people were not asking themselves who would make the best movies, Bill Clinton or Bob Dole.

Q. Re your review of *A Perfect Candidate*, about the 1994 Virginia senatorial race: I was Douglas Wilder's communications director during his 1994 Senate campaign, and was very eager to see the documentary. I wonder what you think about all the playing to the camera that went on in this film. Personally, I didn't allow the film crew to observe our strategy sessions. They asked to film our last debate preparation session—only a few hours before the debate. By then, all of the strategy had been decided. We spent the last two hours before the debate playing poker, trying to keep Doug loose. But if a camera had been in our face, the campaign manager and I would have tried to act like geniuses. Maybe people would have thought we were brilliant and given us credit for Doug's brilliant performance. Or maybe we might have messed up his rhythm, and the filmmakers would have lost some of their best moments of drama. My point is, you can't expect media-savvy egotists to act natural in front of a camera. I know it is a problem for all documentary filmmaking, but it is especially a problem for films about politics. Our job is to spin reality—and the more attention put on us, the less effective we are for our client. In a way, films like *A Perfect Candidate* don't just record history, they alter history. Any candidate who allows his staff to be filmed like this ought to have his head examined. (Daniel M. Conley, Chicago)

A. People are so blinded by the attention of a television camera that they will sometimes permit the most amazing invasions of their own privacy, and some revealing documentaries have resulted. In the case of the 1994 Virginia contests, both the Oliver North and Charles Robb campaigns presumably thought they'd come out looking good. What the film revealed is that both sides unhesitatingly placed style ahead of substance, and grew steadily more cynical as election day approached. I agree the candidates should have had their heads examined—and, hey, that's just on the basis of *seeing* the film.

Q. Being in the United Kingdom, I wasn't aware that Dole slammed *Pulp Fiction* and *Trainspotting* for glamorizing the use of drugs. I wonder if he considered the film *Nixon* to have glamorized the life of a convicted criminal? (Brian Walker, London)

A. Brian, Brian, Brian. Nixon was never convicted of anything. It does strike me as strange, however, that the GOP candidate for president would have attended, so far as we know, only one movie in recent months, *Independence Day*. Wouldn't you think sheer curiosity would have driven him to see *Nixon*?

Q. I was disappointed by your comment about an "Ayn Rand wet dream" in your review of *Richard III*. Whatever your beliefs about her philosophy or her fiction, Rand is rapidly becoming one the foremost thinkers in recent American history. As such I would think the author of *Atlas Shrugged* would command a little more respect. I am probably being oversensitive but I find there are so few people in this world who honestly deserve respect that I will vehemently defend those who have actually earned it. (Jason M. Fortun, Minneapolis)

A. I wrote in the review, "Many of the scenes are placed inside and outside a vast 1930s art deco power station, which looks like the set for an Ayn Rand wet dream." If you have ever been to London and seen Bankside Power Station, with its single towering chimney, you'll know what I mean. Ayn Rand would probably have enjoyed the line.

Popcorn and Candy

Q. Do you sneak candy into the theater like me because the cost of movie theater candy is so outrageous? (Ryan Thompson, Albany, Oreg.)

A. No. While I agree with you that the price of movie candy is high, there is a reason for that: The refreshment counter provides operating expenses and the margin of profit at most theaters, where in the early weeks of the run of a big movie, 90 percent of the ticket price goes to the studio.

Q. Why do you think we eat so much candy and popcorn in the movies? (Harold Gasper, Chicago)

A. The movies make their great first impression on us when we're small children, and a link gets established between oral and cinematic gratification. That link explains why adults so often choose children's candies at the movies (you rarely see an adult in everyday life eating red licorice ropes). As adults, when we eat candy in the movies, it is part of the calming and pacifying process by which we shut down the left brain and allow the right brain to take over. Once our initial supply is exhausted, we never go out into the lobby to buy something else, because we are now successfully in the right-brain movie reverie.

Product Placement

Q. I am the general manager of a theater chain, and a question has been asked of me for years. Are movie companies paid a fee from manufacturers to get their product on the screen? For instance, in *Home Alone 2*, Coca-Cola can be seen repeatedly. Is it safe to assume that Coca-Cola paid the production company a fee to get Coke, not Pepsi, on the screen? If so, are we talking hundreds or thousands of dollars? (Steve McCaffrey, Albuquerque, N.Mex.)

A. Thousands.

Q. I just saw *House Guest*. The movie seemed like a two-hour-long McDonald's ad. I really feel like this is going too far and that we should not have to pay to watch movies that are made just to sell Big Macs, Cokes, or Sonys. Isn't there some sort of law against such practice? (Frederic Morin, Montreal, Canada)

A. "Product placement" is so common in the movies that it's becoming a distraction. Every movie cop has a big Dunkin' Donuts box on his desk. Characters call for beers by name. The top filmmakers refuse to engage in the practice, but some lesser films actually recruit product placement revenue!

Q. McDonald's did an advertising tie-in with *Jurassic Park*, and I think it was irresponsible of them to link up with such a film. McDonald's generally positions itself in the marketplace as a child-oriented restaurant. I think this slant tends to rub off on the perception the public forms about movies like *Batman* or *Jurassic Park*, through the McDonald's co-op advertising. I heard several comments about *Batman* from other parents, saying they wish they had not taken their children to see it because of its violence. How many children, who love cute and cuddly dinosaurs, are now going to have nightmares after they beg mom and dad to take them to the movie depicted on their McDonald's beverage container? (Loring Fiske-Phillips, San Bernardino, Calif.)

A. And how about the nightmares suffered by executives at Burger King, who did an expensive tie-in with *The Last Action Hero?*

Q. I recently saw the preview for *Batman Forever.* Val Kilmer, as Batman, delivers the cute little line, "I'll get drive-thru" as a response to his butler Alfred's question, "Shall I make you a sandwich?" McDonald's was using the scene in television commercials before the movie had even been released. Do you think this scene was written into the movie as part of a promotional deal? I know that product placement in films is becoming increasingly common but, in this case, it is obvious to the point of distraction. Even before seeing *Batman Forever,* the preview and the McDonald's commercial have left me believing that Batman's enemies in the movie will not only include The Riddler and Two-Face, but The Hamburglar as well. (Murray James-Bosch, Scarborough, Ontario, Canada)

A. McDonald's and Batman have been a coosome twosome for years. It was, in fact, their original association that led to the definition in *Ebert's Little Movie Glossary* of the Four Glass Movie: "Any movie with a plot that can be summarized on four soft drink containers from McDonald's." Given the lead time for TV commercials, it's obvious the scene found its way to McDonald's ad agency early in the filmmaking process.

Q. In a recent Answer Man, you wrote: "McDonald's and Batman have been a coosome twosome for years." Then you said their original pairing inspired the "Four Glass Rule" in *Ebert's Little Movie Glossary.* Actually, *Batman Forever* is only the second Batman film to be merchandised by McDonald's. The thirty-two-ounce plastic cups featuring 1989's original *Batman* were from Taco Bell (with free refills and a sample of "cinnamon Bat-Wings"). The McDonald's connection began with *Batman Returns.* And, as I recall, it only took *three* McDonald's cups to sum up *Who Framed Roger Rabbit?* in 1988. (Thomas Allen Heald, Rapid City, S.Dak.)

A. Were those bat wings served with ranch dressing?

Q. I don't usually watch movies overseas, but I had endured a seven-hour flight to Oslo, sitting among a group of friendly and earnest Herbal Life salesmen, returning to their homeland after a conference in Atlanta. To adjust to the time zone I went to *Demolition Man* and saw Sylvester Stallone in a scene with Pizza Hut food. But here in Pennsylvania, in the same scene, it was fare from Taco Bell. These are simple differences, but are there ever more substantial changes, such as in plot or ending, in films shown on the Continent and elsewhere? (Jeff Ward, Allentown, Pa.)

A. What often happens is that dialogue is softened, simplified, or "cleaned up" in the dubbed or subtitled versions of American films, to suit local audiences. This is, however, the first time I have heard of "product placement" being fine-tuned to the local market. I have two questions: (1) Does this mean there are no Taco Bells in Norway? (2) Did Herbal Life compensate you for the product placement in your letter?

Q. I've been wondering, how do they decide which fast-food restaurants get tie-ins to which movies? Currently, Burger King has *Toy Story*, Taco Bell handled the first *Batman* movie but McDonald's took over the next two. Subway has been stung twice—with *Coneheads* and *Beverly Hillbillies*, but rebounded nicely with *Ace Ventura: When Nature Calls*. (Willie Holmes, Chicago)

A. Studios have marketing departments that strike deals with the ad agencies of the fast-food chains. Big money is involved. Sometimes a chain guesses right, sometimes wrong. The benefits go both ways: The chain plugs the tie-in products in its ads, and moviegoers (especially kids) want to collect the Batman mugs, or whatever.

Pulp Briefcase

Q. In view of your column about the contents of the mysterious briefcase in *Pulp Fiction*, I thought you might be interested in the *Toronto Star*'s recent contest to decide what was in the case. Of two hundred entries, the most popular were: (1) the Oscar that Quentin Tarantino hopes to win; (2) a human head; (3) the ear from *Reservoir Dogs*; (4) O.J.'s other glove; (5) Michael Jackson's other glove; (6) the diamonds from the *Reservoir Dogs* robbery; or (7) Rudolph's nose. The winner said it was a homage to Robert Aldrich and Mickey Spillane, who made a B movie named *Kiss Me Deadly* where a briefcase glows because it contains a small nuclear bomb. (Eric M. Davitt, Toronto, Canada)

A. I believe the winner was right. *Kiss Me Deadly* (1955), recently rereleased on home video, contains a briefcase scene similar to the one in *Pulp Fiction*, and Tarantino, who is famous for having studied countless movies while working in a video store, undoubtedly saw it.

Q. Continuing the discussion of what's inside the mystery briefcase in *Pulp Fiction*. When I saw the movie, I took the glow coming from the briefcase as a reference to Robert Aldrich's *Kiss Me Deadly* (1955). Mike Hammer chased around after that briefcase, which glowed when opened (and exploded if opened for too long) because it contained a nuclear bomb. Also there is a reminder of the glowing briefcase in *Repo Man* (1984) if I'm not mistaken. (B.F. Helman, Chicago)

A. The briefcase question will not go away. Your classic movie citations are persuasive, considering that the authors of the story, Quentin Tarantino and Roger Avary, grew up in video stores and would probably have seen *Kiss Me Deadly*.

After previous Answer Man discussions of the briefcase, I received the following from Avary himself: "Originally the briefcase contained diamonds. But that just seemed too boring and predictable. So it was decided that the contents of the briefcase were never to be seen. This way each audience member would fill in the 'blank' with their own ultimate contents. All you were supposed to know was that it was 'so beautiful.' No prop master can come up with something better than each individual's imagination. At least that was the original idea. Then somebody had the bright idea (which I think is a mistake) of putting an orange lightbulb in there. Suddenly what could have been anything became anything supernatural. Didn't need to push the effect. People would have debated it for years anyway, and it would have been much more subtle. I can't believe I'm actually talking about being subtle."

I received copies of the following Internet posting from at least a dozen readers, all of whom are excited that the mystery of the glowing briefcase in Pulp Fiction *has been laid to rest. Here it is:*

"Through a friend of a friend of a friend who had a two-hour conversation with Quentin Tarantino himself, I now know the key to the film. Remember the first time you were introduced to Marsellus Wallace? The first shot of him was of the back of his head, complete with Band-Aid. Then, remember the combination of the briefcase lock was 666. Then, remember that when anyone opened the briefcase, it glowed, and they were in amazement at how beautiful it was.

"Now, bring in some Bible knowledge, and remember that when the devil takes your soul, he takes it from the back of your head. Yep, you guessed it. Marsellus Wallace had sold his soul to the devil, and was trying to buy it back. The three kids in the beginning of the movie were the devil's helpers. And remember that when the kid at the end came out of the bathroom with a 'hand cannon,' Jules and Vincent were not harmed by the bullets. 'God came down and stopped the bullets,' because they were saving a soul. It was divine intervention. Pretty cool huh?"

Sorry, but I'm afraid this is nothing more than a widely distributed urban legend given false credibility by the mystique of the Net. Like all urban legends, it is of course atttributed to "a friend of a friend of a friend." Quentin Tarantino has said many times that the briefcase contains "whatever you want it to contain," and see Roger Avary's answer to the previous question.

Pulp Fiction

Q. Why do the photos of Samuel L. Jackson in the *Pulp Fiction* ads show him with short hair, instead of the giant, curly 'do he wears in the movie? (Joanna Brandon, Chicago)

A. I wish my answer was more intriguing, involving marketing decisions about whether a conservative haircut sells more tickets than a Jheri-Curl, but the truth is: When they were shooting the publicity stills, they couldn't find the wig that Jackson wore in the movie.

Q. Regarding *Pulp Fiction*, the character Jules played by Samuel L. Jackson recites a Bible passage twice in the movie. It's bogus, but no reviews have remarked on this. Have I missed something or do film critics regard this sort of thing as detail-mongering? (Ken Nichols, Grand Terrace, Calif.)

A. Tarantino-watcher Paul Chapman of London, England, tells me: "Jules says he's quoting from Ezekiel 25:17. But he isn't. The second half of his speech corresponds closely to the biblical text, but the rest seems to be a mishmash of invention, expansion, and interpretation. The text of this speech was transmitted on a BBC radio program, which I recorded. Here is what he says:

The path of the righteous man is best on all sides by the inequities of the selfish and the tyranny of evil men. Blessed is he who, in the name of charity and good will, shepherds the weak through the valley of darkness, for he is truly his brother's keeper and the finder of lost children. And I will strike down upon thee with great vengeance and furious anger those who attempt to poison and destroy my brothers. And you will know my name is the Lord when I lay my vengeance upon thee.

"My theory is that Jules did once know the passage verbatim, but it has become corrupted in his mind and infected with black political sound bites (two mentions of the word "brother," for example) and the need to justify his profession to his conscience."

Q. Doesn't Amanda Plummer shout out *Reservoir Dogs* during the final segment of *Pulp Fiction*, after she leaps onto the restaurant table? I'm convinced I heard that line. (Michael Deckinger, San Francisco)

A. "That's the first time I've heard *that* question," says director Quentin Tarantino, who says people are analyzing his film as closely as the Dead Sea Scrolls. "The answer is, no."

Q. After screenwriters Roger Avary and Quentin Tarantino picked up their Oscars for *Pulp Fiction*, Avary said, "I have to take a pee." While this acceptance speech was admirably short, I found it somewhat lacking in propriety. Did he really have to take a pee, or was there some deeper message? (Ronnie Barzell, Chicago)

A. Although the Academy's members awarded many of their

Oscars to *Forrest Gump* and *Pulp Fiction,* they apparently didn't pay attention during either movie, or they would have made the connection that Avary's line occurs in both films—most memorably in the scene where Gump says it to President Kennedy. I put your question to Roger Avary, who replied: "I guess there's a little Forrest Gump inside of all of us—including the writers of *Pulp Fiction.*"

Q. I recently saw *Weird Science,* and the short dance sequence reminded me of the twist scene in *Pulp Fiction.* The song is the same, and the girl is doing the twist with the man, like Uma Thurman and John Travolta. I am wondering whether anyone else noticed this similarity, which may owe itself to Tarantino's video rental store days. (Boris Khentov, New York)

A. *Pulp Fiction* fans have discovered so many quotations, homages, and cross-references between the film and Tarantino's years of total immersion in videos that I wonder if we should reclassify *PF* as an anthology.

Q. The cigarettes John Travolta and Uma Thurman smoked in *Pulp Fiction* looked kind of colorful and I was wondering what their name was and where they were sold. Also, where can I purchase the Odorama card for the movie *Polyester?* (Rosemary Escamilia, Chicago)

A. The brand is "Green Apples," but they're for sale only in *Pulp Fiction.* Regarding Odorama: Director John Waters says Scratch 'n' Sniff cards for *Polyester* were supplied by Criterion with the laserdisc edition of his movie, but unless you can get your hands on the disc, they're no longer available. However, if you care to go to the trouble, you can easily find your own roses, gasoline, doggy-doo, etc., and supply your own scents. In fact, it might be fun to have a *Polyester* screening and scavenger hunt.

Q. I love *Pulp Fiction,* and have seen it repeatedly. I wonder if anyone else has noticed the great profusion of the number 3 within the film. There are three stories within the movie, three discussions of hamburgers or hamburgers on screen, John Travolta goes to the bathroom three times; the third time he dies. Mia Wallace snorts drugs three times; the third time she overdoses. We have three different cars careening around corners in each story (Travolta's Malibu, Willis's cab, and Wolf's Acura). Buddy Holly the waiter is on screen exactly three times, as is Ed Sullivan. Jackson speaks his version of Ezekiel 25:17 three times; the third time he doesn't kill anyone. I wonder if it is just the superstition of the number or whether Tarantino had something else on his agenda. You could even go so far as to mention that three actors from *Reservoir Dogs* are in the cast of *Pulp Fiction.* I admit, it gets ridiculous, but the more you see the film, the more threes you notice. (Christopher G. Telcont, Columbus, Ohio)

A. If you add in the twos and fours, it gets even more amazing.

Quotes in Ads

Q. I notice that the advance ads for *Tank Girl* quote Jeff Craig of *Sixty Second Preview* as saying, "This movie kicks major butt!" As a critic, what is your reaction to his review? (Susan Lake, Urbana, Ill.)

A. Jeff Craig's name in a movie ad is a one-second tip-off that the distributors are desperate. They would not use him if they had more legitimate critics to quote. According to *People* magazine, Craig provides rave quotes for virtually every movie he considers—even though he doesn't see most of the movies he "reviews," depending on eight staff members. (Funny: I actually find time to see all the movies myself.) Craig's payoff is seeing his name in print in a movie ad. In the case of *Tank Girl,* it's a good question whether *anyone* from Craig's staff even saw the movie, since United Artists strictly embargoed all preview screenings until the Tuesday before it opened—several days after Craig's "major butt" quote first appeared.

Q. I just got back from seeing *Dumb and Dumber.* To say that this is the worst movie I have ever seen would be a gross understatement. The four people who saw it with me were all ready to walk out, but I kept them there by saying, "Roger Ebert said he laughed so loud, he embarrassed himself—so it must get better." I was wrong. This movie gets a "worse-than-*Darkman*" rating in my book, and having just lost a parakeet that my wife and I have had ever since we first met three years ago, I wasn't thrilled with the parakeet joke either. (Robert S. Fish, Columbus, Ohio)

A. I did indeed write "I laughed so loudly I embarrassed myself." Then I added: "But because I know that the first sentence of this review is likely to be lifted out and reprinted in an ad, I hasten to add that I did not laugh as loudly again, or very often."

Q. Not sure if you've seen them, but ironically enough, you were right about being misquoted in the ads for *Dumb and Dumber.* They quote you as saying, "I laughed so hard I embarrassed myself," even though you only gave the movie two stars. Are you going to do anything about this, take any revenge on them, or whatever? (Francis Rogers, New Rochelle, N.Y.)

A. I'm not really mad, because in a way I was asking for it. I *am* ticked off, however, that they took my words "laughed so loudly" and substituted the subliterate "laughed so hard."

Q. You have written in the past about obscure critics who are quoted in TV ads because they praise every film, often before seeing it. Here is a new twist: The ads for *Judge Dredd* are filled with rave quotes—but there is no attribution at all under them! They are quotes that *nobody* has said! (Ashley St. Ives, Chicago)

A. I would trust nobody before I would trust *Sixty Second Preview.*

Q. Can you stand one more comment regarding *Sixty Second Preview?* I run a fantasy league game based on Hollywood box office results (sort of like fantasy league baseball, only you bid on upcoming releases instead of ballplayers), and one of our largest penalties is a $3 million fine to any film that is praised by Jeff Craig and his team of happy-go-lucky noncritics. (Kevin Burk, Bonney Lake, Wash.)

A. Fabulous! Great! I loved it! One of the year's best letters!

Q. During Letterman the other night I saw the big woo-wah teaser for *Waterworld,* the one with all of those rave reviews quoted in it. This was before any "real" reviews had appeared anywhere.

All the ads were attributed to call letters, and I imagined the following scenario:

The hosts and hostesses of *AM Springfield* and *Good Morning, Delaware!* and *Boise Coffee Hour* and *The WKSH Movie Minute* and *Fort Lauderdale Senior Circuit* get air tickets and hotel reservations in their mailboxes. They fly to L.A. They swim in the pool. They eat wonderful meals. They get their pictures taken with Kevin Costner! They get a *special* advance screening of a summer blockbuster! They are driven back to the airport and before being thanked one last time and boosted onto their planes, the producers ask them if they'd be so kind as to fax their impressions of *Waterworld*: "Oh, good or bad—just be honest!—because the boys in marketing will be preparing the *national* ads in the next few days." Am I close? (Andy Ihnatko, Westwood, Mass.)

A. Basically, what you're reading are the opinions of people more interested in getting celebrity interviews than in expressing an honest opinion of a movie. The ads always put the raves in giant type and the source of the quote in the same size of type they use to inform you of possible adverse side effects in the use of patent medicines.

Q. The marketing whizzes for *Showgirls* must be desperate for quotes in their ads—they quote you on Elizabeth Berkley's "fierce energy," which isn't too surprising, but they also include, and I quote, "Sometimes it's hilarious." The way they present your quote leads one to believe that the film was *meant* to be funny, as opposed to its hilarity being unintentional. (Michael Dequina, Los Angeles)

A. Funny how they overlooked the word "sleazefest" in my first sentence. But I *did* write, "Sometimes it's hilarious," so I can't complain. I wonder, though, if the filmmakers are pleased to have their film described that way. While I'm at it: Their *Basic Instinct* was hilarious, too.

Q. In the ads for *GoldenEye*, someone named Bonnie Churchill of something called the National News Syndicate is quoted as saying, "On a scale of one to four, *GoldenEye* gets seven stars!" What is your reaction to this new critical math? (Charlie Smith, Chicago)

A. If Ms. Churchill ever sees a great movie, she's going to blow a gasket.

Q. The movie *Twister* opens in my town the day after tomorrow and I have yet to read a review of it. I presume this is because the studio does not want adverse comments before the opening and they do not have faith in the picture. Would you say the length of time before the opening of a movie that critics are permitted to view it is decreasing? Perhaps this length of time in days would be a useful statistic to go into the review. (Dane Rigden, Merrimack, N.H.)

A. *Twister,* which scored a scorching $37 million opening weekend, was not withheld from the critics, but it wasn't previewed until the last moment because its complex special effects went right down to the wire. Although some movies are ready for advance screenings days or months before their opening dates, many of the biggest ones, including summer blockbusters made with lots of effects, arrive in theaters dripping wet from the lab. Another big summer opening, *Mission: Impossible,* also delayed its preview screenings because of deadline postproduction tinkering.

Q. I read an interesting article by Gary Dretzka in the *Chicago Tribune* about trailers of coming attractions. In his lead, he quotes several lines from a review by a "prominent national critic" that is framed on the wall of New Wave Entertainment's offices in Hollywood. The review is of *Sister Act,* the 1992 Whoopi Goldberg movie, and concludes, "whoever edited the trailer has a much better idea of what's good in this material than the man who directed the movie." Any idea who the "prominent national critic" could be? (Charles Smith, Chicago)

A. Why, golly—it's me! I wrote it in the *Chicago Sun-Times,* a newspaper published not a million miles from the *Trib*'s own Gothic bunker. I am sending the *Tribune* a free copy of my book *Roger Ebert's Video Companion,* to aid them in researching the sources of brilliant quotes in movie articles.

Q. I saw something disturbing today. One of those ads plugging *The Spitfire Grill* splashed several unattributed quotes on the screen.

Phrases like "Oscar-caliber performances," "Four Stars," "the feel-good movie of the summer," and the like. Mixed in with these—as if to add legitimacy—were quotes from some of those critics who seem to love everything from *Schindler's List* to *Jury Duty*. You know who. But since when are studios using unattributed quotes? "An incredible experience?" Sez who? (Bruce Maiman, Monterey, Calif.)

A. That's a common practice in TV ads, where they hope the words will flash by so quickly that viewers won't check for the attribution. Any film ad that uses unattributed quotes of praise is highly suspect. For example, if an ad says *Four stars!* but does not attribute the stars, that is another way of saying, "We could not find a single critic anywhere in the world who gave this movie four stars."

Q. As I cashiered tonight, I sold a copy of the video of *Hoosiers* to a satisfied customer. As the receipt printed out, I looked at the back of the video and saw a quote that said "Hip Hoop Hooray! Four stars—Roger Ebert." It didn't sound like something you'd say, and when I looked at it closer it was attributed to a Roger Ebert of the *New York Post*. I'm sure you have no problem endorsing the movie as you really did give it four stars, but I doubt you would want to be stamped with a quote you didn't say from a newspaper you don't write for. (Rhys Southan, Richardson, Tex.)

A. Actually, my syndicated reviews did appear in the *New York Post* for several years. I would never, however, be capable of writing such a moronic phrase as "Hip Hoop Hooray!"—or even "Hip Hip Hooray," for that matter. My guess is that the film's distributors are quoting the *headline* from the *New York Post,* which is unethical, since critics do not write their own headlines.

Recipes

Q. Do you have a recipe for timpano, the special dish in the movie *Big Night?* I can't find one in my cookbooks, from Italian friends, or on the Internet. (Joan Phillips-Sandy, Waterville, Me.)

A. You are referring to the lovingly-prepared dish which, when it is sliced open at last, causes the audience to emit a collection "ahhhh!" Rysher Entertainment, which is distributing the film, says codirector and star Stanley Tucci and his cousin have deliberately *not* released a recipe for timpano because they are writing a cookbook in which they'll include that recipe.

Religion

Q. I was stunned that you gave *Priest* one star and *Major Payne* three stars. I am a Catholic priest currently inactive in ministry. I felt that the portrayal of the two priests epitomized the angst that afflicts most priests I know. I even know ones like the first chap who took a crucifix to the bishop's home, and the last old chap who was so rigid and stale. I knew those scenes of personal torment. I felt that the film lingered on the pain and struggle without flinching. While I was troubled by the serial endings that plagued the latter half of the movie (I kept thinking, 'okay, now it's over. No? Whoops, here we go again'), I thought it was a powerful portrait of the privatized hell of public religious icons. I can at least say that I saw it in full rather than condemn it out of hand without seeing it like some bishops. (Daniel L. Conditt, Long Beach, Calif.)

A. Star ratings are of course relative, not absolute; if you tried to make stars consistent across genres, you'd go nuts. In *Priest*, the film's message was: These stupid church rules prevent priests from having sex, but permit it to child abusers. Yet the whole confessional subplot (the vow of secrecy that prevented the priest from stopping the child abuse) was a gimmick with a hole in it, since the priest could have gone to the cops with what the girl's father told him. The younger priest takes the vow of secrecy seriously because that is convenient to the plot, but doesn't take any other vows seriously, nor does he hesitate before attempting suicide. Many people valued the film because it mirrored their own beliefs or feelings. That makes it important to them, which is certainly valid, but does not make it a good film.

Reviews Favorable and Not

Q. You are a kind and generous man. Giving a two-and-a-half-star rating to Arnold's last movie is surely a sign of impending madness. It was the most tedious and disjointed piece of movie-making I have ever seen. I knew it was going to be bad, but nothing prepared me for the awful truth. Please see it again and revise your rating or else get off Arnold's payroll. (George Kuiper, Lawrenceville, Ga.)

A. You know, it was sort of touching, the way Arnold explained to me that with his budget already up over $80 million, he could only afford enough of a bribe for a negative review.

Q. You rate a movie with stars. The way I rate a movie is as follows. If, after the movie is half-over and I am conscious of the fact that my rear is sore for sitting for an hour, it is a bad film. Otherwise, the movie was worth the money! (Mark Dub, Warren, Mich.)

A. In other words, your rear has feelings which are separate from physical reality, and exist entirely on a subjective mental plane. I have heard of holy men who meditated for years to attain this state, although not necessarily in the place where you have developed it.

Q. I have to tell you about a recent moviegoing misadventure. My wife and I saw that you gave *Thirty-Two Short Films About Glenn Gould* four stars. That was good enough for us, so we trundled down the theater. It didn't take long to figure out that *Thirty-Two Short Films* was like one of those Moroccan dishes with calf's brains and honey. To some, it might be a delicacy, but to others it's just, well, calf's brains. So we sneaked across the hallway of the megaplex to the other movie starting about that time: *Renaissance Man.* I've never seen a more illogically constructed, bogus piece of celluloid tripe since *Last Action Hero.* The point of this note is to suggest you add an intelligence grade for each of your reviews, based on the one-to-five scale. We could call it the Ebert Highfalutin Quotient (or EHQ). For example, *Thirty-Two Short Films* would then get a four-over-four (4/4), whereas *Die Hard* would get a four over one (4/1) and *Renaissance Man* would rate a 1/1. Please, take pity on those who don't know the difference between *film noir* and pinot noir. (Mark Firmani, Seattle)

A. In other words, the first number represents how good I think the movie is, and the second number represents how smart I think you are?

Q. Why is it that the awful reviews are always so much more fun to read—I'm speaking in generalities, here—than the equally positive ones? (Andy Ihnatko, Westwood, Mass.)

A. Because it's difficult if not impossible to be funny about something that's good. The equation seems to run:

bad = funny
good = serious
great = solemn
masterpiece = zzzzz

Q. I was interested in the writer who found your negative reviews more interesting than your positive ones. I, for one, skip your reviews entirely when they fall below two and one-half stars. Why would I waste my time reading about a mediocre film any more than I would listen to bad music or read a dull book? Although I appreciate your humor at times, I'm really basically looking for a guide to good films. (Al Carli, Chicago)

A. Hey, if I have to waste my time seeing them and writing about them, isn't it the least you can do to read about them? Besides, in my reviews of *North, Black Sheep, If Lucy Fell,* and *Little Indian, Big City,* the writing, if I may say so, redeemed the subject matter.

Rumors

Q. I feel silly asking this question, but I promised my ten-year-old son I would. There is a rumor floating around the fourth grade that in *The Wizard of Oz* a shadow of a man can be seen being electrocuted after Dorothy, the Tin Man, and the Scarecrow begin their walk down the yellow brick road together. We reviewed our tape and did see some unusual movements in the background—but is there any truth to the electrocution theory? (Mara O'Neill, Pittsburgh)

A. *Wizard* expert David J. Bondelevitch replies: "The man in the background is a sound man (a boom operator, to be precise). He was not electrocuted, he was simply stupid and got in the shot when he shouldn't have."

This was the Urban Legend that would not die. A year later, I got another question.

Q. I read your Movie Answer Man entry about the mysterious man who can be glimpsed in the forest scene in *The Wizard Of Oz.* Somebody wrote you with the rumor that he was a stagehand who hanged himself. According to the new *Ultimate Oz* laserdisc, the "man" is one of the blurry exotic birds roaming in the background of the forest. Either that, or the studio is deliberately trying to suppress the fact that the corpse of a suicidal stagehand is plainly visible in the grassy knoll of Munchkinland Forest, within something they're trying to pass off as children's entertainment. (Andy Ihnatko, Westwood, Mass.)

A. The dead stagehand rumor is sweeping the country. I get asked about it constantly. I think it's fairly unlikely that an MGM production number could be filmed with everyone in the set somehow failing to notice a dead man hanging from a tree. There are guys who get paid just to look for stuff like that.

Q. There is a rumor that in *Three Men and a Baby,* in one shot you can see a man behind the curtains, and he is the ghost of the original inhabitant of the apartment where they shot the movie. Is this true? (Ashley St. Ives, Chicago)

A. What you are seeing is a crew member who thought you couldn't see him, but was wrong.

Q. There's a rumor circulating around Vancouver's Lower Mainland that I thought you might find amusing. The story goes that last April Fool's Day, you and Mickey Rooney were at Elizabeth Taylor's house and were playing Truth or Dare. Apparently the dares escalated to where Mr. Rooney was dared to sneak the horse they use in *Black Beauty* over to Elizabeth Taylor's home. Once there, apparently one of you challenged the other to "streak" across her backyard on Black Beauty. The story goes that you both stripped, poured baby powder over yourselves, and proceeded to get on the horse and gallop through her backyard. I overheard the story in a Starbuck's Coffee on Robson Street in Vancouver. I couldn't see you involved in something like this. (Greg P. Groat, Vancouver, Canada)

A. Oh, what a night it was!

Sandra Bullock

Q. In your review of *The Net*, you wrote dubiously about Sandra Bullock: "She has an ultra-high-speed modem connection, I guess, since Internet stuff pops up the moment she hits the return key." You are behind the times. Bullock undoubtedly has an ISDN phone line and modem that will transfer data at 128kbps, and establish connections within milliseconds—quietly. ISDN is a digital technology developed in the early '80s, about the same time as the Internet. It is available to the public. Speaking of Bullock, in *Demolition Man,* she delivers dangerously silly throwaway lines with unassuming deftness and cuteness, lighting up the screen. How does a peon like myself go about, in a sly fashion, getting invites or tix to world premieres of films in Hollywood and New York? (Gregory Soo, Beaconsfield, Quebec, Canada)

A. Why don't you start by offering to install Sandra Bullock's own ISDN line? But first explain to me how she got an ISDN line into that hotel room where she was hiding out, when it took me two weeks on the phone to even find a telephone company representative who knew what I was talking about.

Q. I can't imagine *any* screenplay with the following attributes . . .

— "preposterous dreck"
— "situations in search of a story"
— "the plot . . . [is a] series of excuses for the director"
— "This stuff is so concocted . . ."
— "scene may seem absurd"
— "not exactly plausible"

. . . that could be saved even by a Helen Hayes let alone a pedestrian actress such as Sandra Bullock. I'm afraid your favorable review for *The Net* must have been influenced by some organ other than your usually facile brain! (Richard D. Hyman, Alamo, Calif.)

A. I put everything into each of my reviews.

Scams

Q. I noticed a classified ad for persons to review movies for pay. I wrote for more information. They said that if I was selected as a local reviewer, I'd get $11 per completed movie review, if done according to their directions. They claimed they would sell the information to movie studios. The catch is that they wanted some cash up front: $28 for a deposit on an instruction kit, which is refundable if one is not selected as a reviewer, plus $4 for shipping (which isn't refundable). Having $32 in my pocket, and being a movie buff, I decided to take a chance. I'm waiting for their reply, which is promised in two to three weeks. This outfit is named Audience Response. Have you ever heard of them? Do you think I fell for a scam? (Mike Saeger, Minneapolis)

A. You fell for a scam. And, yes, I have heard of Audience Response before. I'm surprised they're still in business. The Answer Man exposed them more than a year ago, after a studio spokesman told me they had "absolutely no need" for amateur reviews written weeks after a movie has opened.

Q. Well, you were right. Audience Response, the company that offered to pay people for their movie reviews, was a total scamola. One month after I mailed it, my *Apollo 13* review was returned by the post office as undeliverable. Those rascals are probably living it up in Mexico on everybody's $32.40 deposit. I'm just glad I saw your article exposing the fraud. Elsewise, I might have filled out that excruciating fifteen-page review form several more times. (Kristen Kirkham, Seattle)

A. Hey, if people want to write movie reviews that badly, they can just send me their $32.40.

Schindler's List

Q. In *Schindler's List*, what was the significance of putting stones on Oskar Schindler's grave? (Marilyn and Raymond Kabat, Cicero, Ill.)

A. Rabbi Mordicai Simon of the Chicago Board of Rabbis replies: "Flowers are considered more of a decorative item, and thus not for mourning. Instead, a rock or pebble is used to say, 'I've been here.'"

Q. In the final shot of *Schindler's List*, I think the man shown in silhouette was Steven Spielberg himself, but wasn't quite sure. Can you confirm this? (Kelly McHugh, Chicago)

A. That was not Steven Spielberg's silhouette in the closing graveside sequence of the film, but Liam Neeson's.

Q. In the credits for *Schindler's List*, I noticed a slash bridging from one letter through the next letter, which is always an "A." Do you know what this means and why they did it? (David Lyell, Pala Alto, Calif.)

A. Blair Finberg of Universal says there's a "slash bridge" from the letter preceding an "a" to the "a" because that's the way the Polish write it. The credits were done in Polish fonts.

Q. At what point in the film do you feel that the Oskar Schindler character's motivation changed to one of saving Jewish lives instead of just making money at the expense of these people? (Graham Kerr, Edmonton, Alberta, Canada)

A. There is no specific scene where that happens—no stereotyped Hollywood scene where Schindler makes a big heartfelt speech. One of the strengths of the film is that he and his motives remain mysterious.

Q. I know that rating movies is difficult, because in a sense, it's rating art. How many stars would you give the *Mona Lisa*? But I am curious to know if you have ever felt like giving a movie like *Schindler's List* some kind of special rating, to signify that it's a very special movie. Perhaps a fifth star? (Steven H. Schlesinger, Chino Hills, Calif.)

A. Any movie rating system is of course arbitrary and silly, but the only way to make it useful is to play by the rules. There is a critic in Los Angeles who says things like, "On a scale of one to ten, I give it a twenty!" That way madness lies. For me, "four stars" means a movie is truly excellent. Of course, some "four star" movies are better than others, because no two movies can be quite the same, but I think most readers understand that.

Science Fiction

Q. I am getting weary of the glut of movies that show the twenty-first century as a desolate, angry, warring place where only the Terminator and mutant Stallones survive. Is there a way to get Hollow-wood to start being a bit more responsible about these portrayals? They create a sense of hopelessness in the national psyche that seems to be playing out all over the country in increased violence, pessimism, and doom. I notice they don't show any movies about how to go to a Hollywood set and kill off all the producers, editors, and camerapeople. (Beth Terry, Honolulu, Hawaii)

A. Actually, there are almost as many movies about murder on movie sets as about the coming apocalypse. But your point is a good one. Not many movies see the future as a time of increased happiness. In the nineteenth century, there were many utopian novels predicting that increased human knowledge would solve our problems. Now we seem to fear knowledge. To give you an idea how deep the pessimism runs, in the movie *Barb Wire*, set in the year 2017, mankind's best hope is Pam Anderson.

Q. I'd like to respond to the Answer Man item concerning the grim, dangerous, unpleasant futures in most science fiction movies. As someone who's written several novels set in that kind of future, I'd point out that a negative future offers more dramatic possibilities than a happy future. The audience can watch how he overcomes all the bad stuff in order to achieve his goal. And those dystopias serve as settings in which the writer is able to satirize or exaggerate present-day situations and trends, and satirize, parody, mock, and warn about the social ills that trouble him in his own society. I think that's one of the most important functions of SF. Just look at *Invasion of the Body Snatchers.* Jack Finney wrote that not as sci-fi horror, but as a commentary on McCarthyism. (George Alec Effinger, New Orleans, La.)

A. You make perfect sense: Conflict is at the heart of all fiction, and in a utopia life might, by definition, tend to be happy but uneventful. But here's a related question. Why does science fiction so often depict visitors from other worlds as hostile? Steven Spielberg has given us two movies *(Close Encounters of the Third Kind* and *E.T.)* in which the aliens were wise and benign, but most movie SF provides bug-eyed monsters with ray guns. Is it because violent invaders are no-brainers for a screenwriter, but it takes real creativity to imagine beings from a superior civilization?

Q. In *Species*, when Sil, the alien, drives the stolen car laden with gasoline into the electric transformer, her abductee is tied and gagged on the passenger side. She hopes the authorities will think it is her. Assuming the body was supposed to be burned beyond recognition, wouldn't authorities have noticed that the body had moved, gagged, and bound itself? Moreover, I couldn't for the life of me figure out why Sil cut off her thumb and put it in a briefcase in the car; if the fire was enough to consume the body of her victim, then it would have consumed the case and thumb as well. (Elliott Norse, Redmond, Wash.)

A. A smarter alien would have known that. But Sil is the star of a movie in which an alien species figures out a way to establish itself on Earth, and then does nothing with that triumph except to jump out from behind stuff and scare people. Here is another problem with the same movie: If the alien grows so rapidly that she changes from a preadolescent girl into a sexy twentyish swimsuit model within a few days, why does she then stop at that stage, instead of continuing to mature until she looks like Ma Kettle? Could it have anything to do with the movie's reliance on plenty of topless scenes?

Q. In your *Species* review, you have the plot wrong. The alien DNA does *not* duplicate the species of those who sent it, but is tailored to create a weed-eater to clear humans off the planet. After all, their culture wasn't transmitted via their DNA and Sil didn't know who or what she was. (J. Walker, Nashville, Tenn.)

A. In other words, they use radio waves to send us a DNA that will create monsters to destroy us, and then they come in, clean out the monsters, and relax next to *our* swimming pools, eating out of *our* refrigerators, and enjoying *our* sunsets? The slimy SOBs! We should immediately devote all of our resources to sending them the DNA code for Pauly Shore.

Seeing-eye Man

Q. My wife and I were listening to the radio when you offered five bucks to anybody who could show you a movie where a woman noticed things first and got to point them out to a man. My wife pointed out (no pun intended) that this happens quite a bit in *The Pellican Brief,* where Darcy Shaw continually has to point things out to various men in the movie. My wife says you owe her five dollars. (Bob Pardee, Columbus, Ohio)

A. You are referring to the "Seeing Eye Man" rule in *Ebert's Little Movie Glossary,* which states that in almost all movies where something is spotted, it is the man who spots it, and points it out to the woman. But there is no movie named *The Pellican Brief.* Perhaps you meant *The Pelican Brief.* Unfortunately, I can process only one request from any individual reader.

Sequels, Remakes, and Ripoffs

Q. Some time ago there was a movie on one of the cable networks in which a character got trapped in a time warp, and kept repeating the same day over and over again. I went to see *Groundhog Day* with Bill Murray, and it uses the same gimmick. What gives? (Ronnie Barzell, Chicago)

A. You are thinking of a thirty-minute movie named *12:01,* written and directed by Jonathan Heap, which played many times on Showtime and was an Oscar nominee in 1991. The film was based on a story by Richard Lupoff that was published in the December 1973 issue of *Fantasy and Science Fiction* magazine. Lupoff is an old friend of mine, and I asked him about the resemblance. Turns out he is much upset, mostly on behalf of Heap, whose film contains sequences that seem to find uncanny parallels in *Ground-*

hog Day. On the other hand, Harold Ramis, who directed the Bill Murray movie, told me it was a case of the same idea being in the air all over Hollywood. Lupoff said he and Heap would like to sue, but don't have the resources to challenge a major studio. Meanwhile, their *12:01* is being made into a Movie of the Week for the Fox network. "For all the grief this has brought me," Lupoff said, "I would like to have a time machine so I could go back to 1973 and simply not write the story."

Q. I read that Sir Anthony Hopkins has cooled to the idea of a sequel to *The Silence of the Lambs,* due to media criticism in the United Kingdom that his portrayal of Hannibal the Cannibal glamorizes serial killers. Do you think Sir Anthony is serious or just bluffing? (Cynthia I. Sole)

A. Hopkins was deeply disturbed by a case in which a small boy was abducted and murdered by two other youngsters, and has been giving deep thought to the possible connections between violence in the media and in society. However, Hannibal Lecter was the role of a lifetime for him, handled so brilliantly it won him the Academy Award, and it is likely that he will not pass over the sequel without carefully weighing the screenplay.

Q. *Jurassic Park* is just a remake of an old Japanese film. Am I the only one to remember it? Unfortunately, I have forgotten the title. Godzilla and all the other monsters were kept on an island under scientific supervision. As you can imagine, they escaped to terrorize the world. (Dorothi St. Ives, Chicago)

A. You may be thinking of *Godzilla on Monster Island* (1972), which was, of course, the first movie in which Godzilla talked. The original twist in the Spielberg film was the idea of cloning the dinosaurs from ancient DNA. Also, all of the actors could speak much better than Godzilla.

Q. Recently I saw the movie *Heat,* and a couple of scenes reminded me of a TV movie I watched a few years ago. When I got home I located the tape and watched it, and it was the same movie! The TV movie was called *L.A. Takedown,* and starred one of my favorite TV actors, Alex McArthur. Michael Mann wrote and directed both this movie and *Heat*. (D. Jackson, Chicago)

A. It appears you are right. George Cifrancis of the Internet current films newsgroup observes: "*L.A. Takedown* is virtually identical in plot and some dialogue to *Heat*. There is the armored car sequence at the beginning with the guys wearing hockey masks, the scene in the bookstore where the women asks the thief what book he is reading, the scene where the cop and robber go have a cup of coffee together—and all the parts in between are pretty much the same as well."

Q. Can anyone explain the thinking behind the idiocy of remaking classic movies? I can't think of a single remake of a classic that was an improvement. *Born Yesterday* is a case in point. Gentlemen, if it ain't broke, don't fix it! On the other hand, if Hollywood has a property that bombed because it was poorly done but had an excellent story line, go ahead and give that another shot. But this doesn't mean to remake *Lost Horizon* as a musical. (A. Frisch, Chicago)

A. I don't know how to break this to you, but they *did* remake *Lost Horizon* as a musical.

Q. What was the first movie sequel? (Joshua A. Leichtung II, Tempe, Ariz.)

A. D.W. Griffith made a series of films about a character named Mr. Jones from 1908 to 1910, according to Ephraim Katz's admirable *Film Encyclopedia*.

Q. I hear there's a remake of *Casablanca* in the works with Kevin Costner and Demi Moore in the Bogart and Bergman roles. True? (James Portanova, Fresh Meadows, N.Y.)

A. According to Rob Friedman of Warner Bros., there is indeed a new version of *Casablanca* in the works—but with no Kevin Costner or Demi Moore. It will be titled *Carrotblanca*, and will star Bugs Bunny.

Q. Haven't seen *Judge Dredd*, but as one of the fourteen or fifteen writers on the movie, I had to wade through the final draft for the arbitration of screen credits. Personally I felt that the script captured little of the satire of the highly original comic books, which is their charm. Anyway, I just wanted to comment that it was *Mad Max* that ripped off *Judge Dredd*, not vice versa. The comic preceded *Mad Max, Blade Runner, Terminator* and all the second-class SF stuff like *Cyborg* that shows a Dredd influence. (Jan Strnad, Los Angeles)

A. I *knew* you were going to say that.

Q. Your review of *To Wong Foo, Thanks for Everything! Julie Newmar* made it sound interesting enough to see, but you made no mention of the fact that it seems to be an American version of *Priscilla, Queen of the Desert.* I enjoyed the Australian version, and it seems the story lines are exactly the same: (1) An adventure from home through the rural heartlands; (2) stranded by vehicle in a town that doesn't get many "queens"; (3) chaos ensues as they take the town in sequins' and high heels; (4) no sex between the men, etc., etc. Isn't this just a ripoff? (Scott Matichuk, Edmonton, Alberta, Canada)

A. So it would seem, but Jeffrey Graebner of Los Angeles replies: "Neither is really a ripoff of the other. In fact, they were in production at about the same time. *To Wong Foo* sat on the shelf for nearly a year before Universal finally released it. The delay probably was to keep it from coming out too close to *Priscilla.*"

Q. Is *Batman Forever* the first movie sequel in modern times that features none of the major stars from the previous movie? (Paul "Funn" Dunn, Bloomington, Ill.)

A. Just about. There's been a complete turnover at *Batman,* proving that the property itself is the real star. They had an opportunity to bring back Billy Dee Williams to reprise Harvey Dent (a.k.a. Two-Face) from the first film, but went instead with Tommy Lee Jones.

Q. This summer sees the release of *Mission: Impossible.* Other recently released films include *Sgt. Bilko* and *Flipper.* What is your opinion of the spate of popular television shows being made into major motion pictures? Is Hollywood beginning to run out of fresh ideas? (Mark Dayton, Costa Mesa, Calif.)

A. The titles of old TV shows work like presold trademarks, making the advertising pitch that much easier. In the fierce competition of the summer movie season, instant name recognition is an advantage. Look at the success of *The Fugitive, Batman, The Flintstones, The Addams Family*, etc.

Seven

Q. This weekend I saw *Seven*, and I'm writing about your disappointment with the ending. I thought it was a fairly clever and creative resolution. If the writers intended a surprise, then there was little "set up" work that could occur before the viewer learned that the bad guy chose to victimize [name deleted] for sin number six, Lust. In my opinion, any greater emphasis on [that character] would have removed any element of surprise whatsoever. My only suggestion to alleviate the anticlimactic end would've been to cloud the issue by casting doubt on more of the characters (i.e., Morgan Freeman throwing knives in the darkness of his room with that scary look). I really don't see how else to conclude *Seven* than by having Pitt commit Wrath. (Greg Robinson, Winston-Salem, N.C.)

A. The ending wasn't really bad, but somehow it didn't complete the film for me at the same level it began. I thought perhaps if a way had been found to force one cop to murder the other one (in particular, if the strong cop, played by Freeman, had been forced to kill his partner), that would have been more consistent with John Doe's demonstration that evil lurks in all of our hearts. It would also have made the ending terrifically difficult for audiences, of course, although as it now stands it's not exactly easy to take.

Q. There's been a lot of discussion about the success of *Seven*. One thing really sang out to me. The picture was written not by a committee but by a single writer, and one who obviously had some education. This is in sharp and dire contrast to the usual run of bang-bang movies in which musclemen with oiled pectorals blow hoods away with dialogue on the order of, "**** you, *******." I grew up on films written by real authors, including Hecht and MacArthur, and, like most novelists, I cringe at the "Hollywood-speak" of so-called screen "writers." The writer of *Seven* deserves an Oscar nomination. (John Jakes, Hilton Head Island, S.C.)

A. I agree that Andrew Kevin Walker's screenplay was original and literate. And I think much of the success of *Get Shorty* is because Elmore Leonard's original dialogue was retained wherever possible. (Because you are a famous writer, I would like to assure readers that the asterisks are mine; you quoted the bad guys accurately.)

Q. *Seven*, like many other films of the serial killer genre, has been awarded high marks by you and other critics. Do you enjoy movies about depraved weirdos, or is it simply the craftsmanship you find so worthy of mention? Personally, I am dismayed by this type of film, if for no other reason but that to make an entertainment of torture cultivates the worst we have within us, resonating perhaps to some effect within our society. (Andrew Paquette, Portland, Me.)

A. The art of all civilizations deals obsessively with the themes of violence and tragedy. One of the functions of art is to help us process the dismay we feel while regarding the hard realities of the world. A society that did not produce art dealing with such subjects would, possibly, be one that did not produce worthy art at all—a dead society. The purpose of such art is not only entertainment but catharsis; it provides a means of vicariously dealing with our fear. I can enjoy the craftsmanship alongside the purpose, while not forgetting they are two different things.

Sex and Morality

Q. I'm interested in your opinion of this situation. Man meets woman. Man is attracted to woman and asks her out. They have a nice time. By third date, man is sleeping with woman, a few doors down the hall from his twelve-year-old daughter. Behavior continues for two months. Man is sharply criticized for his behavior. Man is appalled that his sexual behavior could in any way be linked to his character. Man attacks his critics as "lacking character," since after all his girlfriend is "hard-working" and they are "in love." I have just described the story line of *The American President*. To me, this movie is a wolf in sheep's clothing. The comedy is priceless, but the moral message is distressing. The message is that sexual behavior has nothing to do with character, and those who think otherwise are the bad guys. What do you think? (Deena King, Santa Monica, Calif.)

A. I think we have to decide about the character of the man and woman on the basis of what we learn about them in the movie, and the movie is written in such a way that we approve of them and think they are good people. Their courtship does seem to proceed rapidly as you describe it, but "screen time" is a strange and elusive thing, and most of the audience was probably not thinking that they slept together on their third date; they were sensing it was about time for the second act to begin.

The sexual behavior of the man and woman mirrors the behavior of a great many people in this country, which was the point: The president is not allowed to be like other people. The presence of his daughter down the hallway is a more serious problem. I assume in the White House greater privacy is possible than in most people's houses, and I gather from the movie that both the father and the girlfriend were sensitive to the daughter and her feelings. I hope so. She seemed to be handling the situation better than her dad.

A few decades ago this entire movie would have been forbidden by the Production Code, but as things go in modern politics, the Michael Douglas character in *The American President* is actually a pretty good guy. Your letter is quite illuminating in the way it shows how mainstream opinion on this behavior has changed to such a degree that the sexual behavior in the movie was not controversial for most audiences.

Q. In your review of the movie *Dead Man Walking* you turned a neat little phrase. You said of Susan Sarandon's character that she would not behave according to "the pieties of those for whom religion, good grooming, polite manners, and prosperity are all more or less the same thing." I can think of several individuals and groups that might fit that description. To whom were you referring? (Joe Dempsey Sr., Ridley Park, Pa.)

A. I guess I was thinking of an earnest young man who once informed me that Scorsese's *Last Temptation of Christ* did not have a sufficiently devout attitude because the characters were always wearing dirty clothes. I told him that people in those days might sometimes only be able to afford one outer garment, and that biblical characters probably looked more like bearded, unwashed hippies than like the freshly-scrubbed saints on holy cards. He said that, even so, the movie "sent the wrong message." I am also amused by the televangelists who talk about how prayer has made people into rich businessmen; you can watch those shows for a long time without ever hearing a peep about the camel getting through the eye of the needle.

Q. Joe Eszterhas, that literary giant, while talking about a new script that he is peddling, said, "There is no sex in this piece; no sex between men and women, men and men, women and women, men and animals or women and animals. I think Bob Dole or Roger Ebert would like it, assuming Dole could understand it." Please advise. (Bret Hayden, Thousand Oaks, Calif.)

A. I still hold out some hope for sex between insects and plants.

Siskel & Ebert

Q. In the opening credits of your TV show, Siskel buys a *Tribune.* You buy a *Sun-Times.* Both of you turn to your own columns, and then engage in a spirited discussion. Why are you arguing about what you wrote in your own columns? It would make more sense for you to read each other's reviews. (Adam Ritt, Evanston, Ill.)

A. We are not arguing. If you read our lips, you will see that I am saying, "This is a brilliant review," and Siskel is saying, "I wish I could rewrite mine now that I've seen yours."

Q. I am writing in response to your criticism of Nick Nolte's accent in *Lorenzo's Oil,* on your television show. I was dialectician for *Lorenzo's Oil,* and having worked extensively with Mr. Nolte in the development of his accent, I can assure you that he created the real

Augusto Odone exactly! Augusto is a northern Italian. They speak their Italian differently, and when they speak English they speak it the way you heard it in the theater. Mr. Siskel was correct in accepting Mr. Nolte's accent as essential to the story. (Bill Dearth, 12/31/92)

Q. Please accept my apology for confusing you with your partner Mr. Siskel in my earlier letter. I was actually quite impressed with your reaction to Mr. Nolte's performance and his accent. Mr. Siskel was the one who I felt was unfair. (Bill Dearth, 1/4/93)

A. You put me through a pretty rough four days there.

Q. I saw you on Letterman with Gene Siskel. You were discussing *Free Willy* when you made a cutting remark about Gene's weight being similar to the killer whale's. Was that a media thing? (Jim McNeely, Fresno, Calif.)

A. Yeah, it's a media thing. But you have us confused. It was *Siskel* who made the remark about *my* weight. I was the one who used admirable restraint in *not* observing that Gene should have identified with Willy because they are both large hairless mammals.

Q. In the *TV Guide* article about your big fight with Gene Siskel over the secret of *The Crying Game*, Siskel was asked if you came to blows, and replied that you "lacked the motor skills" for a fight. How did you feel about that? (Harold Gasper, Chicago)

A. What Gene meant to say was that I lacked the speed to catch him.

Q. Please answer a question that my friends and I have about your TV show. How come we never get to see the left side of Gene Siskel's face? My friends say the reason is that Siskel doesn't have a left nostril. (Ben Oelsner, San Francisco)

A. That is in fact the left side of Gene's face you are seeing. Do you have us confused? Both of us have left nostrils.

Q. Is *Two Thumbs Up* a copyrighted phrase? I'll tell you why I ask. This past weekend I joined a new video store here in Ontario, and noticed that certain video cases had stickers affixed to them with two Mickey Mouse–type cartoon thumbs pointed up, and a phrase that said "two thumbs up—critics' choice." Are these in fact official Siskel & Ebert choices, or is my video store trying to pull a fast one on me by capitalizing on the goodwill associated with you and your esteemed colleague's critiques? (Mark Solomon, Toronto, Ontario, Canada)

A. The video store is pulling a fast one. "Two thumbs up," as applied to movies, has indeed been registered by Siskel and myself, and although filmmakers are free to apply it to films that have been so honored, we have not licensed any video stores to do an in-house promotion, and we don't authorize any stickers.

Q. Did you notice that the military school commandant in *The Ref* is named Siskel and even looks a little like Gene? (Rich Elias, Delaware, Ohio)

A. The movie was written by Richard LaGravenese, whose screenplay for *The Fisher King* was selected by Siskel as the worst Oscar nomination of 1991. In *The Ref,* the character is blackmailed by one of his students, who has photos showing "Siskel" with topless dancers. Such revenge has historical precedents. After critic John Simon panned the Broadway debut of Bob and Ray, they made him a running character on their radio programs, where he invariably gobbled a giant sandwich very loudly.

Q. In the latest issue of Detective Comics, the Joker offs two movie critics who happen to have an uncanny resemblance to two movie critics on TV. The Joker is making a movie *(The Death of Batman)* and these two critics offend his artistic sensibilities. (Felipe A. Vicini, New York)

A. It is a little-known fact that when Gene Siskel was an undergraduate, one of his favorite pastimes was dressing as Batman and running through the school library. What goes around, comes around.

Q. I'm going on a second date with a woman who says she prefers Gene Siskel to you. Do you think I ought to pursue a relationship with such a person? (Joseph Kaufman, Hollywood, Calif.)

A. Does she prefer Gene to you?

Q. So okay, what's the scoop on you and Gene appearing on that controversial Jay Leno show where Howard Stern interrupted you and disrupted the entire show with his hijinks with the two bimbos in bikinis? Were you offended? Amused? (Susan Lake, Urbana, Ill.)

A. We could have handled the situation easily had we only been able to turn ourselves into a heavy metal rock group.

Q. I have noticed movie ads with the blurb, "Thumbs Up— Roger Ebert (or Gene Siskel)." Doesn't it seem to you that this is one of the *most* lunkheaded things that could be included in an ad? After all, if you *both* like a movie, they're going to trumpet that fact proudly. But if they cite just *one* of you as liking it, they're implying that the other did not. (James Campbell, Arnold, Mo.)

A. "Thumbs Up—Siskel" I agree with you about. But "Thumbs Up—Ebert"—now *that's* a recommendation.

Smoking

Q. In your review of *The Hunt for Red October* you asked how come the Russian sailors smoked so much when they should be watching their on-board oxygen supply. Modern subs have plenty of oxygen. Fresh water is pumped into an oxygen generator. Electricity separates the hydrogen from the oxygen. Hydrogen is pumped overboard and oxygen is bled into the sub's atmosphere as required. (Alex Phillion, Montreal, Canada)

A. Just do me a favor. Don't break this news to the cast of *Run Silent, Run Deep.*

Q. What bothered me about *Reality Bites* was that all of the people in the movie were smoking. And they were smoking badly, the way people who don't really smoke in real life smoke when they have to for a movie. I'm not saying that all movies should be smoke-free; people smoke, and movies often need to reflect that reality. In this case, however, it adds nothing to the movie, and is just another message to impressionable teens that smoking is cool. (Dale Kingsbury, St. Paul, Minn.)

A. The danger is that impressionable teens will watch the movie and learn to smoke the wrong way. At least with a Bogart movie you knew you were studying under an expert.

Q. I've just watched *Batman Returns* again on video. Two of the Penguin's famous trademarks are his cigarette holder and his monocle. But in the movie, the holder was only in one scene and in that scene he had spit it out! Was this a sort of antismoking message? (Mark Garoutte)

A. The Penguin was played by Danny DeVito, who has chain-smoked in two recent roles (*War of the Roses* and *Hoffa*). Leaving out the holder may simply have been a way to avoid messing up the Penguin's complicated and time-consuming makeup. I doubt it was an antismoking message. A recent British study of the top ten Hollywood films in the United Kingdom so far this year showed smoking in eight of them (the exceptions were *Honey, I Blew Up the Kid* and the rerelease of *The Jungle Book*). However, in only one of them *(The Bodyguard)* was smoking given a positive image. In the others, smokers were seen as losers, criminals, prostitutes, or villains. On the other hand, the British found, there might have been a more subtle message: Smoking was portrayed throughout as a tactic for dealing with stress. I get letters all the time from people with dark suspicions that the tobacco companies pay to have characters smoke in movies. Given the frequency of paid "product placement" for many other commodities (Pepsi, Dunkin' Donuts), this is not inconceivable. But if they pay, do they mind that the smokers are usually villains?

Q. Why do actors in movies not wear seat belts ? (Wayne R. Wilken, Fairbanks, Alaska)

A. For the same reason they smoke.

Q. Any idea why there isn't more media coverage of the tobacco industry's practice of paying to have stars—particularly those appealing to teenagers and preteenagers as "adult role models"—smoke onscreen? Seems to me this topic has been treated in a "hands-off" fashion when it comes to reviews and coverage, as nobody wants to let out the dirty little secret of how all that money is moving around in the movie industry. From what I've heard among friends in the business, however, this is the most effective strategy the tobacco industry has undertaken in decades, and is largely responsible for the recent explosion in teen smoking. Your thoughts? (Thom Hartmann, Marietta, Ga.)

A. Product placement is commonplace in movies, and Sylvester Stallone has recently denied reports that he accepted $500,000 to smoke Brown & Williamson products in his movies. However, has the practice of smoking *itself* been included in movies after payments by the tobacco industry? Such a practice, while not illegal, would certainly reflect badly on any studios or stars who took the money.

Q. My wife and I saw *How to Make an American Quilt* at a benefit showing in our town, where a lot of the movie was shot. What irked me most was the smoking! Most of the main characters smoked frequently, and that distracted me from the telling of the story. (I'm a family doctor, so perhaps I'm more sensitive on this issue than most.) We ought to let the people who make movies realize how offensive smoking can be, even when you can't smell the smoke. If the smoking had some function in the development of a character, or in the movement of the plot, I wouldn't object. The marijuana in this film, for example, might be offensive to some, but I can at least see how it was intended to tell the viewer something about the two sisters. (Robert Bourne, Redlands, Calif.)

A. In the economic and social bracket of the characters in *American Quilt,* most people don't smoke, and those who do, especially in California, are forever going through apologetic behavior about it. It's possible, though, that the student (Winona Ryder) would be a smoker, since some students smoke as a kind of death-defying statement. I understand that in real life Ryder is a smoker. I hope her agent tells her about those little wrinkles she's going to be getting around her lips in about ten years.

Q. I've heard rumors that cigarette companies pay moviemakers to show sexy stars smoking in movies. That might account for the persistence of smokers onscreen despite all the recent negative press. I am personally offended by this. I can understand it if the movie depicts bygone eras when smoking was common. But why do modern films continue to depict smoking as "cool" while the rest of us tend to label any of the younger generation who smoke as "low lifes"? (Darren McBride, Reno, Nev.)

A. Good question. Another one: Why don't you ever see anyone in a movie objecting to anyone else's smoking?

Q. Regardless of what influences the tobacco industry may have on the movie industry, and regardless of what you or I might think of smoking, it is *in fact* cool again among teens and young twenty-somethings. If a film is to portray or appeal to this age group, smoking is one of the costume accessories. Urging censorship of portrayals of this self-destructive behavior is no more virtuous than any of the other censorship cries being leveled against movies today. (Robert G. Haynes-Peterson, Boise, Id.)

A. I suppose you're right. Here's an acid test, however, of whether product placement is at work: Smoking among young African Americans is at an all-time low, recently estimated at less than a third of the rate of smoking among whites of the same age. If we were to see a lot of young blacks suddenly smoking in the movies, that might set off an alarm bell.

Q. You wrote in a recent Answer Man, "I have never or rarely seen anyone in a movie objecting to anyone else's smoking." Have you forgotten that scene from *RoboCop 2* where the hero goes haywire and nearly blasts an innocent bystander for lighting up? Our local theater used the scene as a "No Smoking" announcement for a (blessedly) brief time. (Lucius P. Cook, Chicago)

A. Before he aims his death ray, does RoboCop say, "Thank you for not smoking"?

Speak Up!

Q. My wife and I both suffer from some hearing loss. It is difficult for us to filter the dialogue from background sound. This makes it impossible to enjoy a film where the background volume is higher than the dialogue. All too often, the sound technicians place a mike within inches of a running stream, to show how wonderful they are at picking up sound. The audience can hear every tiny bubble in the stream as it bursts and the gurgle as the water passes over every pebble. Big deal! Night scenes are even worse when they manage to crowd the sound of every frog, cricket, and mosquito within ten miles onto the sound track. (Mary and Bill Richards, San Ramon, Calif.)

A. I agree that many movies are hard to understand—even for those with good hearing. Surround sound doesn't always help; stay away from the side speakers, since all the dialogue comes only from the center speaker behind the screen.

Q. My wife and I are often disappointed when viewing a movie on TV because we can not understand much of what the actors are saying. It seems they make a minimum effort to enunciate. When we watch an old movie, vintage 1930s and '40s, it is a joy to listen to the actors speak and be understood. In addition to the mumbling there is often background noise that drowns out much of what is being said. Have you noticed this yourself? (E. John Berger, Mission Viejo, Calif.)

A. I have indeed. So has David J. Bondelevitch of Studio City, California, who writes: "One reason that dialogue intelligibility was so high in the '30s and '40s was that virtually everything was shot on a sound stage. Now, for realism, virtually everything is shot on location, so you get a lot more background noise."

And here is a response from an actor, Ed Hooks: "I have appeared a lot in front of the camera. The sound you hear on the final print is actually built, layer by layer. Take, for instance, a scene in a nightclub. If I have dialogue with another actor at a table and, in the background, there are people dancing and music playing, etc., they will actually have everybody mime their actions and move silently, so the dialogue at the table can be recorded. Then they will separately record the music and the crowd noises and then, in the mixing room, put it all together. Coupled with all of the technical wizardry there is the added element of actors who do not enunciate clearly. Anyway, your perception is correct. The sound on your VCR is only semi-okay."

Q. In recent columns you addressed the problem of digital sound systems in movie theaters and how difficult it can be to understand the dialogue. This problem is academic to me and others who view movies by renting or buying tapes. When I rent a movie, I want to pop in the tape, adjust the volume, and sit back and enjoy it. But I find I either have to constantly adjust the volume or play the entire movie at a raised volume and hope I can hear what's being said. What are we supposed to do? (Maria A. Slivka, Chicago)

A. It's ironic that when you rent an old movie, you can hear every word on the sound track, but the new movies with state-of-the-art sound tracks are sometimes unintelligible. The reason, I suspect, is that sound engineers and even directors (who learn the dialogue by heart during the editing process) get carried away with their bells and whistles and do not place the intelligibility of the dialogue above all other considerations. I have received so many letters on this subject that I suspect large numbers of moviegoers are unhappy with the new high-tech approach to sound.

Q. In *Barcelona* the character played by Taylor Nichols seems to stumble over some of his lines. Isn't that unusual? Everybody in films is always articulate, unlike real people. No? (Alexis Bakaysa, San Antonio, Tex.)

A. The character has a slight speech impediment. For me, this added to his interest. It always seems a little strange that in the movies nobody ever pauses to search for the right word. John Wayne used to make a style out of coming to a halt halfway through every sentence ("You'll never stop . . . Genghis Khan!") and it gave him a curious believability.

Q. Could we suggest to Dolby, et al., that when promoting their fancy-schmancy sound systems at the start of features, they *not* use sounds that make us cringe, like the "knife sharpening" sound, for instance, that practically sends me running from the theater with my hands over my ears? Shouldn't this promo be a *pleasant* experience rather than something that makes you wish you'd stuffed your ears with sealing wax? (Jan Strnad, Los Angeles)

A. Either that, or they could change their slogan to, "The Audience Is Cringing."

Q. I arrived at *Clueless* a bit late and did not get the dictionary definition for "SF." Comparing notes with another moviegoer, I recalled that "SF" was mentioned over a dozen times, but my friend cannot recount a single mention. What is the meaning of "SF"??? (Alexander P. Safer, Chelsea, Mass.)

A. That's how Alicia Silverstone says "As if . . . !"

Special Effects

Q. My wife and I went to see *The Beverly Hillbillies* and, while I'm no expert on special effects, it seemed that the scene in which Dolly Parton entertains at the Clampett's party was strung together using a blue-screen technique, and that Parton was not really there for most of it. Am I right? (Ted Bridis, Tulsa, Okla.)

A. No, you are wrong. According to Nancy Meyer of Twentieth Century Fox, Dolly Parton was present for the filming of the entire scene. ("Blue screen," by the way, is a process in which different shots can be combined into one. TV weathermen use it to seem to be standing in front of maps.)

Q. The opening tracking shot in *Ed Wood*, which takes us from a miniature of the Hollywood sign during a storm to a live-action shot in front of a theater, pays respects to the famous tracking shot through the skylight in *Citizen Kane.* I assume this was intentional since Ed Wood in the film worships Welles, whose character makes an appearance late in the story. (Larry Gross, St. Louis)

A. I think you're right. The movie's opening is an astonishing display of visual confidence by director Tim Burton.

Q. Does it strike you that some movie sound effects are overdone? I've noticed in recent years that when a movie couple gets passionate, their kisses sound like they're sucking a peach. If I kissed my wife that sloppily, she'd wipe off her face and send me to the guest room for the night. And what about movie punches? Movies have been overdoing fight sound effects for years. My most vivid memory of *Rocky III* was of Sylvester Stallone and Mr. T beginning their fight with punches that would kill the average person. Do you feel that sound effects are as clichéd as some of the other areas you cover in your *Little Glossary?* (Steven Bailey, Jacksonville Beach, Fla.)

A. I don't know if they use peaches, but I remember visiting the sound effects session of a Charles Bronson movie named *Hard Times* and watching them tape-record themselves beating the hell out of a Naugahyde sofa with Ping-Pong paddles.

Q. I work at Mission Control for the shuttle program, and am impressed by the realism of *Apollo 13.* That control center in the movie is dead-on. To me, the whole thing looked and felt real, which is the highest compliment I can give. There are some minor technical things that only insiders would know (Mattingly stands too close to the launch, the crane was facing the wrong way in the Vehicle Assembly Building, the paint scheme was a little off, the phases of the Moon and the site shown on the Moon were not correct), but those are just nitpicks. I'm glad the American public is going to see it in such numbers. (Michael Grabois, Houston)

A. It's ironic that the movie's effects are so good that many people don't realize they're effects; sequences like the lift-off look so real that viewers assume they're watching archival documentary footage—not models, computer animation, etc.

Q. In Jean-Claude Van Damme's *Sudden Death,* don't you think that helicopter defied the law of gravity in how it fell? Wouldn't the propeller movement force the helicopter upside down? I mean, it fell perfectly into that hole in the roof. (Odell Henderson, Jersey City, N.J.)

A. It's hard to explain (maybe *Mystery Science Theater 3000* fans will understand), but I relish certain kinds of phony special effects, because in their oddness and implausibility they create an effect that merely "realistic" effects do not. I like the f/x in the original *King Kong* better than in the high-tech remake, for example, and the parting of the Red Sea in *The Ten Commandments* better than the much slicker wall of water in *The Abyss.*

Q. After seeing *Mr. Holland's Opus,* my brother insisted that Richard Dreyfuss's image was computer-altered for the scenes of him as a young man. I hadn't read or heard anything like that, but I did think he looked just like he did fifteen years ago. Do you know if a computer was used to give Richard his youthful look? If so, is this now a typical practice? (Sherry Mabry, Kansas City, Mo.)

A. Hairpieces and makeup (and good acting) were used, but no computers. Dreyfuss has always had an uncanny ability to change his apparent screen age. In *American Graffiti,* he played a high school student when he was already almost thirty.

Q. Special effects have almost completely taken over the movies lately. As you mentioned in your review of *Twister,* the actors were along for the ride while the special effects put on the show. My wife rented *Jumanji* for the kids the other day. They were watching it, while I was in the office pounding the keyboard. I didn't watch it, but just hearing the incessant *screaming* by small children and adults in that movie almost drove me *nuts.* Anyway, I've come up with a test for an ASEF (annoying special effects flick): Don't watch, just listen to a movie. If all you hear are screams and explosions, and the most sophisticated line of dialogue is "Look out!", then it's an ASEF. In *Twister* I can't recall a single interesting line, except maybe "I think that's the same cow." Will the rest of the summer be riddled with ASEFs? (Matthew J.W. Ratcliff, Villa Ridge, Mo.)

A. You bet! Summer has become the prime season for stunts, explosions, special effects, sequels, and film versions of TV shows. Distributors with serious, thought-provoking movies hold them until autumn, which is when the Oscar Season unofficially begins.

Q. The latest movie spin-off industry is the production of TV shows explaining how movie special effects are done. Magicians don't let the audience know how their tricks are accomplished, and I think Hollywood should keep their procedures a secret. It would make the effects seem more special! (Paul "Funn" Dunn, Bloomington, Ill.)

A. Although I gave a favorable review to the documentary *Special Effects,* I think you have a point. Now that I've seen doc footage of technicians blowing up a model of the White House, every time I see the *ID4* TV commercial, I think, "There's that model again" instead of "Jeez, I hope they were able to save Socks." Magicians have an old saying about their secrets: "The trick is told when the trick is sold."

Q. What was the one best special effect that you saw in the movies this summer (1996)? (Frank Bellantoni, Danbury, Conn.)

A. It's not in *Independence Day, Twister, The Rock, Eraser, Escape from L.A., Mission: Impossible,* or *The Phantom.* It's in a much smaller film named *Basquiat,* the biography of a New York artist, and it shows surfers riding the waves in Hawaii in the sky above Manhattan skyscrapers. The reason I chose this special effect is because it shows something that is *not* intended to look "realistic." Some modern special effects are so realistic you don't even realize they're special effects; quite often, for example, the sky in *Twister* is given clouds or ominous coloring at times when twisters are nowhere in sight. Other special effects are obvious, but we're supposed to believe them: The helicopter chasing the train in *M:I,* for example, or the flying saucers in *ID4.* What I liked about the effects in *Basquiat* wasn't how good they were (they weren't all that great) but that they were original and thought-provoking. They used an artificial image to reflect the character's state of mind, and left it up to us to interpret it. In other words, the effects are the tools of the director's vision, when in the other films the effects essentially *are* the director's vision.

Speed

Q. What happened to the other passengers on the subway train in *Speed?* Saw it twice, still haven't figured out if they all bought it when the second and third cars jumped track, or if they just slipped out the back door at 60 mph when no one was looking. (Terry Ryan)

A. They're called "extras" for a reason.

Q. I read your column where a reader asked about the fate of all the other people on the subway train when it derails in the movie *Speed* with only Keanu Reeves, Sandra Bullock, and the (dead) train operator accounted for. Your answer was "that's why they call them extras." But I'm not sure that answered the question. I just watched the movie on my laserdisc. Dennis Hopper leads Sandra Bullock (wrapped in explosives) onto the train; he begins firing his gun into the air and screaming at the passengers on the subway to evacuate the train, which they do rapidly. As such, the train has no "extras" on it when it derails. (Adam Weisler, Roslyn Heights, N.Y.)

A. That Dennis Hopper, he's all heart.

Q. A great scene in *Speed* was the first view of the approaching fifty-foot gap, *with a flock of birds in flight* between the elevated sections of highway! This struck an extra chord of fear. I can't believe the cameras rolled for hours until these birds happened to be "caught" on tape. Were these not trained pigeons? (Jim Carey, New Lenox, Ill.)

A. Not only were the birds inserted with an optical effect, but— *so was the gap!* The special effects experts began with a shot of a section of highway under construction, and altered it to make it appear there was a gap.

Q. I felt compelled to write after reading your glowing praise for the movie *Speed.* I am all for checking my brain at the box office, but there is a limit to how much unbelievability I can accept. 1) No bus can make such turns at high speeds. 2) Does LAX have the longest runways in the history of airports? They must, because the bus never had to make a turn while Keanu Reeves was trailing underneath by a thin wire. 3) Why could Keanu accelerate the train, but not decelerate it? Doesn't every car on a subway have emergency brakes? 4) If the bomb were attached to the front wheels of the bus, wouldn't it have exploded as the bus was flying through the air? After all, the front wheels only move when the back wheels are propelling the bus. 5) No bus, and I mean no bus, could make that jump! (Peter Kahl)

A. What makes you think a bus couldn't leap a fifty-foot gap in a highway? Martin Vasko, a San Francisco expert on the laws of physics, has supplied me with this analysis: "The landing area would need to be at least six feet and two inches below the takeoff area for a reasonable chance for success. On the other hand, if the bus took-off at an angle, the landing area could be level with the takeoff area. At 55 mph this appears to require an angle of 7.2 degrees, which sounds small, but is rather steep for a road except in the middle of ramps, overpasses, and mountain passes. The odds are much better at 70 mph: you'd need at least three feet and ten inches or at least 4.4 degrees. Higher speeds would be even better, but maintaining control upon landing might get hectic."

Q. Am I the only one who has noticed, Roger, how many times, Roger, that the name "Jack" is called out in the movie *Speed?* Roger, it ruins the movie for me. That constant name reference, Roger, gets on my nerves. Also, Roger, in *Indiana Jones and the Last Crusade*, Harrison Ford calls Sean Connery "Dad" one thousand times, Roger. (Jeanie Wagner, Park Ridge, Ill.)

A. Jeanie, Jeanie, Jeanie.

Spoilers

Q. This is a cry of frustration: Why do they keep making previews that give away the entire plot of the movie? The recent film where Peter Falk plays an eighty-year-old man leaves little to expect from the movie itself. I notice on the AMC movie channel that in the old days, previews used to be a come-on, to lure people in. These days I sometimes don't attend a movie because I already know what's going to happen. It is especially bad in the case of romantic movies, where you see the couple meeting, their initial dislike, how they start to love each other, etc. The worst example was *Speechless*. The film was okay, but I would have enjoyed it more if I hadn't already heard *every* good line in the previews. (Richard Hubbell, Arlington, Va.)

A. You mean like when she says, "Shall we speak the unspoken language of love?" And he says, "You mean the kind only dogs can hear?" And they crawl under the sheets and bark?

Q. Can you suggest to studios that when they release a movie on videotape, previews for *other* movies are okay, but ads for the sound track of *this* movie that include clips from the film (giving away plot twists, punch lines, endings, etc.) should be moved to *after* the movie. That way, when someone rents the film, key ingredients aren't given away even before the opening credits start to roll. (John McCartor, Portland, Oreg.)

A. This makes such good sense that I am amazed the studios haven't thought of it themselves. On second thought . . . not very amazed.

Q. Why must trailers and ads be misleading or give away some of the movie's surprises? In *Courage Under Fire* part of the story revolves around an investigation to determine if Meg Ryan's character will be awarded a medal after she is killed in battle. In the TV ads Denzel Washington is seen placing a medal on a tombstone, which seems to imply that Meg's character does indeed get the medal. Another example was the movie *Terminator 2.* In the beginning of the movie James Cameron is very careful not to reveal that Arnold's terminator is the "good" one; on the contrary, he leads us to believe that Arnold is still the "bad" terminator. However, the trailers for this movie talked about the "kinder, gentler" terminator, and essentially told us that Arnold was the good guy. If *Citizen Kane* had been made today, the TV ads would start with a shot of the "Rosebud" sled. (Gary Currie, Montreal, Canada)

A. And the ads for *Psycho* would show Norman Bates having tea with his mother. Let's not even think about the ads for *The Crying Game.*

Star Wars

Q. Was David Prowse the only actor to ever play Darth Vader in the *Star Wars* movies? I know James Earl Jones was used as the voice, but did anyone "stand in" for the image of Vader's face? This will settle a lively discussion in our family! (Fred Urrutia, Livermore, Calif.)

A. David Prowse, an English actor, wore the Darth Vader costume but was not seen on screen. If you want to see what he looks like, rent Russ Meyer's *Blacksnake.* When we finally see Vader's face, in *Empire*, he is played by Sebastian Shaw.

Q. What is the deal with the new *Star Wars* movies coming out soon? Do they take place before or after *Return of the Jedi?* (Craig Foster, Wilmington, N.C.)

A. Jeffrey Graebner of Los Angeles reports that George Lucas's plans for another *Star Wars* trilogy are still rather tentative: "I would be surprised if the movie showed up before the turn of the century." The new trilogy will be parts one, two, and three, and Lucus eventually plans to do parts seven, eight, and nine.

Q. I read that you recently did a workshop at the Hawaii Film Festival comparing the work of Buster Keaton and Jackie Chan. One walks into a Jackie Chan film to escape reality and watch a master performer amaze you with physical acrobatics and creativity, and thrill you with eye-popping stunts. Jackie Chan has repeatedly said that he would love to be in a Spielberg or Lucas film, that he'd love to see what would happen with his action and their special effects. Wouldn't the perfect role for Chan be as a Jedi knight in the new *Star Wars* trilogy? (David Hunt, Springdale, Ark.)

A. In the workshop, we used stop-action laserdisc to look at some of Chan's great action sequences. I was impressed once again by his physical grace and agility, and the way so much of what he does is touched with humor. He could be a fascinating addition to the *Star Wars* mix. Of course, with the glacial progress of Lucas's new trilogy, Jackie may be retired by the time filming begins.

Steven Seagal

Q. Is it just me or is Hollywood changing the male/female relationships in films? Example: In *Under Siege*, Erica Elaniak's character was more of a helper to Steven Seagal than a lover, and except for one of the minor characters who referred to her as "Miss July," it was as if no one figured out she was female until the film was almost over. It was the same in *A Few Good Men* (Demi Moore and Tom Cruise) and *A League of Their Own* (Geena Davis and Tom Hanks). I am guessing that it is more '90s now to do this. Do you agree? (Michael R. Bowman)

A. I was trained in earlier decades, and guessed that they were female almost immediately.

Q. I just watched *Under Siege* on videotape and noticed that the bad guys spend most of the movie building an overhead railway through the narrow, twisty corridors of the battleship so that they can steal the *Missouri's* fifteen-foot-long cruise missiles. Never mind the fact that if the navy loaded the missiles deep in the ship, they must have had an easy way to get them down there. The real goof is that at the end of the movie, the missiles are actually found in canisters on the *deck of the ship*! This has to be one of the stupidest plot devices I've ever seen. My question is, what's the stupidest one you recall? (Mark Blanchard, Norwalk, Conn.)

A. Hmmm. How about the decision to end *Lambada* (1990), a movie about a Latin dance craze, with a climactic scene involving a trigonometry contest?

Q. Regarding Steven Seagal's sanctimonious speech about the ecology at the end of *On Deadly Ground*: He probably released more toxic fumes into the atmosphere during the making of this film than the Hertz fleet could over the course of a year. I wish that somebody would assess the environmental impact of a blockbuster movie (landfills of paper waste from refreshments and merchandising tie-ins, emissions from cars commuting to and from the theater complexes, etc.) and put one of these rich, hypocritical "environmentalist" stars on the spot. (Jeff Levin, Rochester, N.Y.)

A. Seagal originally wanted to make his closing speech twenty minutes long, which might have rivaled the atmospheric effect of bovine gas emissions.

Stone and *Nixon*

Q. Once again the Golden Globes blew it, by failing to nominate Oliver Stone's brilliant *Nixon* as one of the best-directed films of the year. What gives with this group? (Jordan Marsh, Chicago)

A. Anthony Hopkins was nominated for Best Actor. But Oliver Stone may have lost the "director" nomination for himself. In behavior that seemed positively Nixonian, he took personal control of the preview press screenings of the movie, insisting on approving every name. In most cities he allowed only a handful of "leading" critics to attend. The Golden Globe membership is made up of Hollywood foreign correspondents—few of them on Stone's A-list. Since ten actors are nominated (five for comedy, five for drama), enough Globe voters saw the movie to nominate Hopkins. But in the more competitive director category (only five names), Stone's policy may have aced him out of a nomination. Ironically, the Globe voters have historically supported Stone; they gave him their "Best Director" Globe for *JFK*.

Q. I was just watching the David Brinkley show on *Nixon*. I'm a literary critic, not a film critic, but I have to say, whether it's a film or a book or a play, it would be impossible for any artist to produce a quality piece of work without some degree of empathy for the subject. One thing that particularly annoyed me about the Brinkley show was the commentary of Nixon's biographer. He seemed to believe that any filmmaker who addresses a historical subject should be compelled to make a documentary. *Nixon* is not a documentary. It is film drama based on the life of an influential political figure. Similarly, Shakespeare's history plays were not meant to be read as actual representations of the events that inspired them. I'm not sure why so many people believe Stone should be a historian first and a filmmaker second. This is the same sort of mind-set that got Welles into so much trouble with *Citizen Kane*. Thankfully it did not prevent him from making the greatest film of all time, and it's certainly not cramping Stone's style. (Don A. Renicky, Durham, N.C.)

A. Agreed. *Nixon*, like any movie biography (from *Patton* to *Butch Cassidy and the Sundance Kid*) is a work of the imagination, an attempt by an artist to understand his subject. I am particularly impatient with Stone's critics who say, "But what about all the people who will believe this is the truth?" My answer is: If they're that impressionable, they (a) probably won't be interested in the movie in the first place, and (b) they must bear responsibility for informing themselves. *Nixon* is psychological and artistic *opinion* in a work of fiction, and any adult should be sophisticated enough to view and evaluate it on that basis. That is what an education is for.

Q. The AP's movie report last weekend was centered around the fact that Oliver Stone's *Nixon* didn't place in the top ten. It didn't mention that it was still in limited release, and actually doing very well on a per-screen basis. How can you account for this total dishonesty? I'm not saying the film will do the kind of box office *JFK* did, but I am saying that media like the Associated Press are trying to influence people to not see it. What is so terribly stupid is there is so much crap put out by Hollywood, and AP usually cheers it. (Vickie Weimar, Norman, Okla.)

A. Oliver Stone's sin is that he is the only major American director who consistently tackles controversial political issues, and has the temerity to do so from his own point of view. The "box office winners" lists are meaningless unless you understand that a film on two thousand screens is obviously going to outgross a film on four hundred screens. Young moviegoers turn out in hordes over Christmas for *Jumanji*-type movies, but the adult audience for a movie like *Nixon* builds more slowly. If all movies are required to do blockbuster business the instant they open, we'll get nothing but movies for teenagers.

Q. Where can I find the real identities of the Texans played by Larry Hagman, et al., that Nixon came to visit in Texas, in *Nixon?* (L.J. Jensen, Liberty Hill, Tex.)

A. There are no "real" Texans behind those characters. The scenes represented, in a general way, the influence at the time of the John Birch Society, and Nixon's disinclination to deal with them. They show Nixon as more moderate than some segments of his party.

Strange Questions

Q. The year 1996 marks the fiftieth anniversary of the release of *It's a Wonderful Life*. Would you send me your favorite scene from the film? (Rich Bysina, Lombard, Ill.)

A. I like the scene where Donna Reed loses her bathrobe, and Jimmy Stewart ends up talking to the shrubbery.

Q. *Goldfinger* was on television the other night and I would like to settle a couple of questions about this movie. (1) I recall this movie being released with Goldfinger's jet pilot being named "Tushy Galore" instead of "Pussy Galore." Is this true and why was the charactor renamed? (2) Is there any truth to the rumor that when

Goldfinger steals the gold from Fort Knox, that influenced President Nixon to have the United States get off the gold standard?
(Jack Ferguson, Rockaway, N.J.)

A. (1) As I recall from seeing the film, the character was indeed
named "Pussy Galore." I cannot for the life of me think why the
character would be renamed. (2) No truth at all. Actually, what
Nixon wanted was to hire Odd Job as an aide.

Q. I just saw *Under Siege* and really enjoyed it. As with most action flicks, I frequently find myself wondering if what is done on
screen is actually possible or is it just part of the magic of movies.
For instance, when Steven Seagal mixes two ingredients in a glass
and places it in the microwave on high for several minutes, it created a powerful little explosion, almost like a pipe bomb. Is that really possible and if so, what ingredients do you think he used? (Steve
McCaffrey)

A. I don't know, and I don't want to know.

Q. My wife and I were browsing the Microsoft Cinemania movie
guide and noted that it claims you were born June 18, 1962! If this
is true, did you really write the screenplay to *Beyond the Valley of
the Dolls* at age eight? (Craig Renwick)

A. Seven.

Q. Who is Dita Parlo, and why has Madonna engraved her initials on her new gold tooth? (Charlie Smith, Chicago)

A. You have actually asked two questions. (1) Dita Parlo is remembered as the star of two of the best French films of all time,
Jean Vigo's *L'Atalante* (1934) and Jean Renoir's *Grand Illusion* (1937).
In the Vigo film, she was heartbreaking as the woman who fell in
love with a handsome young bargeman, only to become separated
from him and spend much of the movie fearing they could never
find each other again. (2) Madonna may have engraved the initials
"D.P." on her new gold tooth, but we have only her word for it that
she had Dita Parlo in mind. She might also have been thinking
about Dolly Parton, Debra Paget, Dorothy Parker, or Don Pardo.

Q. What are your ten all-time favorite Women in Prison films? (M. Scott Partee, Peachtree City, Ga.)

A. Before I complete my list, I'm waiting for *The Leona Helmsley Story*.

Q. I've often wondered why there isn't an award ceremony for some really great acting by the child stars of the movies. (Judy Benton, Akron, Ohio)

A. Just the thought of such a program boggles the mind. The Jean Hersholt Award for humanitarian lifetime service could go to an old-timer like Brooke Shields.

Q. As it's been very hot this week in the warehouse where I work, many of the men have taken to working shirtless. This practice was accepted until a couple of the women decided it would be okay to remove their shirts and work in their bras. Needless to say the topless women have created a controversy. Why can men get away with toplessness in the workplace and women can't? Has anything like this ever happened at the newspaper where you work? (James D. Frey, Oakland, Calif.)

A. Not here at the *Sun-Times*, although I understand it's quite a problem over at the *Tribune*.

Q. I've been thinking about this for years, but a recent revival of *Dr. Zhivago* made me write. *Zhivago* takes place in Russia. The characters are Russian. But we hear English, of course, since this is an English-speaking movie. Now that we've settled that point, I ask: If we're *hearing* English, why aren't we *seeing* English? Why are all the signs and newspapers written in Russian? Shouldn't the sight be consistent with the sound? (Richard Covello, WNIB radio, Chicago)

A. Two reasons. (1) I think we're supposed to forget we're hearing English, and assume the characters are talking Russian, so of course they would read Russian. If that seems shaky, try (2), which is that since the movie will be dubbed or subtitled into dozens of other languages, you'd have indignant French or Japanese audiences looking at English signs in Russia and complaining of cultural imperialism. Better to leave the signs in Russian, so they'll play convincingly in every market.

Q. Why, do you think, a lot of comedies start off funny and end off serious? Why aren't they consistent and start funny and end funny? Of course there are some comedies that aren't funny throughout. (Bill Millard, Colorado Springs, Colo.)

A. You can hardly even call those last ones comedies.

Q. I have just noticed that they always show things in a movie as they would appear on a map. Whenever an airplane flies from New York to Los Angeles, it will always fly from right to left, and when Columbus discovers America, he always finds it on the left side, coming from the right. You could show those things in the opposite way, since it all depends on where the camera is. If the plane from New York to L.A. was filmed from the other side, it would seem to fly from left to right but would still go in the same direction. (Vincent Assmann, Heidelberg, Germany)

A. On the other hand, *Flying Down to Rio* didn't have the plane crashing into the bottom of the screen.

Q. Which of the following do you think would end up being the better movie? (1) a movie written by the world's *worst writer* and directed by the world's *greatest director,* or (2) a movie written by the world's *greatest writer* and directed by the world's *worst director?* (Joey Berner, Houston, Tex.)

A. The better movie would be the one by the *greatest director,* because so much depends on visuals, editing, composition, tone, and other matters not influenced by the work of the *worst writer.* On the other hand, a great script can easily be mangled by the *worst director,* as I have been told many times over the years by people describing themselves as the *greatest writers.*

Q. Is it a fact that the most-often uttered phrase of movie dialogue is "Let's get out of here"? (Bo Bradham, Charlottesville, Va.)

A. It probably ranks right up there with "Look out!" "Take this!" and "****!"

Q. I'm reading the weekend movie returns, including the number of theaters and returns per theater, and I'm thinking, the average blockbuster now plays in 1,500 to 2,000 locations in the United States and Canada. That's a lot of film stock! What happens to all those prints at the end of the run? Do they send them overseas, destroy them, what? (Robert Haynes-Peterson, Boise, Id.)

A. Prints in good condition are used in English-speaking overseas markets and in discount houses, and later on the campus, military, and revival circuits. Foreign markets where dubbing is used get new prints. As prints wear out, they are recalled by the studio and destroyed.

Q. Is the nose ring that Anna Paquin wears in several of the scenes in the latter half of *Fly Away Home* real? I would find it odd that the filmmakers would include the nose ring themselves as part of her character. It's especially distracting since she is wearing it in some scenes and not in others. (Michael S. Zey, Austin, Tex.)

A. A spokesman for Columbia tells me the nose ring that Anna Paquin wears in *Fly Away Home* is not real, but only a clip-on. She wore it to the set one day and the filmmakers decided to include it in the movie.

Q. I am following the installation of a new elevator at work, and I am sorry to say that it is now mandatory (in Ohio anyway), that the overhead doors in the roofs of elevators are locked! Movies will suffer as a result of this. Heroes will no longer be permitted to climb through the top of the car to escape before the car crashes to the bottom of the pit. On the other hand, the villains will now have more difficult access to the riders of stranded cars. I will do my own research over the next year to see how the movie death toll is affected by this legislation. At this writing, I have not heard of any laws requiring guardrails around fruit stands, so that one is still safe. (Scott Moff, Marietta, Ohio)

A. What will they think of next? Making the drivers in chase scenes wear seat belts?

Stunts

Q. In your *Assassins* review you mentioned using a table for protection from an explosion. In almost every action film ever made, there is at least one scene where someone takes cover from gunfire behind an object completely inadequate for the task. (Usually an overturned table, frequently an interior wall next to a door.) Bullets easily pass through these objects if a villain is taking cover, but are magically stopped in the case of the hero. (Larry Jones, Ontario, Calif.)

A. Yeah, in cop movies they always draw their guns and stand on either side of the door—so they won't get hit if the desperado inside shoots through the door. If the bad guys had any brains, they'd shoot through the walls.

Q. In a recent Answer Man, a reader noted a problem with the movie portrayal of head-butts. He wrote, "Whenever a head butt is delivered in a movie, the receiver of the butt is sent reeling into a semiconscious stagger with all manner of hideous facial contusions, while the deliverer of the butt doesn't even wince, even though his own head has just received an identical impact." As an aging rugby player, I have had the distinct displeasure of receiving my share of head-butts (and given a few). Your correspondent is more a student of physics than of hard-scrabble street maneuvers. The point of a head-butt is to strike the soft part of your opponent's head (e.g., nose, filtrum, mouth) with the hard part of your head (e.g., forehead). If you do that correctly, you will likely hear a noise similar to a walnut cracking. If you do it wrong, both of you will stagger away looking like Moe after Curly nails him with a two-by-four. (Mark Firmani, Seattle Rugby Football Club)

A. Now that we know how you do it, how did Curly do it?

Subliminal Sex, etc.

Q. I agree that people spend too much time digging for subliminal sex in cartoons while ignoring the more blatant examples all around us. And I agree that any Disney animator caught adding such scenes likely would wind up as crocodile bait. But the key word is "caught." I recently heard an interview that animator Chuck Jones, who invented Yosemite Sam, did with Terry Gross of National Public Radio. In it, Jones described how he and other Warner Bros. animators took great delight in adding one-frame naughty bits to cartoons, then screening them on a movieola for studio execs they enlisted to "find the glitch we're having trouble with." According to Jones, the execs invariably turned purple and demanded the offending frame be removed, to which Jones replied, "Oh, but it's finished, and to redo it will cost too much and besides, it's only ¹⁄₂₄th of a second. No one will ever see it." Jones says they did it out of sheer boredom. Kind of makes you wonder what might be written in those clouds of dust raised after Wile E. Coyote is squashed by a boulder, doesn't it? (Dave Molter, Pittsburgh, Pa.)

A. I'm starting a campaign to replace the Road Runner's "beep-beep" with "(bleep)-(bleep)."

Q. Is it true that certain *Little Mermaid* videos are going to be collector's items because of the cover art? A video store owner told me that the artist included an obscene detail in the towers of the castle. The picture does kind of look like what people say it looks like. I heard they changed the art on later cassettes and so the early cassettes will be valuable. (Jayne Kranc, St. John, Ind.)

A. Thank you for enclosing a Xerox copy of the offending castle turret. You are right. It does kind of look like what people say it looks like. As yet there is no collector's market for it, however.

Q. I heard that the animators sneaked some secret frames into *Who Framed Roger Rabbit?* Would you happen to know where the offending scenes are on the laserdisc? (James LaRosa, Long Island City, N.Y.)

A. One such moment occurs when Baby Huey stalks off the set in the cartoon that precedes the actual film.

Q. The American Life League, a right-wing Christian activist group, wants Disney to withdraw *The Lion King* from video stores because they think a bit of animation in it briefly forms the word "sex." The group was alerted to the "hidden message" by a woman whose four-year-old son noticed it. According to them, if you watch the scene where Simba flops down on the cliff edge, the cloud of dust swirling up briefly spells the letters S, E, X, each letter fading as the next appears. What's your reaction? (Jon Woolf, Beavercreek, Ohio)

A. I wonder what kind of parents would teach a four-year-old how to spell "sex," and that it was a dirty word.

Q. Those wacky boys at Disney are at it again! Apparently the infamous Tower of Tumescence on the cover of *The Little Mermaid* video wasn't enough to satisfy their phallocentric obsessions— now they've desecrated an archbishop! Take a close look at the scene where Ursula is about to marry Prince Eric—it'll soon become obvious just how excited the clergyman is. (Chuck Mathias, Steilacoom, Wash.)

A. This and other recent rumors about hidden sexual content in Disney movies have been sweeping the country. They were brilliantly tracked down to their sources in a article by Lisa Bannon in the *Wall Street Journal.* In one case, the Christian magazine *Media Guide* printed a retraction of its report (that Aladdin whispers: "All good teenagers take off their clothes") after subjecting the suspicious phrase to digital analysis in a recording studio and finding that it actually sounded more like "Scat, good tiger, take off and go." Many of those spreading the rumors could not find the references for themselves, but passed them on because they made a good story. I am sad that the rumors are being spread by those who, in the name of family values, are destroying childhood innocence by encouraging kids and their parents to look for nonexistent filth. These days, my guess is that a Disney artist caught sneaking *anything* unauthorized into a movie is likely to be turned over to Captain Hook and fed to the crocodiles.

Q. In a recent Answer Man about the "subliminal sex messages" in Disney cartoons, you forgot about one inescapable fact, which completely undermines the family organizations' intentions. Whenever somebody discovers and makes public this subliminal sex, every man, woman, and child will seek out the nearest copy of said film with the freeze-frame button ready. Trying to deter children from Disney films by pointing out this alleged smut is tantamount to protecting a picnic from ants by forming a barricade of honey. (Michael S. Zey, Austin, Tex.)

A. The real purpose of the antismut crusaders is not to fight smut in *The Little Mermaid,* but to create a heightened paranoia among their followers, as part of the general strategy of portraying a world filled with sinful dangers. That helps promote the bunker mentality crucial to cult groups. Another benefit is the publicity. There is so much real smut available that to concentrate on imaginary smut in Disney family films requires a skewed mentality.

Q. A message from the Rev. Donald Wildmon, head of the American Family Association, is making the rounds of the Internet. In it, he attacks Disney, writing: "In *Toy Story,* rated G by the ultraliberal MPAA, the main characters, 'Woody'—note sexual reference—and 'Buzz'—note drug reference—are owned by a child in a single-parent household in which the father is noticeably absent. 'Woody' and 'Buzz' have equally disturbing toy friends, including a sex-obsessed talking potato, a sex-obsessed Bo Peep doll who cannot keep her hands (or lips) off 'Woody,' and an Etch-a-Sketch whose 'knobs' must be 'adjusted' to produce results."

Don't you think this is carrying things to extremes? (Name Withheld)

A. I withheld your name because you merely forwarded a message that had dozens of other recipients in its header. It sounded fishy to me, so I contacted the American Family Association, and its spokesman, Scott Thomas, said, "This message is a hoax. It was sent by someone who doesn't like AFA, and apparently doesn't mind using others to express his view, since he has manipulated many (about one hundred so far) into writing us on his behalf. The message purports to come from Don Wildmon, who doesn't even have a modem, let alone an e-mail address. Nor does the AFA maintain any electronic mailing lists."

Q. I recall a rumor that *The Exorcist* used subliminal messaging to affect the audience. When I saw it on its initial theatrical release, I passed out at one point—and I don't faint easily. It was early in the film when she was having her brain X-rayed: The scene showed Regan with a needle on the end of a tube stuck in her neck, and there's a gyrating X-ray machine and the machine gun–like sound of sheets of film rapidly advancing. I recoil at the thought that a movie could have such an impact on me without some kind of unfair advantage. Maybe the hype surrounding the film and the crowded theater set me up for it. When I came to, I noticed that I'd slumped down and jammed my shins against the metal edge of the seat in front of me. They were cut and bleeding. Probably one of the few times that watching a movie led to physical injury. (Tom Norris, Braintree, Mass.)

A. A couple of years ago at the Hawaii Film Festival I did a frame-by-frame analysis of *The Exorcist* with Owen Roizman, its cinematographer. Using freeze-frame on a laserdisc, he revealed two single frames in which a satanic face is superimposed over the face of Linda Blair, who played Regan. The audience was pretty impressed, but there were no injuries.

Superman versus Batman

Q. Who would win in a fight to the finish? Batman, or Superman? (Steve Kass, Chicago)

A. Superman, of course, since Batman is only human and the Man of Steel has superhuman qualities. If Batman used kryptonite, however, that would of course tilt the balance. But the Answer Man began wondering about *other* superheroes, and when your question was presented to famed science fiction creator George Alec Effinger, he responded: "I was a Marvel comics writer back in the early '70s, and there was (and may still be) a definite hierarchy of who could beat up whom. Thor was tops, being a god, and then it went (if my memory is right) Hulk, Spiderman, Thing (and so on; Hulk and Spiderman may have been reversed). I used to match up the Marvel and DC versions of similar characters: Batman versus Daredevil, Submariner versus Aquaman (oh boy, spot Aquaman two touchdowns and a field goal), Hawkeye versus Green Arrow, etc. Then I became much too literary to care about such things. Sure, you bet."

Q. Regarding your recent Movie Answer Man item about whether Superman or Batman would win in a fight: In *The Dark Knight,* by Frank Miller, Batman and Superman have a "fight to the death," and Batman (using his brain and kryptonite) wins the battle. Well, he almost wins; check it out. Which I guess goes to show, brains will always beat brawn, eh? (Joe Long, Redmond, Wash.)

A. Like I said, brains—and kryptonite. Superman always has seemed a little dim to me. I checked out the book, and see what you mean by "almost." I think it still counts as a victory, though.

Q. After viewing *Batman Forever,* I immediately began speculation on what villain might appear in the fourth *Batman* installment. The traditional ones have all been used. Then I remembered that just after Robin escapes on his motorcycle, Batman comments, "He's probably halfway to Metropolis by now." That city is the residence of Superman! I think it would be interesting to see Batman meet Superman in a movie, perhaps as enemies. Then your question about which one would win in a fight would finally be resolved. Does Batman keep kryptonite in his utility belt? (Brian Moore, Hanover Park, Ill.)

A. Superman and Batman have met over the years in comic book adventures, and it's possible they could meet on the screen; the films of both superheroes are produced at Warner Bros. After the two franchises have run out of steam, your idea might look attractive. In the meantime, you'll have to be content with *Jason meets Freddy,* New Line Cinema's match-up of the villains of their *Friday the 13th* and *Nightmare on Elm Street* movies, now in preproduction.

Q. Will Warner Bros. try at some point to revitalize the Superman franchise through a Batman film, à la *The Dark Knight Returns?* I think it would be interesting to see. (Francisco L. Mendez, Dallas, Tex.)

A. Warner Bros. says it has no such plans, but in my opinion it's only a matter of time. The tradition of having one superhero visit the world of another is well-established in comic books, where it was originally started as a way of encouraging "sampling" of a new character by the fans of an older one. At the present moment the Superman series has run out of box office steam, while Batman is Warner's most valuable franchise. But eventually Batman, too, will need a retread, and the idea of a combined Batman-Superman adventure will be seductive. One obvious story line could star Christopher Reeve as a Superman whose mental acuity is untouched but whose body has been immobilized by kryptonite. Harnessing his remaining powers such as X-ray vision to a Virtual Reality computer program, Superman could act as an adviser and ally for Batman. I can even imagine a subplot in which Bruce Wayne uses his scientific knowledge to try to aid the paralyzed Clark Kent—little realizing Clark is actually Superman.

Talking in the Movies

Q. For the past few weeks I've been dating a woman who is smart, kind, attractive, and genuinely fun to be with . . . *but who talks loudly in movie theaters.* Must I throw away this fine, fine woman because of her one (albeit serious) social shortcoming? I have, unfortunately, determined that she's beyond rehabilitation. Quiet *sshhh!*s lead only to her talking just as loudly, but right into my ear. (Andy Ihnatko, Westwood, Mass.)

A. Try this. Obtain a joy buzzer. Hold her hand loosely. Every time she talks during a movie, squeeze it. Let me know how it works.

Q. Patrons of Sony theaters now have an opportunity to spot the talkers in the audience before the movie starts. Just wait for the *shhhh!* card to appear on the screen. Every talker in the theater, unable to pass up a chance to display contempt for the Social Contract, will read the card out loud. It's as good as having an electric sign over their heads saying, "I'm a pinhead. Better change your seat." (Barry Schechter, New York)

A. Look at it this way: At least the early warning gives you time to get up and move before the feature starts.

Q. Why do people clap at the end of a movie? A play, I could understand, they can hear you. Do people really think anyone that has anything to do with the movie is going to hear them clap? (Bacel Lewis, Baltimore, Md.)

A. All noise in a movie theater is a form of communication, in which the audience tells itself what it thinks of a movie. The audience laughs, for example, to confirm that something is funny; if you were watching the same movie alone, you might not laugh aloud, because there would be no one to hear you. Applause, likewise, is a way to tell others what you think. People who talk inappropriately in movies are telling others that the movie is not worth paying attention to, and in my experience noisy talkers tend to shut up during a movie that is really working.

Q. Thought you might be interested in this listing in the morning paper for the Logan Theater in Chicago: UNDER 6 YRS OLD NOT ADMITTED TO R RATED fiLMS AFTER 6 P.M. Quick! Somebody notify Jack Valenti. (B.F. Helman, Chicago)

A. Actually, I've received several requests over the years for just such a policy, from moviegoers who don't like the noise that restless children make during movies that don't interest them.

Q. You recently wrote, ". . . movies get pretty much the audience they deserve. People tend to be quiet for good movies, and noisy during bad ones." Recently we went to see *Fargo* (a great movie) at the Sony in Rolling Meadows, and had to move seats because the ladies behind us were discussing their eyeglass purchases during the first twenty minutes. We had been anxiously awaiting *Richard III* (another great movie), and settled into our seats at the York Art Theater in Elmhurst—but the talking audience affliction had struck there, too! Not only were the three people behind us treating us to a continuous description of what Shakespeare meant, ad nauseam, but three people across the aisle were chatting, too. We don't know where you go to the movies, but please let us know these locations. (Charlene Chapman and Henry Sadowski, Itasca, Ill.)

A. I'm not always so lucky. I once got so mad at four guys talking during a movie at the Webster Place that I told them I was going to ask the manager to call the police. They got a good laugh out of that. They *were* the police.

Q. What do you do when the lights dim and someone within earshot won't shut up? (Chip Castille, Tampa, Fla.)

A. Move.

Q. I attended *Demolition Man* recently, and had the least enjoyable time I've ever had at a movie theater. A couple next to me chatted away long into the movie. There was a family with two small kids behind me, who talked at full volume throughout the movie, as if they were at home. I didn't know what to say without being totally rude myself. (Gerald R. Hogsett)

A. Why *not* go ahead and be totally rude yourself? Many moviegoers are, frankly, too afraid of noisemakers. Why not seize the initiative? Turn around and say, slowly and distinctly, "The next person who talks while I'm listening to this movie goes home in a box." Let me know what happens.

The Tarantino Watch

Q. I read that whenever Quentin Tarantino is getting interested in some woman, he shows her *Rio Bravo* and "she better like it." My own particular litmus tests for prospective Significant Others isn't a film, but a format. If she tells me she prefers colorization to the original black and white, I tell her to close the door from the outside. (Michael Zey, Austin, Tex.)

A. An excellent early-warning strategy, because anyone who prefers colorization to the original black and white is eventually going to reveal serious character flaws in a number of other areas.

Q. Any idea what a *Reservoir Dog* is ? (Carl F. Staaterman, Wilton, Conn.)

A. Quentin Tarantino sometimes says the title has no meaning, sometimes says he doesn't want to reveal it.

Q. I've seen commercials for the movies *Desperado* and *Lord of Illusions* quoting Quentin Tarantino as he praises the movies. Has it always been the practice to use popular filmmakers this way, or is it just because it's Quentin Tarantino? (Sean Goodrich, Trophy Club, Tex.)

A. It's just because it's Quentin Tarantino. In his unflagging attempt to be the den mother for a new generation of filmmakers, he finds he cannot make cameo appearances in every one of their movies, much as he would like to, so he writes blurbs for their ads.

In the case of *Desperado* he also appeared in the movie, where he was shot dead in the middle of a sentence. Only cynics would say there was no other possible time to shoot him.

Q. I am a Quentin Tarantino fan and was pleased with your TV special on him, where you mentioned that one of QT's favorite films is *Blow Out*, by Brian De Palma. Two nights ago, my friends from school and I rented *Body Double*, another De Palma film. At the end of the movie the villain's dog leaps into a reservoir. Is it just possible that this is the origin for the title of the film *Reservoir Dogs?* (Jesse Cohen, Potomac, Md.)

A. Tarantino steadfastly refuses to discuss the meaning of the title. That makes your theory as good as anybody's. Maybe better.

Q. A while ago, I read that Quentin Tarantino claimed to have acted in Jean-Luc Godard's *King Lear.* Now I recently read that he only put that on his résumé to try and sneak his way into getting an acting job. Yeash! (Mike Hatch, North Kingston, R.I.)

A. Funny, how with a hot young director, something like that is seen as colorful chutzpah, while with a political candidate or company official, it would be cause for dismissal. I'm sure Tarantino would agree with King Lear in Act IV, Scene 7: "Pray you now, forgive and forget."

Q. On the Revolving Thumb segment of your TV show, you guys said that Quentin Tarantino should just get going and direct another movie. By chance I overheard QT himself talking about the subject. He said he's "nailed the door shut" on his apartment in order to concentrate on writing, giving himself an entire year for the project. (He lives, by the way, in the same duplex that he's had since before he became a success.) Personally I admire him for working this way on the script. In an era where most films are rushed into production, Quentin is respecting the importance of the writing process. Certainly whatever comes out of his self-imposed exile will be better than if he jumped into something just to get another film going. (Joseph Kaufman, Hollywood, Calif.)

A. Good news. Tarantino has the stuff of genius, but I hope he doesn't burn himself out by playing the public role of one. (I note that even after he nails himself into his apartment, he is still careful to be overhearable.) As to whether he's rushing into the next movie, I am told by QT-watcher Michael Dequina of UCLA, "Quentin is currently writing an adaptation of Elmore Leonard's *Rum Punch*, which he will direct."

Technical Questions

Q. In the film *Blink* there's a St. Patrick's Day scene in a bar. Then we see, in what feels like only a day later, Madeline Stowe and Aidan Quinn watching a Cubs game from a rooftop across Sheffield Avenue. Last I checked, Opening Day isn't until the first week in April. Any clues? (Matthew Mendelsohn, Arlington, Va.)

A. It is not unknown here for people celebrating St. Patrick's Day to find themselves on rooftops, imagining they are watching a baseball game.

Q. Tommy Lee Jones, the mad bomber in *Blown Away*, has his secret headquarters on a beat-up old abandoned boat. Yet his TV picks up a cable channel, "Arts and Entertainment." This is obvious from the large overpromotion of its logo in every shot. How did Jones get cable in his secret hideout when I can't even get the cable company to come to my house? (Eric M. Davitt, Toronto, Canada)

A. Have you tried bomb threats?

Q. I was watching *Judge Dredd* on video, and I noticed something. You know those glare spots on camera shots of cars' headlights, etc., that appear on the screen? Well, film technology technique has managed to almost weed them out entirely. Then I notice that on occasion where a computer-generated light source is filmed, those spots are artificially added! That's not the only time I've seen this, either! Why add such a flaw on purpose? (Matt Perry, Rocky Hill, Conn.)

A. The purpose is to make the film look, in a subtle way, more real. Although reflections and highlights are a function of the film itself, we are so used to them that when they're missing we subconsciously register it. In *Toy Story*, which was entirely done on computer, one of the brilliant touches was the use of room reflections on the helmet visor of Buzz Lightyear. Check out the trademark logos that studios use at the beginning of films. One of the popular clichés has a wave of light reflecting over the letters, and then a little flashing "ping" of light.

Q. I'll tell you how David Copperfield made the Statue of Liberty disappear if you tell me how they went from a seamless helicopter track-in to a dolly-in into the building for the opening shot of *The Birdcage*. (Greg Alexander, Coos Bay, Oreg.)

A. Gladly. The shot is not seamless. It appears that the camera zooms over the ocean, the beach, and the boulevard, and right inside Robin Williams's nightclub. But it doesn't. Look carefully for the almost-invisible quick dissolve hiding the cut between the helicopter shot and the dolly shot that takes you inside the club. (When I told you this via e-mail, you made good on your promise about Copperfield. So the base we see without the statue on it is a model, eh? And the audience was on a turntable?)

Q. Just saw John Ford's *Stagecoach* and was reminded again of a question that occurs to me every time I see a Western. There must be a reason why the wagon wheels seem to turn backwards, but what is it? (Susan Lake, Urbana, Ill).

A. There is a reason, which has been explained to me countless times, after which all I remember is, "That's the way wagon wheels look when they're photographed." This is not a helpful answer, and so I was happy to pick up an issue of *Discover* magazine, and find a concise explanation: "Were the film speed perfectly in sync with the rotation of, say, a wheel being filmed, the wheel would complete a rotation whenever an image of it occurred, making it appear stationary. As it happens, though, a wheel of a moving vehicle often lags slightly behind the film speed, so that a spoke has not quite returned to its initial position at the moment an image is taken. As we focus on a spoke's original position, the forward-moving wheel appears on film to turn backwards."

Q. In a recent Answer Man you explained why wagon wheels sometimes appear to be moving backwards in the movies. There is an easy way to conduct an experiment at home, and see how this phenomenon works. If you have a ceiling fan, put it on its slowest setting. Lie back and blink your eyes at varying speeds. You can get the ceiling fan to appear to stand still, move backwards, or forward even more slowly, because you're only producing "stills" of each image of the fan your brain receives. A twenty-four-frame-per-second movie produces the same effect. (Robert Haynes-Peterson, Boise, Id.).

A. Lacking a ceiling fan at home, I went to a nearby Starbucks coffee shop, laid flat on the floor, and performed your experiment, first explaining to the clerks that I was doing important cinematic research.

Q. What is the length of time of a "reel"? Is that term still being used in the business? (Gary Currie, Montreal, Canada)

A. In the old days, films used ten-minute reels because that was how much would fit in the camera. Then reels became twenty minutes in length, dictated by how long the old carbon arc lamps would last in a projector. Today, movies are shipped in twenty-minute reels, but at most theaters they're spliced into one continuous length of film while being projected, and then broken down again for shipping.

Q. Saw and enjoyed *Bound.* I found the parts where they "laundered" the bloody cash a stretch—$2.176 million in $100 bills means 21,760 individual bills. Running them through a washing machine is probably possible, but hanging up 21,760 bills to dry, as depicted in the movie, would require over 6,600 feet of line (more than a mile and a quarter), and one would also need 21,760 clothespins. As for ironing the bills, assuming the ironer can do one bill, both sides, in ten seconds, with no rest—that would take fifty-five hours. Yet the syndicate group was on its way from the airport during that time. Someone was way out in leftfield on this one! (Ronald J. Moran, Lake Forest, Ill.)

A. I'm still wondering how the cops failed to notice the dead bodies stacked in the bathtub.

Teenagers

Q. In the movie *Evil Dead III: Army of Darkness*, the "magic words" used are the same ones spoken by Michael Rennie in *The Day the Earth Stood Still* (1951). You mentioned that this movie must have been targeted for fourteen-year-olds, so I wonder if the movie writers thought this also. Only adults (or sci-fi–addicted adolescents) would get that tongue-in-cheek reference. (John D. Patrick, Champaign-Urbana, Ill.)

A. *The Day the Earth Stood Still* was also targeted for fourteen-year-olds. That is a compliment. Most Hollywood movies are targeted for twelve-year-olds.

Q. I am thirteen and disappointed in your continual bashing of teenage moviegoers. I'm getting tired of hearing our generation has bad taste. Personally, I thought the best movies of last year were *Dead Man Walking, Get Shorty, Heat,* and my favorite family film, *Babe.* By far the best movie this year is *Fargo.* If someone were to make a list of my movie rentals without knowing me, they might describe me as a middle-aged man with a passion for the movies of his youth. (Jason M. Buck, St. Charles, Ill.)

A. If more thirteen-year-olds had your good taste in movies, there wouldn't be a problem. But I don't really mind teenagers who choose movies like *Black Sheep, Ace Ventura: When Nature Calls* and the endless slasher sequels. When I was thirteen I liked trash, too. The problem is with the way Hollywood reads box office figures. All the emphasis is on "winning" the opening weekend. Since teenagers have free time, they're able to race to movies on opening night. Adults need to plan ahead. As a result, movies oriented toward teen audiences open strongly, and more mature films get blasted out of the theaters before they have time to develop their audiences. It's a vicious circle. The media are partly to blame, for publicizing the "box office top ten" every Monday morning, even though they know the numbers are supplied by the studios themselves and are subject to manipulation.

Q. I was wondering about a claim you make in the last paragraph of your review for *The Long Kiss Goodnight.* You say the target audience is apparently fourteen-year-old boys. That's practically impossible, since the film is rated R. Is this like outrunning a fireball?! (Robert Burns Neveldine, Seattle, Wash.)

A. It's a lot easier for a fourteen-year-old to get into an R-rated movie than to outrun a fireball. But perhaps I should have written "for audiences with the maturity and taste of fourteen-year-old boys."

Telephones

Q. I enjoy watching movies because doing so lets me forget my own reality. The one thing that absolutely destroys this reality displacement is to hear a reference to a telephone number beginning with 555. When I hear this, it is like a wake-up call that suddenly reminds me that I am watching a movie. I know that attempts have been made to mask the 555 thing. For example, some movies use KLondike-5 as a telephone prefix. Why can't production companies just pay for a few real phone numbers and use them in their movies? (Rodger Ellis, Anchorage, Alaska)

A. The "555" prefix is used, of course, because no real numbers begin with those digits. One movie that *did* hire a real phone number was Phil Alden Robinson's computer caper, *Sneakers* (1992). If you called the number, you got a fake answering machine message.

Q. In the movie *Sneakers,* the girl gives a telephone number. I called it, and got a recording of two women named Mary and Deanna. They acknowledged the movie by mentioning "all you Sneakers fans." I did not receive a return phone call from them, however. Do you know what this is all about? My curiosity needs to know. (Michael Grigsby, Palmdale, Calif.)

A. *Sneakers* director Phil Alden Robinson had the studio buy the number for people who like to call the numbers they hear in movies. Sorry, but I can't tell you a thing about Mary and Deanna.

Q. At the end of *The Pelican Brief,* Denzel Washington makes a bunch of phone calls. How do you suppose anyone was able to hear him when he was talking with the phone's mouthpiece tucked firmly under his chin? I guess he tucked it under his chin to show off his smile, since he wasn't using one of those phones the White House characters used—with the smaller mouthpiece that doesn't obstruct the actor's face but does proudly show off the AT&T logo. (Dan Margules, San Diego)

A. You have raised a favorite topic of my friend Rich Elias, a film critic from Delaware, Ohio. He often writes of "Mabel," the omnipresent phone supplied to movie companies by AT&T's product placement department. "You don't have to dial it," he writes, "and you don't have to speak into it. All that's required is that the AT&T Death Star logo be aimed toward the camera and, presto! your call goes through." He's got a point. Ordinary phones don't have logos on the mouthpieces, but since he pointed this out, I've noticed AT&T logos in countless movies.

Q. Just saw *Die Hard III* and here's my question: When is Hollywood going to figure out that the phone company can trace a call instantaneously? Once again we see that tired old cop cliché, "Hold him on the line long enough for me to trace the call!" Is Hollywood the only place they haven't heard of Caller ID? Everyone in America can trace a call these days; you'd think the New York cops could, too. (Mark Blanchard, Norwalk, Conn.)

A. I put your question to the Answer Man's expert telephone consultant Rich Elias, of Delaware, Ohio, who is both a film critic and a training specialist for AT&T. He responds: "Blanchard is correct. The technology which enables Caller ID allows an instantaneous trace on incoming calls. The reason is that the telephone network, which nowadays uses digital electronic switches, separates signaling information (including originating number) from the voice path. One consequence is that all signaling information is available throughout the duration of a call and is easy to query.

"The scenario in *Die Hard*—'Keep him talking! We've almost got his number!'—hasn't been accurate for years. In the old days, when central office switches were electromechanical (not digital), a call trace required a switchman to step backward across a physical circuit—from the terminating phone to the switch module to a trunk, etc. This took time. Nowadays, all such information is part of the signaling information that sets up a call. You can forget the 'Keep him talking!' scenario."

Q. In the HBO movie *The Late Shift*, did anyone else notice the large number of instances when angry agents and network execs slammed the mouthpieces of their cell phones closed, akin to slamming down the receiver of a normal phone? And did anyone notice that when someone angrily slammed shut their cell phone, the person on the other end always looked shocked, staring at the phone as if hearing a dial tone? Folding the mouthpiece shut on a cell phone has absolutely no effect on a connection. (Mark Firmani, Seattle)

A. If anyone should know how to use a cellular phone, it's an agent. And if anyone should know how to hang up, it's a TV executive.

That Jug Problem

Q. This question comes from the Answer Man himself. In the movie *Die Hard With a Vengeance*, the mad bomber sets the heroes a task: Using only a three-gallon jug and a five-gallon jug, they need to measure out precisely four gallons of water, in order to defuse a bomb. As I wrote in my review: "I was not quite clear how they used the three- and five-gallon jugs to measure exactly four gallons of water; a fourth-grader can probably enlighten me." I have now received countless solutions to this problem. Some of them cheated by requiring a third empty jug. One required the heroes to find a handy bathtub. Here are two different answers:

A. From Stan Peal, St. Paul, Minnesota: "Fill the five-gallon jug and pour the contents into the three-gallon jug until full. This will leave exactly two gallons in the five-gallon jug. Empty out the three-gallon jug. Pour the two gallons of water that are in the five-gallon jug into the three-gallon jug. Refill the five-gallon jug. Pour water from the five-gallon jug into the three-gallon jug. It will accept exactly one more gallon of liquid. Exactly four gallons of water will remain in the five-gallon jug."

From Michael Bermant M.D., of Utica. New York: "Fill the three-gallon jug. Empty into five-gallon empty jug. Fill up three-gallon jug and fill remaining two gallons left of five-gallon jug (the five-gallon jug will contain five gallons and the three-gallon jug will have one gallon left). Now empty the five-gallon jug and fill it with the one gallon left from the three-gallon jug. Fill the three-gallon jug and empty into the five-gallon jug that had one gallon in it. This will give you a five-gallon jug with four gallons in it."

Q. Earlier in the summer several readers gave solutions to the problem in *Die Hard With a Vengeance*, where the heroes were given three- and five-gallon jugs and told to measure exactly four gallons of water. After deep thought I have come up with a simpler solution, which uses one less step.

Fill the five-gallon jug to the top, tip it 45 degrees so that the water is level with one top edge and the opposite lower corner of the jug. The water that remains in the five-gallon container is 2.5 gallons. Now do the same with the three-gallon jug. The water that remains is 1.5 gallons. Dump the contents of the three-gallon jug into the five-gallon jug and the five-gallon jug will contain four gallons. (Charles Eglinton, Rochester Hills, Mich.)

A. Your solution is the most elegant yet, and does not include, as one reader's did, the instruction, "First, borrow a bathtub."

Q. *Die Hard With a Vengeance* recently came out on video, and after watching it I reread your review and the Answer Man discussion about how they solved the water jug problem (starting with a three-gallon jug and a five-gallon jug, they had to obtain exactly four gallons of water to disarm the bomb). Your readers sent in many different solutions to the problem. But no one watching the movie seems to have questioned this moment of dialogue: "McClane, that truck you're driving contains $13 billion worth of gold!" I did a little math. At $350 an ounce, that comes to a weight of slightly over 2,200,000 pounds. That's a heck of a truck. Do you think it would run into problems at the state highway patrol weighing station? (Don Howard, San Jose, Calif.)

A. Details.

Theaters from Hell

Q. Saw your item complaining about American theaters. For your reference: In Taiwan, in most theaters, they turn the projector off and the lights on as soon as the movie is over. They cut the credits so they can empty the theater and get the next crowd in as soon as possible to increase profits. Sometimes they even send the noisy cleaning crew in to start their work *before* even reaching the climax or ending of the film!!! Also, before each movie begins, they play Taiwan's national anthem, which they are constantly updating so it'll stay fresh. It's been jazzed up so many times that it now has a reggae beat! (I am on the radio in Japan and Taiwan as "Kamasami Kong.") (Bob Zix, Honolulu)

A. Even as I decided to run your letter, I started to cringe. Many American theater owners may be inspired to adopt these practices. Our own national anthem, by the way, apparently has the lyrics, *Know what time it is??? It's refreshment time!!!*

Q. I have been following the comments about moviegoing experiences in America, Taiwan, etc. As a Brit, having just completed a trip to New York City, it amazes me why your cinemas are so backward compared to those in London. Why do Americans tolerate such awful service? We Brits are told how much we can learn from the service industry in the United States, but the simple task of seeing a film can turn into a nightmare! Examples: (1) Why do New Yorkers enjoy queuing up for forty-five minutes to purchase a ticket? (2) Once you've bought your ticket, why do you have to queue up again to wait for the cinema to open the house doors? (3) Then, when it's open, there's an almighty rush to find the best seat, and then you have to wait another half-hour before the film starts! By contrast, in going to the movies in London, we: (1) Telephone cinema and book tickets on credit card. Best available seat numbers are given. (2) Get to cinema five minutes before film starts, collect tickets, go into the auditorium, usher takes you to your seats and film starts. Simple as that. No queues. No hassle. (Darren Tossell, London)

A. What you have observed is a uniquely New York phenomenon. Moviegoers in the rest of the United States do not usually line up for tickets, except, of course, in Los Angeles. The reason in both cities is the same: These cities are filled with exhibitionists who resent the fact that they cannot be seen in the dark. Accustomed to being televised from their ringside seats during Knicks and Lakers games, they go to fashionable movies early in order to display themselves in the queue. If the theaters presold tickets and let everyone in quickly, they probably wouldn't go at all.

Q. My husband returned from the movies this weekend upset by a notice that had been posted at the ticket booth for *Toy Story*, saying that even though this film had been showing for nine weeks and was prone to breakage, the splicing itself only took a minute to fix and no one was entitled to get their money back because of the above-mentioned technical problems. My husband feels that moviegoers should see a film with good technical quality or get their money back. I think this cineplex is being cheap in not acquiring a better copy. (Irene Ford Hyatt, Asheville, N.C.)

A. Anyone paying first-run prices deserves to see a first-run movie. When prints show signs of wear and tear, they are usually replaced by the distributing studio. The fact that such a notice was posted in the theater suggests they're having chronic problems, which may mean it's their projector that needs replacing, not the print.

Q. It appears to me that movies are getting darker and darker, in terms of physical light. The most recent example was *Tombstone*, where even when the sun was shining and there were no clouds, the sky was darkened. Do I need new glasses? (Kent Livingston, Bloomington, Minn.)

A. The problem may be right there in your local theater. Some major movie chains have been known to instruct their projectionists to turn down the power level on the $4,000 lamps in the projectors. Director Martin Scorsese, who travels with a light meter and likes to take readings from movie screens, says in some theaters the light intensity is as much as a third less than the recommended levels.

Q. Recently I had my worst moviegoing experience at the Cineplex Odeon in Orland Park. I waited months in eager anticipation of seeing *Sense and Sensibility*. The movie was wonderful, but imagine my disappointment and outrage when the projectionist *did not run the credits!* I was furious. I rushed to the manager to report this crime against movie fans, and she said he had done this before, but not with the approval of the theater. Why does he still have a job? (Cindy Beberman, Orland Park, Ill.)

A. It is sad to encounter someone who has no sympathy for the meaning of his work. Not only are the closing credits themselves of intrinsic interest to many moviegoers, but they also often include full performances of one or two songs from the sound track—plus, in some comedies, additional outtakes or in-jokes. Not only should the full closing credits always be projected, but if the theater has curtains, they should not be closed until the final copyright notice appears.

Q. I went to see *Richard III* in a Syracuse suburb that has one of the few "art houses" in the area. The film started to roll. I thought, "The screen is too small for this film." Everything on the right side of the frame was chopped off. The name credits came up. Then the title: "RICHARD." I laughed out loud. The dramatic impact of the tank crashing through the wall was lessened by the too-small screen. I wouldn't want to see *Richard III* on video, but I certainly resent being duped by this theater! (Valerie Gigliatti, Syracuse, N.Y.)

A. The screen was not too small. What we have here is still another example of a projectionist too untrained or lazy to frame the picture properly. All movies arrive on the same size 35mm film. It is the projectionist's job to "frame" them in the projector so that the correct part of the picture area is seen, and the rest is not. Earlier I wrote that when you see the microphone at the top of the picture, the movie has been framed too low. It is much rarer to screw up the horizontal framing of a movie, but your projectionist managed it.

Time Compression on Video

Q. I was watching *The Sons of Katie Elder* on TBS a couple of weeks ago, and some of the fight scenes looked like the Duke had watched too many old silent movies. He was moving *really* fast. Last night, I was flipping channels and noticed a message that said, "This film has been time-compressed to fit in this time slot." Just what, exactly, is "Time compression"? Is it the same as "this film has been edited for television," or just another one of Ted Turner's "innovations," like colorizing? (David Little, Baton Rouge, La.)

A. Time compression is a technique for speeding up film in a way that is allegedly not noticeable to the audience, so that a few more seconds or minutes can be crammed into a time slot. TBS claims they don't do it. The technique is used all the time for commercials.

Q. I recently saw *Gone With the Wind* on TBS and after five minutes, I felt I was on amphetamines. Actors were scurrying up and down staircases like mice. Vivien Leigh was reciting her lines so fast she sounded like a chipmunk. The entire tempo of the movie was much faster than I ever saw it in the past. I know that rock stations speed up their music to give their shows punch, but I've never heard of a TV station playing a movie at a faster speed. Is it possible or am I on drugs? (J.L. Abrams, Chicago)

A. I cannot speak for your body chemistry, but Bill Cox, vice president of programming at TBS, says, "We did not edit or electronically alter the film in any way."

There is an ongoing controversy in the video industry, by the way, about "electronic compression" that squeezes movies into time slots where they don't quite fit. Time compression and other changes in an original film (colorization, pan-and-scan, etc.), will soon be labeled for both home video and broadcast use, under MPAA guidelines adopted in response to a threat of congressional legislation.

Q. You wrote about whether the Turner cable operation uses "time compression," which you described as "a technique for speeding up film in a way that is allegedly not noticeable to the audience, so that a few more seconds or minutes can be crammed into a time slot." This was in response to a question about characters seeming to fly around in *Gone With the Wind,* and you said Turner claims it doesn't do it. Shortly after you mentioned this, TBS began running a disclaimer at the beginning of many movies saying they had been time expressed or time expanded to fill their slots. (Bob Rusbasan, Lafayette, Ind.)

A. A TBS public relations person says he hopes to have a statement "soon" to clarify their policy. I guess time compression is what we should expect from the same Turner folks who colorize classic black-and-white films like *Casablanca,* and are now trying to muscle American Movie Classics off of cable systems. AMC never compresses and never colorizes; here's another example of the bad driving out the good.

Q. Regarding your discussion about Turner Broadcasting's alleged use of time compression to squeeze movies into shorter time slots: I spent a dozen years as a broadcast engineer, and can tell you what to look for. Digital compression throws away one frame of the picture for every few frames it shows. If you want to see this effect, wait for a character to do a "crossing move" at a moderate speed and watch to see if they seem to jump slightly ahead every so often. This is an absolute giveaway. A little harder to see, but just as reliable, is to look for a horizontal line in the frame, and put your finger right at the line. Now count how often you see the line bounce up and down. Each bounce is one frame lost. Count the number of bounces in one minute and use this formula: *Percent of compression equals bounces per minute divided by thirty-six.* Knowing this, they will never be able to fool you again. (Bill Becwar, Wauwatosa, Wisc.)

A. This is going to make me the life of the party.

Toy Story

Q. You said in your *Toy Story* review that the launching in *Apollo 13* was done entirely by computer animation. Actually, the launch was a killer catalog of special effects techniques. The ground was a digital stitch of aerial photos, the smoke and other particle effects were 100 percent computer animation, and the rocket was a ¹⁄₉₆th scale model (an off-the-shelf Revell model, interestingly enough). The whole kit and caboodle was composited digitally, of course. I gotta say, though, that I'm offended by ads that refer to *Toy Story* as a Disney film ("More Warm, Heart-Touching Classic Disney Magic!"—Debbie Stylingel, KSYA). Disney taking credit for *Toy Story* is like Ford Motors taking credit for the NFL superstar who was conceived in the backseat of a Mustang. (Andy Ihnatko, Westwood, Mass.)

A. The movie's animation was done outside the Disney shop, by Pixar, a company started by George Lucas and later purchased by Apple pioneer Steve Jobs. Steve Lasseter, the movie's director, works at Pixar. But Disney was deeply involved in fine-tuning the characters and story.

Q. I thought *Toy Story* was phenomenal. Do you think it will make future audiences think of traditional cel animation as "old-fashioned" and "inferior" in the same way that a previous generation preferred Talkies over Silents? Could this be the watershed moment in the history of the animated film? (Ed Slota, Warwick, R.I.)

A. My experience in talking to "ordinary people" who saw the film was that they didn't much notice that the animation was different, and just related to it as an animated film, period.

Q. Just saw *Toy Story* and agree that it is a wonderful film. However, I kept thinking that the humans and the dog looked no different from the toys, and they should have. Do you think that the humans should have been played by human actors (and the dog by a real dog), à la *Roger Rabbit?* (Rob Solomon, Sylmar, Calif.)

A. It was necessary for everything in the movie to look like part of the same visual universe. *Roger Rabbit* was about humans who coexisted with 'Toons, so of course they looked different. But *Toy Story* is not about two different worlds. It is about one world, in which toys are intelligent.

Q. I am continually fascinated by the little political digs on your show. Tonight, you compared the sadistic and mean character Sid from *Toy Story* to Bill Gates, a brilliant software engineer and entrepreneur. This comparison is lost on me, yet your motivation to disparage a prominent businessman is not. (Mike Sadlowski, Camarillo, Calif.)

A. You should have listened more carefully. I was suggesting that although *Toy Story* makes Sid into a villain, it is likely that a kid smart enough to take his toys apart and put them back together in an improved way has the potential to grow up to be a Bill Gates. Kids who just sit there and play with their toys will end up buying "Windows 95," instead of selling it.

Q. While the computer-generated animation in *Toy Story* is superb, it scares me a little, as do other movies making extensive use of computers, such as *Jurassic Park*. Now I can't always tell whether something is real, or created from zillions of bits. Last night I watched *My Darling Clementine*. I knew those mountains and rock outcroppings were real. Yes, backdrops were sometimes used (I don't care for that method either, but it's easier to spot). I hope the movie industry doesn't go overboard with chips and trickery. Don't get me wrong: I am all for technology, in part because I'm a quadriplegic. I'm typing this on a Mac. Before working on them, I thought computers were anathema, but now they have opened up countless worlds for me. (Robin L. Rogalski, Glendale, Wisc.)

A. I hear what you're saying, but the movies have used effects right from the start, and many "real" scenes in the past were actually all trickery. When the seaplane takes off in *Indiana Jones and the Temple of Doom*, for example, the plane, the water, the land, the town, and the sky are all separate effects. Pauline Kael's *Citizen Kane Book* reveals how many of the shots in that great film use special effects—including shots where you don't suspect a thing, as when Kane is finishing Jed Leland's review.

Trailers

Q. I went to see *Falling Down*, and what a surprise! It's a drama! All the previews I've seen are promoting this movie as a real laff-aminit comedy. Have you noticed how often serious films are being promoted this way? If a film has even the slightest element of comedy, those scenes are spliced together, provided with a jovial voice-over to form the trailer, and sent out to fool unsuspecting audiences. (Frank Scalfano, Fort Walton Beach, Fla.)

A. Yeah, judging by the trailers you'd also think *Swing Kids* was a musical, and *Jack the Bear* was a hug-me, feel-me family movie. I guess the marketing experts believe the public can't handle the idea that a movie might really be about something.

Q. When a movie is released on videotape, why isn't the original movie trailer included on the videotape? Sometimes the trailer you see in the theater is more interesting than the movie itself. Or, like the trailer for *Citizen Kane*, almost as interesting. (Steven Siferd, Alpine, Calif.)

A. Increasing numbers of movies do include the previews (and some include previews for other forthcoming videos). The determining factor is often the length of a movie, since 120 minutes is standard for both tapes and discs, and if the movie runs a full two hours, there's no room for a preview.

Q. I saw *Dangerous Minds*, which was an okay movie, but could have been better. My question is, what happened to the scene where the students and teacher are playing pool? This scene is a major part of all of the previews and is still in some of the TV commercials. Why did they decide to cut that scene? (David Becerra, San Diego)

A. Movie ads and previews are made from early rough cuts, and often contain shots that are later taken out after test screenings. For example, in the ads for *Batman Forever*, the Riddler says, "The Bat wants to play? We'll play!" Not in the movie. You think that's weird? *Dangerous Minds* originally costarred Andy Garcia as Michelle Pfeiffer's love interest, and his entire character was cut after testing.

Q. Is it ethical to use material in a film's trailer that is not part of the film itself? For example, in the trailer for *Something to Talk About*, in the scene where Julia Roberts stands up at her women's club and asks who else has been sleeping with her husband—in the preview, but not in the movie, someone responds by asking if kissing counts. I think this is a form of false advertising and I'm surprised the studios are allowed to do it. (William A. Cirignan, Chicago)

A. Many movies are in editing right up until the day before the labs start churning out the prints. But the previews, which must be ready weeks or months earlier, are put together from earlier versions of the film. Sometimes they include scenes that are cut from the final print, but I've never heard of a studio deliberately putting scenes in a preview that aren't in the film.

Q. In an Answer Man column you said "I've never heard of a studio deliberately putting scenes in a preview that aren't in the film." According to *Premiere* magazine, the makers of *Patriot Games* shot two versions of the scene where James Earl Jones comes out to Harrison Ford's house to tell him that Sean Bean's character had escaped from prison. One was used in the preview (Jones says "There's never been a terrorist attack on U.S. soil, blah, blah," and Ford replies, "But I killed his brother"). The other, used in the film, was a bit less melodramatic. The director, Philip Noyce, acknowledged that a version was shot specifically for the trailer. (Paul McElligott, Lake Forest, Calif.)

A. This is depressing news. I already knew there were movie critics who supplied their quotes directly to the previews without putting them in a review first. Now you tell me the previews themselves don't always come from the movies. What we're developing here is a parallel art form, with parallel critics to review it.

Q. In the Answer Man recently, you discussed scenes in previews that differ from the same scenes in the final movie print, and whether studios deliberately shoot scenes for a trailer that aren't intended for the film. In the original *Home Alone*, I had a brief role as a grocery store manager. I was in the background at a computer while the cashier spoke to Macauley Culkin. Then the scene was reshot with me standing next to the cashier and speaking the lines. The latter version was used in the movie's trailers, and as a lead-in for TV interviews with cast members. It was even shown on the Academy Awards, as a lead-in to Culkin as a presenter. But it was not in the movie. Whatever their reasons for doing this, I am grateful to the producer and director; the speaking part enabled me to join the Screen Actor's Guild. (Richard J. Firfer, Chicago)

A. I suppose this is a reflection of the larger tendency of studios to make previews reflect the movie they wish they had made, rather than the one they actually did make. Remember the ads for the Richard Gere movie about *Mr. Jones*, which was a tragedy about mental illness? The previews and the TV ads made it look like an upbeat comedy.

Q. I've worked in the medical field for fifteen years but have always loved movies—especially the preview trailers. When I go to a show, if I miss any of the previews I feel like I missed what I came for. I would love to have a part in the production of movie trailers. Any suggestions? (Kimberly Stickels, Buffalo Grove, Ill.)

A. Trailers are made by specialists—editors and advertising people—who emphasize the aspects of a film that are most likely to attract audiences. The music is usually from an earlier film, (1) because the new film will not have been scored when the trailer is being made, and (2) as a subtle way of identifying the new film with an established hit. Sometimes there is a voice-over announcer. Some trailers (especially Disney's) encapsulate almost the whole plot. Any trailer is more likely to reflect the movie the studio wanted than the movie it got. The trailers and ads for *The Cable Guy*, for example, make it look more like an Ace Ventura farce than the black comedy it really is. To get into the trailer industry, you could take film and video editing courses and advertising courses, and then point yourself in that direction.

Q. In *The First Wives Club*, when the women are discussing plastic surgery, Bette Midler says to Goldie Hawn, "Did you have just a little done, or did you get the full enchilada?" If memory serves me correctly (and I'm sure it does), in the theatrical preview containing this scene, Midler says "or did you get the full Ivana?" During the actual film, it is very apparent that they did an audio dub over "Ivana" to replace it. I'm wondering if, considering Ivana Trump was in the movie, they felt that they should change it. (Matt Thiesen, Maple Grove, Minn.)

A. I'd say so. I was going to call the studio and ask, but something told me that on this one I was not going to get a straight answer.

Trailers and Music

Q. Is it my imagination or do advance movie trailers often use the theme music from another movie as background? Recently I've heard the themes from *Willow* used for *Robin Hood, Prince of Thieves, The Rocketeer* used for *Forever Young* and then *Robin Hood, Prince of Thieves* for *Sommersby.* Is this a common practice and do the owners of the original themes approve of and get compensation? (Susan Dunlop, Reston, Va.)

A. You have an excellent ear. Often the earliest coming attractions are released before the music for a new film has been scored, so a studio will reach back to appropriate music it already owns. Everybody gets paid.

Q. What's the deal with the constant recycling of the *Few Good Men* main theme in coming attractions trailers? The aural backdrop to Lt. Caffey entering the courtroom has been used for trailers of *Rising Sun, The Firm, Pelican Brief,* and now *Philadelphia.* (Jim McClure)

A. Studios often make their trailer before the music for a movie has been scored. Or, they feel a movie's actual music won't sell a picture. So they grab music from an earlier hit, hoping it will subtly remind you of a movie you liked. Or, in this case, of trailers you hated.

Q. What movie originated that ubiquitous trailer music that is used for *Rob Roy, A Few Good Men,* and *Clear and Present Danger?* (Cliff W. Rives, Jacksonville, Fla.)

A. It's from the Alan Parker film *Come See the Paradise,* according to Michael Zey of Austin, Texas.

12 Monkeys

Q. I just finished reading your review of *12 Monkeys* and you mention that there is a time-travel paradox in the film. I have wracked my brain and can't for the life of me figure out what and where it is. (John F. Coyle, Tulsa, Okla.)

A. It is apparent that the hero (Bruce Willis) is the little boy who sees himself (as the adult Willis) killed, and that would mean that he exists twice at the same time in the same place, which must be a violation of the law of conservation of something or another, don't you think?

Q. Re your discussion of the time travel paradox in *12 Monkeys*: To understand what's going on, one merely needs to disregard the common perception of time as a linear dimension. The time theory at work in *12 Monkeys* is that time does not start at point A and travel along to point B, but rather that all moments in time occur simultaneously. Time is not like a line, extending, stretching, and leaving a path behind, but rather like a painting, with each point and brushstroke being a different moment in time. At any given moment in time, we only see one little point in the painting, but all the others are still there, including present, future, and past, and together they make up the universe, which is timeless. (Dominic M. Armato, Winnetka, Ill.)

A. Thinking back about the movie, I'm convinced you are right: The Willis character hops, as it were, between points in time, and in a way the "dream" material indicates a leakage of memory, or "paint," from one part of the picture to another.

Q. It appears that with the release of *12 Monkeys* you will have to make an update to the *Cole Rule*. (Rob McKenzie, Stratford, Ontario, Canada)

A. This is the rule in *Ebert's Little Movie Glossary* which states that no movie made since 1977 with a character named "Cole" is any good. I think time is running out on it.

Q. I just saw *12 Monkeys* tonight, and one thing in particular really bugged me about it. Bruce Willis's whiskers were of varying length, throughout the same day. Sometimes longer stubble, then shorter, then longer. Arrrrggghhhh!!!!! (Steve Ferrarini, Paso Robles, Calif.)

A. Give him a break. Here is a guy who is being jerked around in time, from 1999 to 1990 to 1996. He hardly even knows what year he last shaved in—let alone where to set the Stubble-Meter on his electric razor.

Twister

Q. Concerning your comment about "Dorothy," the sensor-delivering machine in *Twister*—I also wondered exactly what all the bells and whistles were for, and why it took interminably long for Bill Paxton to "set it up" the first time, while the next time Helen Hunt flicks one switch and says, "It's ready!" In fact, it would make more sense to me if they got rid of Dorothy completely and just left the sensors spread out across the area. If the tornado can suck up a human being and a cow, it will pick up those little balls just as well. (David J. Bondelevitch, Studio City, Calif.)

A. Quite true, but then the movie wouldn't have a reason why the characters have to dangerously position themselves in the path of the tornadoes. Dorothy functions like one of Hitchcock's "MacGuffins"—the machine provides a reason for the plot to move forward, without really being necessary in itself.

Q. As nobody got hurt, this is kind of funny. While *Twister* was showing at the Cineplex drive in outside Thorold, Ontario, they got hit by a—you guessed it—tornado. It blew the screen apart during a big thunderstorm. I can imagine the audience saying "How did they do that?" or "Obvious fake!" etc. (Eric M. Davitt, Toronto, Ontario, Canada)

A. I can't stand people who talk during tornadoes.

Q. With the exception of Disney's yearly animated features, the movie musical has almost completely vanished. I believe I know what has happened to it. Hollywood musicals were primarily spectacle. People went to see them not for the plot but for the lavish production numbers. Recent films like *Twister* and *Mission: Impossible* have been described by critics in terms that could just as easily be applied to Hollywood musicals. Regarding *Twister* you wrote: "As drama, *Twister* . . . has no time to waste on character, situation, dialogue, and nuance. The dramatic scenes are holding actions between tornadoes. As spectacle, however, *Twister* is impressive. The tornadoes are big, loud, violent, and awesome, and they look great." Well, swap "song and dance" for "tornado" and you've got a pretty good description of a Busby Berkeley musical. It looks as if the big-budget, special-effects extravaganza is adopting the role of the movie musical. What do you think? (Brad Hoehne, Columbus, Ohio)

A. This is an intriguing theory. Certainly the audience expectations are the same: When a musical production number or a special effects sequence gets under way, we suspend our disbelief and surrender ourselves to the spectacle. Such scenes typically involve a central character who is able to transcend time, gravity, and logic while effortlessly maintaining his poise and personality. In other words, Fred Astaire and Arnold Schwarzenegger are doing essentially the same thing.

Q. I recently viewed *Phenomenon* in a new multiplex with the new sound technologies (whatever they are). Anyway, about half-a-dozen times during the movie, I heard a low-pitched rumble, which lasted for a few seconds each time. I kept thinking there was about to be another earthquake. Was this some kind of device to keep viewers alert? (John Ritzert, Indianapolis, Ind.)

A. I was immediately reminded of "Sensurround," the bass rumble effect supplied for the movie *Earthquake*, which had to be turned off at one Chicago theater after it jarred plaster loose from the ceiling. But my fellow film critic Rich Elias, of Delaware, Ohio, thinks it may have been the sound track of *Twister* leaking in from the next theater: "Twister Boom is a major problem at many thin-walled multiplexes."

Waterworld

Q. Here is the sum total of my exposure to the epic *Waterworld*: One *Spy* magazine article, which tells nothing of the plot but discusses its huge budget overruns and the difficulties of the director, and yesterday's arrival of four sample *Waterworld* trading cards in my monthly comix catalog. Based on the cards, I can predict that this film will be a complete flop.

I haven't completely figured out the plot yet, though. The four cards show guys horsing around on a catamaran and repainted JetSkis, and one piercing photo of a shabbily-dressed woman. Therefore, I am guessing that the postapocalyptic world is flooded. Because Cliché number 821 requires that postapocalyptic people must fight over water, I'm going to guess that the key conflict is over an evil despot who controls the *land*. Another complete guess is that an ultimate goal is to find a mythic big land mass where one can finally dry one's socks. I'll also go out on a limb and say that the villain dies at the end. This is based on four trading cards. I'm sure once I see an ad, I'll have the whole thing down scene by scene. (Andy Ihnatko, Westwood, Mass.)

A. If I send you the set of four collector's cups, can you do a job on *Batman Forever?*

Q. Any geophysical scientist will tell you that *Waterworld*, which is about the earth being covered by water, is based on an *impossible* premise. There simply isn't enough water to raise the sea level enough to cover more than one-third of present land. Now if 150 or 200 icy comets were to hit the earth, raising the temperature and providing lots of additional water, then there might be a chance. (Mark A. Reichert, St. Louis)

A. You have just plotted *Waterworld II.*

Q. In *Waterworld,* if the world is covered with water, why is everyone so dirty? (Stacy Horwitz, Schenectady, N.Y.)

A. And where does Dennis Hopper get his cigarettes?

Q. *Waterworld* is like the *Mad Max* movies: We're in the future world with very little in the way of petroleum refining going on, yet there seems to be an awful lot of people on various gasoline-powered vehicles hot-rodding all over the landscape burning up a lot of petrol. (George Alec Effinger, New Orleans)

A. And why is everyone so dirty, and smoking all the time?

Q. In *Waterworld* the Mariner trades 3.2 kilos of dirt for supplies, yet included in the supplies he receives is a tomato plant that
is planted in dirt. Later, he is seen scooping up a handful of dirt at
an underwater city. Why doesn't he bring up bucketfuls and become the Donald Trump of *Waterworld?* (Charles Maze, Northfield, Ill.)

A. I forwarded your letter to the Mariner, who banged the heel
of his palm against his forehead and said, "I am such a *stupe!*"

Q. I am wondering if you recognized the sunken city in *Waterworld* as Denver? I thought I caught a glimpse of the distinctive
skyscraper known locally as "the cash register building" because
of its offset and curved top. Further evidence would be the ski lifts,
although they would have had to swim awfully far to reach the
nearest ski lift. And if it is Denver, then wouldn't the highest mountain (and thus most likely the fabled Dryland) be Mount Evans to
the west and not the south? (Robert Jones, Tigard, Oreg.)

A. If the sunken Denver was close enough to the surface for
Mariner to take the woman there in a diving bell without her getting
the bends, wouldn't that mean the top of the mountain would be visible above the waves? Could all of the problems in *Waterworld* have
been solved if they had just looked in the other direction? My favorite
Waterworld story is the little girl who turned to her mother at the end
of the movie and said, "Mommy, they've landed in Jurassic Park!"

Writers, Scripts, and Deals

Q. What exactly is a "spec" script and how does a "pay or play"
deal work? (George O. Burkhart, Honolulu, Hawaii)

A. A "spec" script is written on speculation by a writer who
hopes to get paid for it. "Pay or play" means the studio agrees to pay
an actor, director, etc., for a film whether or not it is eventually made.

Q. In your movie reviews, you give *Showgirls* and *Sense and Sensibility* the same two-and-a-half stars. Any second thoughts? In
your opinion, who is a better writer, Joe Eszterhas or Jane Austen?
(John Cauman)

A. Eszterhas is definitely the better screenwriter. The thing about stars is, they're relative, not absolute. I thought *Sense and Sensibility* fell just short of its goal of being more than a respectful adaptation of an official masterpiece, and *Showgirls* fell just short of its goal of being a trashy sexploitation film with style. To see movies that succeed in these two genres, I recommend *Persuasion* and *Beyond the Valley of the Dolls*.

Q. In your review of *The Substitute*, you wrote: "I am so very tired of this movie. I see it at least once a month. The title changes, and the actors change and the superficial details of the story change, but it is always about exactly the same thing: heavily armed men shooting at each other. Even the order of their deaths is preordained: First the extras die, then the bit players, then the featured actors, until finally only the hero and the villain are left."

This is sadly true; but have you ever read any of the Old Icelandic "Family Sagas"? Everything you said above certainly applies to, for sample, *Njal's Saga*. This type of story structure is "at least" medieval in origin. The problem is not so much in the repetition of an ancient theme, but in the quality of the execution! (Brad Miller, Ph.D. candidate in English, University of Toronto)

A. Of course you are quite right. In fact, in writing my review of *The Substitute*, I forgot Ebert's Law, which states: "A movie is not about what it is about. It is about how it is about it."

Q. I don't think I have what it takes to be a great screenwriter. I might make a pretty good hack, though, and I was wondering if you have any advice for me. I'm serious. How many pictures come out of Hollywood in a given year? Two hundred? Then doesn't the size of the industry suggest there are lots of people getting paid to write scripts that never get made? That sounds like the perfect job for me. If there really are people who do that, how do they get started? Someone got paid to write *Jury Duty*. Someone gets paid to write those direct-to-video movies that pop up on *Showtime* at 3 A.M. I don't even want to go that far; I'd rather write bad scripts that don't get made than bad ones that do—it would be less embarrassing. All I really want is to go into a meeting with a half-assed idea and come out with a check for a few thousand dollars, enough to keep me in a studio apartment and Ramen noodles until I can sell another one. (Alex Strasheim, via Internet)

A. It's just as hard to write a screenplay that doesn't get made as one that does. And no one writes one without hoping to see it on the screen. That's true even of legendary sci-fi writer Harlan Ellison, who at one point had sold twenty-eight screenplays and seen only one of them (*The Oscar,* 1966) made. But you're on to something. Last year Hollywood made around 350 movies, and the Writers' Guild registered about thirty thousand screenplays. Many of them were written on spec, but lots were paid for. There are people who get rich in "turnaround," shopping projects from one studio to another, getting paid every time. The key is, never admit that's what you're doing.

Q. I am a sixteen-year-old girl and have a passion for writing screenplays. I am currently finishing up the treatment for my first serious one, and am wondering if you could give me advice on where to send it, if I'll need an agent, or if I'll need to copyright it. (Jen Markowitz, Toronto, Canada)

A. I'm not sure about the procedures in Canada, but in the United States a writer would want to register it with the Writers' Guild of America, West, Inc. Yes, you will need an agent; no reputable producer will even open the envelope of an unsolicited screenplay, because of the plague of nuisance suits from people claiming to have had their ideas ripped off. Most agents charge a reading fee, because they cannot afford to subsidize the reading of the thousands of freelance screenplays produced every year. I can't recommend an agent—and, of course, as someone who may be reviewing your screenplay some day, I cannot read it at this stage.

Q. In last week's Answer Man you say, "Most agents charge a reading fee, because they cannot afford to subsidize the reading of the thousands of freelance screenplays produced every year." Actually, reading fees are verboten for Writers Guild signatory agents! They'd be bounced from the biz for charging reading fees! There *are* a lot of fly-by-night agents who charge reading fees, but any agent who would charge you such a fee you wouldn't want representing you! Every year there are over thirty thousand scripts registered with Writers Guild of America, West. Every year there are about 150 to 200 theatrical features made, and 300 to 350 direct-to-video or cable features made. Probably half of all films are assignments or based on novels, plays, or other copyrighted material, and *not* registered with the WGA—making the odds about 120 to 1 that a WGA-registered original script will be made into a movie! Good advice to new screenwriters: Keep writing! Don't show your scripts too soon. It may take writing ten scripts before you finally get a handle on the form. Don't burn a bridge in front of you by sending your work out before it's up to professional standards. I've written twelve produced features and still have no agent. (W.C. Martell, Studio City, Calif.)

A. Thanks for clearing up the Writers' Guild policies for me. I still believe it's true, however, that unproduced writers with no connections have a hard job getting established agents to read unsolicited screenplays. At some point, some kind of networking is helpful.

Yessss!

Q. I heartily agree with your comment in the *Lassie* review about the annoying habit of young characters who hiss a sibilant "yessss!" and do a slam-dunk whenever something turns out their way. Maybe Ronald Reagan started it with his usage of "yes" as a conjunction, e.g., "Yes and health care, too." Whoever started it, it drives me nuts and, unfortunately, it's starting to make its way into Canada. Maybe because whe have an NBA franchise now, who knows. (Rob Heslin, Toronto, Canada)

A. Yessss!

Q. Your comment in your review of *Black Beauty* about tuning into animals' true thoughts reminded me of a Gary Larson cartoon—the one in which a scientist walks down the street wearing a bizarre helmet that lets him hear what dogs are really saying. They're saying, "Hey! Hey! Hey! Hey! Hey! Hey!" and "Hey! Hey!

Hey!" and "Heyyyyyyyy!" In Beauty's case, of course, it would be "Hay!" (Jan Strnad, Los Angeles)

A. Yessss!

Q. You have frequently expressed your impatience with young movie characters who say "Yessss!" when something goes right. Did you know that Marv Albert is credited with creating the phrase "Yessss!"? (Harris Allsworth, Chicago)

A. So *Sun-Times* columnist Jeffrey Zaslow reported in a recent column. But I do not understand why Marv Albert takes the credit, instead of accepting the blame.

Index